HYPERSENTIENCE

also by Marcia Moore

Diet, Sex and Yoga
Astrology in Action
Yoga, Science of the Self
Astrology, The Divine Science
Reincarnation, Key to Immortality

HYPERSENTIENCE

Exploring your past lifetime as a guide to your character and destiny

Marcia Moore

CROWN PUBLISHERS, INC., NEW YORK

Printed in the United States of America
Published simultaneously in Canada by General Publishing Company Limited

Designed by Laurie Zuckerman

Library of Congress Cataloging in Publication Data

Moore, Marcia.
  Hypersentience: exploring your past lifetime
  as a guide to your character and destiny.

  1. Reincarnation. 1. Title.
  BL515.M62 1976.   133.9   76-8199
  ISBN 0-517-52536-4

To Isabel Buell

They say
that memory is an energy of the soul,
and I shall remember your kindness to me
in lives past
and lives to come

Contents

Acknowledgments

This book has been a collaborative enterprise carried on by many loyal friends with and without bodies. Their energy, enthusiasm, and unwavering support have nourished the project from its conception.

To my family, boundless gratitude is due. This includes my parents Robert and Eleanor Moore, my brothers Robin and John Moore, and my children Louisa, Christopher, and Jonathan Roof. Successive drafts of the manuscript were written in the homes of Akeva in California, of Robin and Mary Olga Moore in Connecticut, Wilmon and Katharine Brewer in Massachusetts, Bruce and Isabel Buell in California, and John Dunshee in California. These dear friends have sustained me body, mind, and soul during the times when help was needed. Also appreciated has been the encouragement given by four courageous pioneers of new therapeutic techniques. These are the physicians Shepard Ginandes, M.D., Lloyd Koelling, M.D., Margaret Millard, M.D., and Richard Willard, M.D. A special thank you is also due to the hosts and hostesses who have so hospitably sponsored workshops throughout the United States and Canada.

In particular I want to mention the generous contributions made by many gifted co-workers, including: Akeva, Rita Brite, Ethel Brown, Anne Bowles, Valerie Brock, Maria Comfort, Peter Crane, Lourie Dildane, Gayle Eaton, Lillian Germaine, Carol Griffith, James Hershberger, Eileen Hyatt, Kathleen Jenks, Patty Jenkins, Tony Joseph, Jack Kerollis, Barbara Lee, Michael Matthews, Judy Olsen, Pelu, Arlene Robertson, Juanita Steele, Claudia Barnes Strobel, Amyra Sunevia, Robert Thomas, Joyce Ween; Isabel, Bruce, Ward, and Sterling Buell; Barbara, Bob, Lindsay, Christina, and Gregory Bozzani; Violet and Jack Gillfillan; Neva and Ray Robinson.

To my literary editors Linda Price and Jacob Goldberg, I'd like to express my appreciation for the professional skill and personal sensitivity which have helped to deliver my words into print.

Finally, a special word of gratitude to Lynn Powell, who has done so much to ease the pains of parturition and to bring this labor of love into the world.

It has been a joy to walk the path with so many wonderful companions. I thank you one and all.

Marcia Moore
Ojai, California

Introduction

The purpose of this book is to show that you can recall your former lifetimes and can help others to do likewise. Hypersentience is a method of inducing an altered state of consciousness which affords valuable new insights into the nature of man and the universe. As such, it is very similar to meditation. The technique can be practiced by any open-minded investigator. All that is required is respect for the power of the human mind and common sense. I have tried to impart all that I know of this safe, easy, and uncomplicated system because my experience has shown that people are capable of putting it to good use.

Most of the thousands of subjects with whom I have worked feel that they have achieved a fuller knowledge and appreciation of themselves by means of hypersentience. Their success has enabled me to spend the last two years traveling about the United States regressing individuals, lecturing, and conducting hypersentience workshops. While demonstrating the technique to groups of fifteen to twenty people at a time I have always found plenty of volunteers who were able to recapitulate prenatal existences, even with an audience looking on. Virtually all of them found the experience beneficial.

It should be understood from the start that I am not setting out to prove that reincarnation is a fact of nature, even though I firmly believe that it is. A superabundance of evidence in support of this theory already exists, much of which has been summed up in my book *Reincarnation, Key to Immortality*. Anyone who craves strict scientific validation can study the material published by such authorities as Ian Stevenson, M.D., Francis Story, and Jeffrey Furst. Consequently, I have not felt the need of taking on this task.

Essentially, the problem of verification lies not in accumulating more numerous and stringent "proofs" of reincarnation but rather in persuading skeptics to consider what has already been made known. Having observed that many people's social conditioning makes it impossible for them to survey the evidence for the survival of death with an unprejudiced eye, I have now taken a new tack. It can be futile to try to persuade a blind man of the existence of stars if he is convinced that the sky is a solid black canopy one hundred feet high. To an earthbound nature stars make very little sense. But if an operation could be performed to restore the blind man's sight, further debate would be unnecessary. One could simply take him by the hand, lead him out under the night sky, and say, "Look up."

My mission has been to popularize an operative procedure which enables people to open the eye of their inner vision. Then they may see the truth for themselves and marvel at the beauty of the evolutionary plan which makes man a creature who can aspire to more exalted states of being.

In this respect it is particularly important to emphasize that I am not dealing with a religious issue, The truth or falsity of the reincarnation hypothesis has little to do with religion. It is not a question of faith or belief but of logic, reason, and firsthand experience. Once existing information on the subject has become common knowledge theologians may make of it what they will—as a natural, not a supernatural, phenomenon. People will then find that it seems perfectly natural that they should live forever.

The issue of verifying that the hypersentient impressions which flash through people's minds are memories of actual happenings simply isn't very important at this stage of our research. Too much time has already been lost because skeptics have been so fearful of being deluded that they have refused to look at what would otherwise be acknowledged as an extraordinary capacity of the human mind. In this they have been like silver miners ignoring a uranium deposit because they have not yet learned how to deal with a strange metal.

Even when the images brought to the surface during a hypersensing session are only symbolic they are nonetheless legitimate communications from the subconscious mind. As such, they deserve to be heard. Some accounts take form as dreamlike fantasies while others have an ineffable ring of truth. Some bubble up from just below the surface of daily awareness, while others arise from recondite recesses of the psyche. But each and every offering should be accepted as a meaningful expression of that individual's inner being.

Throughout this text I have refrained from deleting concepts put forth by our subjects, even when details of their accounts seem to involve the violation of accepted physical laws, or contain terms to which we cannot now relate. For example, a description of a long-lost civilization mentions that a "people reproduced by the star system." What that system is, I cannot at this point imagine, but my experience has shown that often these incidental details are confirmed and elaborated by other independent sources. Above all else, I have tried to remain nonjudgmental in attitude as I transmit that which has been said with minimal editing.

For me, the real joy of this work has stemmed from the fact that the development of the system presented here has been a *group* achievement. Virtually all that has been accomplished is the result of the combined efforts of many little-known people without special training or credentials—people like most of you who read this book. We have a right to know who and what we are and to acquire this information for ourselves. We need no intermediaries, no one to tell us what can or can't be done, to fill our minds with needless fears or play upon our lack of confidence. Rather, we need to be strong and bold and free in our pursuit of broader mental horizons.

The search for our own souls may be the most important enterprise we ever undertake. Now, if you will read on, I will try to cast some light upon this process of consciously controlled self-knowing.

HYPERSENTIENCE

1

HYPERSENTIENCE—
WHAT IT CAN DO

A young man who attended one of my hypersensing workshops had long been sensitive about the left side of his neck. When possible he wore a scarf or turtleneck shirt. If anyone touched him in this area, he cringed visibly.

During his regression session we discovered that he had been a wine-guzzling, womanizing captain during the French Revolution. Although he himself was not an aristocrat he had been found guilty by association and condemned to the guillotine. As the knife descended he turned his head to look upward, catching a glimpse of the falling blade just before it hit the side of his neck.

Evidently the shock of the knife-blade's ghastly impact made a deep impression upon the permanent recesses of his soul's memory bank. There the experience continued to haunt his dreams until this persistent ghost of the past was exorcised by bringing it into the light of conscious awareness.

Surprisingly, the simple act of exhuming a repressed memory, either from this life or from a previous incarnation, will in many cases alleviate its adverse effects. Literally, *to relive is to relieve*. This is a cardinal principle of all psychotherapy.

An attractive middle-aged woman once told me that during most of her adult life she had suffered from a gnawing pain in her side. Not until her gall bladder had been needlessly removed did she discover that in a previous life she had been a quick-tempered swordsman who, in a fit of anger, had killed a friend in a duel. As the swordsman, she had run a rapier through her opponent's side, causing him a lingering death. Had she perceived the cause of her discomfort at an earlier date she might have been less insistent in her subconscious determination to induce a surgeon to thrust a blade into the same area of her body.

On the positive side, a fiftyish woman insists that she has no musical talent, yet she practices the piano two hours every morning. Her explanation for this solitary pursuit is that in her next life she wishes to be born with the skill to become an accomplished musician.

Although many people think that they enter life as brand-new human beings, this does not seem to be the case. Like it or not, we are conditioned by submerged memories of prior existences. It is my belief, and the thesis of this book, that thoughtful individuals can redeem the past and create a brighter future by means of the technique to which I have given the name "hypersentience."

TERMINOLOGY

"Hypersentience" derives from the prefix *hyper* meaning "above," "beyond," or "super," and from the word *sentience,* meaning a condition of sensory awareness.

The state of being hypersentient involves a finely tuned capacity for response that transcends the realm of the physical senses. Hypersensory perception includes visual images, emotional reactions, intellectual concepts, and intuitive realizations. It may involve the actual reexperiencing of another existence (as in a vivid dream) or the detached observation of a succession of mentally registered pictures (like watching a movie). In the great majority of instances the subject remains fully aware of his present personality and circumstances, even while opening up to the inflow of impressions from realms of consciousness normally beyond his ken.

Although hypersentience may evoke memories of previous incarnations, it is not exclusively preoccupied with the past. The individual who sets out to explore the uncharted realms of his own psyche, and of the mind of the universe, endeavors to enter a dimension of wholeness which contains the archetypal plan of the kind of human being he may become. He recollects the way he has traveled but he faces the future which holds the promise of his innate potential for self-fulfillment. He is a seed seeking a vision of its own flowering. Thus he looks back to his origins in order to move forward with faith, hope, and the will to actualize his highest aspirations.

The person serving as a guide in this cooperative endeavor is called the *facilitator.* The subject is called the *sensor.* When the sensor enters an altered state of consciousness we speak of him as being in a *meditative posture.*

When the hypersensory reverie involves the recapitulation of bygone times, it has proven convenient to call these probings of the past *regression sessions.* While being regressed the sensor is enabled to recapture memories pertaining to his present life and also to remember the events of what appear to be former incarnations. Because the word "regression" has negative connotations for some people we often use the term *retrocognition.* Thus we speak of taking a *retrotrip* or of a *retrocognitive* experience.

THE PURPOSES OF HYPERSENTIENCE

Why should people want to know who they were in the past—or what they may become? Although no one should have to justify the desire for increased self-knowledge, there are many reasons why individuals choose to experiment along these lines. In brief, the purposes of hypersentience encompass the following overlapping areas.

  a. *Problem-solving*—a method for upgrading the quality of daily living.
  b. *Educational*—a means for increasing our knowledge of history, psychology, parapsychology, and cosmology.
  c. *Spiritual*—a way of consciousness expansion and self-realization.

As I proceed to give a brief overview of the various directions in which our investigations have proceeded, it is of the utmost importance for the reader to realize that hypersentience is a subject which must be approached holistically. In modern culture there is a tendency to classify science, psychology, education, history, philosophy, religion, etc., into separate, mutually exclusive categories. For example, an individual might say, "Well, I am scientifically oriented, and remembering former lifetimes falls into the province of religion. Therefore I want no part of it." Alternatively he might explain, "I want to know who I was but I'm not interested in abstract explanations of why people reincarnate."

Consequently, the following discussion of the practical and theoretical benefits of hypersentience may seem to toss an odd assortment of items into one basket. Beginning with the practical, I will illustrate some of the therapeutic benefits of the system, touching on the uses of the power of suggestion, the development of tolerance and an appreciation of the sensitivity of infants, and the possibilities of spiritual refreshment and recreation. The discussion will then explore the opening up of new vistas of history, cosmology, and exobiology. Moving on to more profound metaphysical issues, we will turn our attention to the eradication of the fear of death and to a brief exposition of the law of karma, speaking finally of the quest for personal integration and spiritual inspiration.

By this time it should be apparent that hypersentience is, and must be, as large as life itself. It is to be hoped, therefore, that the reader will bear in mind that each of the many facets of this discipline acquires meaning in relation to the others because all are aspects of a single whole.

THERAPEUTIC TECHNIQUE

The most immediate application of hypersentience lies in the area of problem-solving. Trying to eradicate certain psychological difficulties without going below the surface of consciousness can be like fighting crabgrass with a lawnmower. Through hypersensory perception an individual can broaden his awareness to include not only the immediate causes of his problems, but also the deeper causes of the causes. Usually, the farther he can dig down to the roots of his ingrained attitudes and expectations the better his chances of benefiting by the knowledge he has acquired. With the help of a sympathetic facilitator, the sensor can achieve a more profound understanding of his present situation and move forward in the light of a greater awareness of the vision and intent of the "high self" which constitutes his primary guide.

The extent to which the sensor uses the information gained to overcome his hangups is entirely up to him. Some are content to gain one small glimmer of illumination, while others aim at nothing less than liberation from the relentlessly spinning wheel of repeated embodiments. For all, the recollection of former existences leads to less materialistic modes of thought and to an enhanced appreciation of the power of the mind.

The world is indebted to the promulgators of psychoanalytic theory for the widespread dissemination of the concept that therapeutic benefits may derive from the recollection of long-forgotten traumas. If a seamstress inadvertently knots a thread, the line will catch with every stitch. Repeatedly the thread must be tugged through the cloth, thereby causing irritation and delay. Usually the only way to remedy the difficulty is to go back and remove the offending knot.

One individual who was enabled to deal constructively with a present problem by delving into the past was an attractive young woman who by current standards can be called a nymphomaniac. During a regression session she discovered that thousands of years ago she had been a priestess in a Middle Eastern fertility temple. Stretched naked upon a fur-covered block of stone, her body a living altar, it was her sacred duty to receive the men who sought her out. Symbolically, she was the earth goddess awaiting the sowing of the seed which would cause her people's crops to flourish. At that time she did her work conscientiously and found it deeply satisfying.

At present she is subconsciously convinced that she has a sacred obligation to bestow her sexual favors on any man who makes a pass at her. She still does the job well, but finds to her dismay that in this profane society there is far less appreciation of the selfless spirit in which she offers her body to all who request her services.

There were, however, other lifetimes during which she was trained to direct her physical energies into dancing, massage, and the preparation of herbal concoctions. By continuing to develop these more acceptable talents she has now found her niche as an assistant in a health spa. Sexually she is still a swinger, but her compliancy has lost much of its compulsive undertone.

The variations are endless, but somehow each soul seems to know which lives to explore in order to cast light upon the problems of the present.

THE POWER OF SUGGESTION

The technique of hypersentience is so easily applied that it can help people to appreciate the importance of introducing positive suggestions into their everyday conversations. When an individual realizes the extent to which words can hurt or heal he becomes more likely to filter and purify his verbal output.

For example, consumers who understand the power of speech will be more sensitive to the effects of advertising. No longer will buyers respond to the false promises of hucksters who promote disease-producing products. At least, such people can avoid being seduced by unscrupulous word merchants, political demagogues, and religious fanatics.

A friend of mine was driving her car over a remote country road when her ten-year-old son fell out and broke his arm in two places. To compound the difficulty, he has a type of blood that does not easily clot. On the long bumpy ride to the hospital, she was able to quiet him by using the same relaxing phrases we had practiced together during numerous regression sessions. By the time they obtained medical treatment the doctor was astonished to find the boy calm and self-possessed.

Sooner or later most people are confronted with tension-producing situations in which it is helpful to have some training in the art of suggestion. A fearful child must be prepared for a trip to the dentist, an insomniac needs a soothing verbal massage, or an irate man must be persuaded not to punch his antagonist in the face. In such situations something more than cheerful banalities are required. To be in command of a method of quieting distraught people and of bringing them to their senses may often be more useful than a closet full of tranquilizers.

SPIRITUAL REFRESHMENT

At one time I conducted a series of hypersensing sessions with a recently divorced woman who was feeling sorely oppressed by lack of money, poor health, a ramshackle house, and three whining little children. The last thing she needed was any more distress. In order to provide a respite we would take retrotrips through some of the more enjoyable episodes of her previous lives. As a means of much-needed recreation it was cheaper and more convenient than going to the movies.

Although hypersensing is a serious business, the technique may be used simply to provide a break from the rigors of life on the mundane plane. Many times I have said to a distraught person, "Let us go back to the time when you were happiest and most successful," and then allowed him to provide his own entertainment. Even in depressed times no one is too poor to open a window to the wonders of the world within by calling upon his powers of creative visualization. A receptive subject can induce a high without recourse to drugs or alcohol. Moreover, this self-induced lift will be followed by an afterglow rather than a hangover.

It is not always necessary to depend on memories of previous lifetimes to see a hypersensory picture show. This account, submitted by Lillian Germain of Kenosha, Wisconsin, shows what may happen when the mind is given free rein.

THE TEMPLE OF LIGHT

Marcia was telling me to go through the time tunnel, and that I would see a light at the end. I did so, and as I came out I looked for someone to guide me. Then I saw a beautiful golden angel coming toward me from the sky. She alighted near me and smiled in a very loving way. She was glowing with an inner light and had a long golden robe that reached to her feet. Her wings were folded and lay over her shoulders and back. She had large luminous green eyes and a benevolent, serene face framed by flowing golden hair. The overall effect was of golden light with the angel at its center.

I asked her if she was my guide and she said yes. She told me to hold out my hand, and as I did so we rose into the air and began flying. There were mountains nearby and we flew into a long dark cave that seemed unending. Suddenly we came out into a blinding light and stopped before an enormous structure that looked like a temple. I asked what it was called and she told me it was the Temple of Light!

The outer facade was glowing like white marble and there were many doors that looked as though they were made of different kinds of metals. They were gold, silver, bronze, and some I did not know. I was very eager to enter, and I heard Marcia ask me if we could go in. The angel smiled and gestured toward the golden door telling me to enter.

Moving on through the opening I was overwhelmed with the sound of sweet singing and a feeling of peace and love. There seemed to be a great hall filled with many beings dressed in various colored robes. Some were conferring with one another in small groups and others were moving toward different rooms that lined the area. Each one was surrounded by an aura that seemed to match the colors of his robe.

Next we went toward an open space that seemed to be a garden filled with flowers and birds. In the center was a fountain where some lovely beings were laughing and talking. As I approached they made room for me and inquired if I was well. I asked them if I was dead and they laughed with a gay tinkling sound and told me I had never been more alive!

I was then informed that this was my home between lives and that I had been here many times before. The reason I had reincarnated was because of ego problems that could only be worked out in an earthly existence. I then asked to talk to one of the high ones and was ushered into a small chapel.

This time I immediately recognized an old and dear teacher and knelt at his feet in quiet peace and respect. This learned one wore a green robe and no longer incarnated on the Earth plane. I was lifted up and we sat in a lovely alcove where we could hear chanting and prayer bells in the background. As we sat and talked I realized how familiar the temple was and began to remember many things about it.

The rooms were of colored light with no walls as we think of them. Many tasks were being carried on by the souls who inhabited this place of light. Healing, teaching, learning, composing, painting, and all the creative arts were being taught.

There was a room of souls who had passed over violently through accidents, suicides, or murders. They were placed on shelves like long drawers and were being tended by some highly evolved ones so that when they awakened they would not be frightened or confused. A sort of sleep learning was in progress and it seemed as though they were using sound or vibrations to produce the desired effects.

There was a huge library of books where many beings were reading and studying. Some of the books were written in symbols and colors. There was no noise or confusion in this area; they seemed to be communicating through thought.

I was attracted to an inner room that glowed with an intense blue violet light and asked my teacher if I could speak with the great one within. He gave his permission and as I entered I realized that what I thought was a being was really only light with cosmic intelligence.

It is very difficult to describe the emotions that swept over me as I stood in the presence of this great force of life. I knew that there was still much to learn and that I would have to go back to the Earth again, but it didn't upset me. This was truly my home and I would always return to this sacred place. The lessons were important for my growth, but the day *would* come when I would never have to leave this Temple of Light.

I am an unending force of life and there is nothing to fear by changing forms or places. The essential core of me is immortal and growing toward this knowledge. There is only life, and it is beautiful!

TOLERANCE

One benefit of a belief in reincarnation is increased tolerance for personal idiosyncrasies. Many apparently irrational attitudes, phobias, fetishes, and compulsions can be explained in terms of previous life experiences. Again and again we have encountered subjects who have converted memories of dying by fire into an unreasoning fear of conflagrations. Indeed, inborn phobic reactions can more often be comprehended in terms of reincarnation than in terms of the prevailing psychological assumption that owing to early traumas the child produced these complexes out of the murky convolutions of the subconscious mind.

Erudite psychologists often insist that such a straightforward explanation is "simplistic" and consequently not to be believed. To us, however, it seems perfectly reasonable that ex-Egyptians should cherish cats, that a man tossed into a snake pit should still fear serpents, and that a child killed by a bomb in World War II should carry over a fear of loud noises.

On the positive side, many affinities can also be traced to prenatal events. Thus it does not seem surprising that a group of reincarnated American Indians should, as hippies, start a movement back to their once cherished land. Indeed, if the hippies *were* Indians, why shouldn't they wear beads, live in teepees, and eschew many of our modern artifices?

Even when a complex appears to have originated in the present lifetime, it may have more distant antecedents. For example, two children are frightened by a narrow escape from drowning. Yet only one retains a fear of the water. It then turns out that the one who overreacted drowned in a shipwreck a hundred years earlier.

One case in which knowledge of the past led to a more compassionate understanding of another human being is that of a young unmarried woman who, despite the easy availability of contraceptive devices, allowed herself to become pregnant by a married man whose affection for her was never more than tepid. On hearing of her condition he immediately washed his hands of the affair. Consequently, she was obliged to go on welfare.

Some people might consider her conduct morally irresponsible, especially in view of the tightening population squeeze and the uncertainties of life in the late twentieth century. What right had she to add to the public tax burden at a time when hardworking citizens are pressed to the limit?

After one retrotrip, however, the issue appeared in a different light. In a previous existence she had desperately wanted a child but had miscarried repeatedly. Owing to her inability to produce an heir, her marriage disintegrated and she was left bereft of companionship. Little wonder, then, that in this lifetime she was willing to sacrifice so much in order to have a baby of her own.

Another instance in which knowledge led to understanding is that of a young woman who is passionately fond of dogs. Although the cost of dog food puts a severe strain on her budget she has two large dogs and would like to adopt a puppy. In view of her modest circumstances some might say this is hardly sensible behavior. However, her first retrotrip cast a new light upon the situation.

In a former life this girl saw herself as a Japanese maiden named Sensu. When we came upon her, Sensu was about to make a three-day journey from the coast where she had been visiting her lover, a fisherman, to her family home in the mountains. The road was rugged and she was obliged to travel alone.

When we told Sensu that she was arriving at her place of residence she insisted, "I never got there." As it happened, Sensu became too ill to travel and collapsed by the roadside. Night was coming on and she feared that she might die there by herself. Then she said, "Someone is coming to comfort me."

"Who is this person? Is it someone you know?"

"It's a dog. He wags his tail and licks my face. He's trying to keep me warm. He wants to comfort me."

Sensu's faithful canine friend remained with her throughout that long, lonesome night until at last she awakened and found herself in the light.

A wasted life, one might think, yet the love of dogs retained to the present has enlarged her soul.

APPRECIATION OF INFANT SENSITIVITY

One of the most important findings to grow out of our hypersensory research is the realization that infants are far more cognizant of the world around them than was formerly deemed possible. On the strength of his work in regression therapy, the psychiatrist Denys Kelsey speaks in impassioned terms of the shock that can be inflicted upon an infant's sensitive psyche by circumcision. According to many accounts, even unborn babies have some awareness of their circumstances and know whether or not they are wanted.

One subject, on being asked to bring up a very early memory, reported that she was in the center of a round red room. After she woke up we questioned her about the experience. "Oh!" she exclaimed, "that was the womb."

A thought-provoking story passed on to us by a colleague is that of a hopelessly autistic child whose alienation from his surroundings was virtually complete. However, one therapist succeeded in establishing enough rapport to regress him to the period immediately following his birth. At this point the child could only writhe and moan, "The light, the light, the light!"

Subsequent questioning revealed that he had been born prematurely and kept in an incubator for several weeks. During the entire time a light was kept shining so that the hospital personnel could keep him under surveillance.

It is now known that constant exposure to light can shatter the nervous systems of hardy adults. This is, in fact, an effective means of torture. Yet in many hospitals vulnerable infants are still subjected to this treatment.

Even the childhood experiences of past lives may exert a powerful emotional impact. When I first regressed my friend Cherokee Gorden, she saw herself in a cradle with her mother bending over her. On being asked what her mother called her she said, "Sweetie." Thereupon she burst into tears.

It turned out that Sweetie's mother had been killed by Indians when the child was still an infant, and somehow the baby knew it. The little girl, whose real name was Kate, died at the age of eleven of scarlet fever. Yet Sweetie's shock and sense of loss were enough to make a mature woman weep two centuries later.

NEW HISTORICAL PERSPECTIVES

A sensor once recalled being a little girl in Tibet whose grandfather showed her a treasure trove of ancient manuscripts stored in a Himalayan cave. No one else knew of this hiding place. Unfortunately, the girl died at the age of fourteen, and with her was buried the secret of the cave.

Again and again we read historical accounts of books being lost, libraries burned, and teachers killed before they could transmit their knowledge. Civilizations have vanished without a trace and whole continents have been submerged. Now, however, we realize that nothing that has existed can ever really be lost. Whatever has been known can be known again—re-created directly out of the mind of the universe.

Traditions become hidebound and should rightly die, but their essence can be reborn. The soul of man's accumulated learning has its own immortality and it too seeks periodic expression through groups of human transmitters.

Often our subjects speak of basking in the light of wisdom, much as a cat might stretch out in a pool of sunshine. On higher levels this perfect understanding can be directly absorbed, thus obviating the necessity to stock the brain with superfluous information.

With hypersentience scholars can acquire many new insights into the past. For example, the noted clairvoyant Joan Grant has published a series of historical novels based upon her intuitive recall of previous existences. The contemporary author Kathleen Jenks is also drawing heavily on her intuitive faculties in composing her three-volume magnum opus on the life of Moses.

While Kathleen was visiting me in Ojai, California, I was able to put her in touch with my friend Isabel Buell, who independently corroborated much of the material about the various women in Moses' life. Coincidentally, I had regressed a young man named Robert Thomas who had spoken of Moses and described the parting of the Red Sea. Here is an excerpt from Kathleen's account of her first meeting with me.

> My mention of Moses reminded Marcia that she had had a subject a week earlier who had been one of the many nameless people on the Exodus. "Not too much of interest came out of that regression," she commented casually. "But he did say one thing which surprised me. He said Moses had blue eyes."
>
> "Blue," I asked blankly, staring at her.
>
> "Yes, blue as a robin's egg, he said. It struck me as odd."
>
> "Oh my God," I said, feeling a sudden excitement surge through me. It was, of course, extremely far-fetched for Moses to have had blue eyes. It would have been plausible at the time of Christ because of the increase in racial intermingling under the Romans. But in Moses' day, more than a thousand years earlier, it was highly unlikely. Yet almost from the earliest versions of my book I had given Moses blue eyes.
>
> I could not explain why. I had not merely *mentioned* that his eyes were blue, but had woven that strange fact in and out of core scenes in my novel. The eyes were blue, the color of a kitten's still-blind eyes. People found it difficult to lie to the shy Moses because of some mysterious quality in his eyes.
>
> Every time I started a revision of the book I determined to give Moses brown eyes. "You've got to get rid of those blue eyes, Jenks," I would lecture myself sternly. "If you don't, you know what *Time*'s literary critic is going to say. Imagine the *scorn* you'll face! He's going to say something like this: 'For openers, Ms. Jenks permits herself the self-indulgent fancy of a blue-eyed Moses. After that, this reviewer finds it impossible to take the rest of her work seriously.'
>
> "That's what they're going to say, Jenks. So get rid of those blue eyes."
>
> So ran my thoughts each time I began a new revision. But after seven years of arguing with myself, Moses still has blue eyes in my novel. So when Marcia mentioned the color of his eyes I felt my trip to Ojai was worth it for that alone.

A year later I met Wilma Cooper from Hull, Massachusetts. In the course of a casual conversation Wilma happened to mention that she had once been regressed and had found herself living at the time when the children of Israel were fleeing from Egypt. Like Kathleen and Bob, Wilma recollected Moses as a shy person of relatively short stature who was not too pleased with the job thrust upon him.

"Was there anything special about his face?" I asked.

"Yes," Wilma replied. "He had remarkable blue eyes. He could influence people because of the look in those eyes."

When I mentioned these coincidences in the September 1975 issue of my *Hypersentience Bulletin* still another report came in from a reader who had also had a subject who spoke of a blue-eyed Moses. Can it be, I wondered, that the original Children of Israel have incarnated as a group here in America? In any event these stories suggest a new approach to the study of the evolution of mankind.

One of our current projects involves the writing of the unknown history of astrology. This material, drawn from many independent sources, will eventually be condensed into a single volume which, it is hoped, will serve as a companion piece to my historical survey entitled *The Astrological Tradition*. Some helpful information along these lines has been given by Margaret Millard, M.D., a pediatrician, acupuncturist, and astrologer currently practicing in Windham, Maine.

Margaret's second retrotrip took her back to an embodiment as an astrologer in a desertlike land in the Near East—presumably Babylonia. She (then a he) and a companion were observing the stars from a conical pyramid whose walls rose high around them so that they were looking out from the depths of an open-topped building. Clad in voluminous white garments as a cover against the dust of the desert, they were making notations with a stylus. With the aid of an instrument resembling a pendulum, they were measuring time by observing the passage of stars over the meridian. In addition, they took careful note of the colors of the stars. Thus, if a child of royalty was born with a red star rising, he was trained to be a warrior. If a yellow star was rising, he was trained to be an intellectual. If a blue star was rising, he was trained to be an administrator.

At the time when this information was given I had never heard of using star colors for prognostication. Later I discovered that this was a common practice among Oriental stargazers.

When we first looked in on these two young men, they were part of a group of about twelve novices who were being trained by the chief astrologer. Ordinarily just one student would be designated to succeed the chief who served as advisor to the king. In this case, however, two were chosen. Owing to his lack of manual dexterity, Margaret's former personality did not achieve the top position. But since he was a superior interpreter he was retained along with another student who had the requisite technical skill. Thenceforth the two worked harmoniously together, each one becoming renowned for his special capabilities.

In her present life Margaret identifies her companion in the observatory with our much-respected colleague Robert Pelletier who has recently published two well received astrological textbooks.

THE ORIGIN OF MAN

For years, those of us who have experimented with regression recall as a means of demonstrating the soul's survival of death have been perplexed by the manner in which subjects kept dragging up reminiscences of exotic civilizations that did not fit in with any known historical epoch. For a while we simply overlooked these maverick memories, but then as we went further back these anomalous cases started to become the rule. Repeatedly, people spoke in detail about Atlantis, Lemuria, and other hypothetical cultures. Frequently their accounts corroborated one another. It appears, for example, that flying machines were well known in the remote past, especially in Atlantis. Indeed, numerous former Atlanteans seem to be in incarnation at this time, presumably because of the many similarities between the era leading to the destruction of that mighty continent and the present world crisis.

Curiously enough, most subjects, when pushed back to the inception of their career on this planet, do not envision hulking humanoids rising out of the kingdom of the apes. More often they speak of angelic "light beings" descending to Earth from higher realms. Several times when the phrase "light being" was used the sensors seemed uncertain whether the second word was "being" or "beam."

When I asked my friend Akeva to go back to the dawn of history he said, "I see lava—everything is covered with lava. Where everything was black it is now starting to be green."

"Now go forward to the time when people appeared."

"Five hundred sixty-two thousand years ago. There seem to be beams of light. The forms are coming down out of these light beams. They come to life when they touch the Earth. All different forms are coming down the light beams. Some are humanoid and some are animals."

A few subjects have traced their origins to a musical note, or to a realm of pure vibratory impulses. Many have spoken of other planets whose cultures cannot in any way be correlated with human history. Often it appears that these alien spheres became unfit to sustain life. Consequently, their inhabitants found it necessary to migrate elsewhere.

We also have descriptions of luminous mist-enshrouded islands whose ethereal inhabitants live close to the heart of nature. Evidently a nostalgic yearning for a golden age of myth and fairy tale still stirs the imaginations of numerous people. From the viewpoint of the physical body Charles Darwin may have been correct in his theory of the ascent of man out of the primordial slime. From the standpoint of the soul, however, our evidence suggests that man is no mere amoeba that made good; he is more like an angel fallen from a high estate to his present puny plight.

Now, as we accumulate data, it is possible to compare notes concerning various prehistoric epochs and to put people who have had similar experiences in touch with one another. We have followed the adventures of the culture-bearers of many lands, explored the pyramids and the Sphinx, observed exotic rituals in Indian temples, Druidic groves, and Peruvian mountain retreats, and have participated in the daily lives of a multitude of ordinary people who have labored obscurely to survive a few years on the face of this planet. Truly, this has been a way to comprehend in the deepest, most poignant sense what it means to be human.

Eventually, systematically compiled historical accounts will utilize the vast wealth of material which can be elicited from the deeper reaches of man's mind. Descriptions of long-vanished cultures will be correlated and out of this mass of information will be refined the pure gold of everliving truth concerning the development of consciousness on Earth.

A NEW COSMOLOGY

The widely demonstrated ability to recollect details of previous lives seems to show that memory is not strictly a function of the physical brain cells. Clearly, the brain must be more than a storehouse; it must also be a radio receiving set. To search for programs inside the apparatus is largely fruitless, even though it does have a memory bank. Basically, however, the state of attunement is far more important than the data fed into the mechanism. A true appreciation of this concept could revolutionize the field of education!

The student of hypersentience is drawn inexorably to the conclusion that the universe itself has a memory—the *akashic records* of which occultists have long spoken—and that this "big computer in the sky" is far more than a passive recording device. Somehow the balance sheet is continually updated so that the past endures to shape the future, even while that which exists as a spiritual potential (like the flower within the seed) exerts its forward pull.

Hence, the realm of causation embraces both the past and the future, that which has been and that which strives to be made manifest.

Some sensors have described the place where the akashic records are stored as a vast multitiered library. Occasionally it is possible to peruse one of the books of lives in which each incarnation is a page, but first permission must be gained either from the subject's high self or from the custodians of the records.

Much of the material in the akashic vaults is classified and can be shown only to those who have earned the right to fathom the deeper secrets of the universe.

The following description, composed by Violet Gillfillan of Oxnard, California, represents just one of the numerous cases in which a sensor identifies the akashic records with an actual place.

A VISIT TO THE CELESTIAL LIBRARY

While working with Marcia Moore I entered a state of consciousness during which I had the sensation of being transported to a familiar place. Yet it was so magnificent, so full of portent, so far beyond my comprehension that I found it hard to accept with my conscious mind.

I was led into a large and beautiful circular room with smooth, stark marble walls. In the center someone was sitting on a dais but the light around this being was so bright I couldn't raise my head to look. I felt like an unworthy interloper.

Then I became aware of a long corridor that appeared to have no ending. On either side of this majestic hallway were tiered shelves, all very neatly and elegantly inlaid with inscriptions describing their contents.

The personage who was serving as my guide was wearing a garment of starry iridescence. She was so lovely and familiar she seemed like someone who had long been dear to me. She was holding a huge volume bound in white and lettered in gold. The words were written in a strange script. The message I received was that this was the Book of Life and that I was being shown the record of human souls.

Although I could read these ancient words they were beyond my comprehension. I was informed, however, that in the future I could return by myself and learn of the events due to take place in our world. This knowledge would come to me in order to be passed on. Little messages like jewels would emerge from my consciousness to be given to the young souls coming in.

My beloved guide reassured me that all would be well. I wanted to go with her but the time wasn't right. Then the light grew brighter as my friend withdrew down the long corridor. I felt the tears on my face as I stretched my arms across the span of space and time. I wanted to sing praises and kneel humbly in reverence to the Holy One. Could I, who am so unworthy, be this privileged? Had I really gone through those enormous golden doors into that celestial library?

Yes, there was a message to be relayed to the light bearers whom we know as world servers.

Thank you, God. Thy universe is a "heavenly place" full of wonders more sublime than anyone can know—until you unlock the Golden Doors to the kingdom within.

If, therefore, the universe has a memory it must also have a mind, a heart, and a soul. Above all else, it must have a Self. It is this vast "I am," with which every self-aware entity can achieve a sympathetic rapport. However, the finer degrees of attunement can come only through the renunciation of personal egotism which enables an individual to identify with the will of the One Creator.

The cosmos is quite capable of knowing what it is doing, and why. The technique of hypersentience is one way of endeavoring to align our small intellects with the intelligence that fabricated the universe. Thus we become conscious cooperators with the design of the larger organism in whom all sentient creatures live and move and have their being.

EXOBIOLOGY

Exobiology is the study of the life that exists beyond the confines of Earth. Formerly, it was mainly a matter of theory to conjecture that intelligent beings might inhabit other spheres or dimensions of the universe. Philosophically many thinkers accept the idea that even the seemingly empty spaces between the stars may be part of the body of an all-pervading Divine Mind. Theosophists have long spoken of a series of "globes" existing both successively and concurrently in subtle planes of matter.

More recently, the publicity given to unidentified flying objects had caused people to wonder if extraterrestrial observers are surveying the Earth. Were there once "chariots of the gods," which at the dawn of history brought in missionaries from other star systems? Did these sojourners instruct and uplift the barbarous human race? Is there, as some occultists claim, a hierarchy of superior beings who guide the destinies of men?

An effective stimulus to the theory that outsiders are even now among us is the attention being paid to an Israeli psychic, Uri Geller. According to Uri's biographer Andrija Puharich, this young man has been chosen as a spokesman by a species of highly evolved entities who keep an eye not only on the Earth but also on a flock of other life-bearing spheres. They are, in a sense, gardeners who cultivate what they find, but who scrupulously refrain from interfering with the inner structure of the living beings under their care. Whether large or small, each divinely conceived organism must grow in its own image. It may be watered and weeded, but should not be arbitrarily manipulated by alien minds.

The most remarkable aspect of the Uri phenomenon is the apparent ability of others to replicate Uri's accomplishments. Throughout the world stories are coming to light about ordinary people, including children, who can bend objects and manipulate watches by the power of their minds. Something mysterious is certainly happening even though there is no consensus as to what it is.

The increasingly widespread practice of regression-recall has also given enormous impetus to the "visitors-from-other-dimensions" theory. Moreover, anyone can set out to explore these inner spaces of meta-awareness, whereas there isn't much that isolated individuals can do to lure in the flying saucers.

Even in the relatively short time we have been working on the subject our research group has accumulated enough material on extraterrestrials (or as we prefer to call them, inner-dimensionals) to fill a substantial volume.

THE ERADICATION OF THE FEAR OF DEATH

We hope that the widespread promulgation of the technique of hypersentience will help to banish once and for all the ancient specter of death which has for so long shadowed human thinking. At last the hour has struck for those who know the truth to step forward and dissipate the sick superstition that existence ends with the grave. The very thought of the progress that could be made once people assume that they are due to move on into higher realms is mind boggling. If this ailing civilization is to be healed of its contagious selfishness and greed, then there must be an appreciation of the fact that every individual is, in essence, an immortal soul who is accountable for his own actions and who will endure to face the positive and negative consequences of all he does or fails to do.

On the physical level the root problem of this planet is overpopulation. Hunger, pollution, aggression—all stem directly from the drive of too many people to compete for the world's dwindling resources. *There can, however, be no birth control without death control.* As long as human beings seek a spurious immortality through the overproduction of progeny, or refuse to limit their families because they fear killing something that has never been born, then war, famine, and pestilence will have to cut them down.

Today, millions of people are laden with guilt because they have found it necessary to condone abortions. Is it fair that a woman should have to think, "I have killed my baby," when there was no tolerable alternative? How much easier it might be for her if she believed that the noble human soul need not move into a wretched hovel where it is not wanted. It can just as easily wait and enter a house where it will be a welcome guest. In this universe of limitless time and space, there is room for all who are willing to work within their proper sphere.

A new perspective on death may also ease the inevitable act of relinquishment which terminates our span of years on Earth. So much of medical science has been devoted not to the prolongation of living but to the prolongation of dying that for victims of terminal diseases and their relatives the final passing is a never-to-be-forgotten horror. Whole families are impoverished by the death and burial expenses of one member, while valuable land is deformed into ugly, nonproductive cemeteries. Too often physically and mentally defective babies are forced to linger on in pain when merciful nature would have permitted them to return to life in healthy new bodies.

During our regression sessions we make it a point to take the sensor through his departure from the body, and often through many deaths. In virtually every instance the immortal self is delighted to be free—so much so that it seems as though people should mourn births and celebrate dying. Not only is the transition from this plane to the next one of our most practiced activities, it can also be our most joyous awakening.

Even children seem not a whit dismayed by the remembrance of a violent demise. Eleven-year-old Gregory Bozzani of Capistrano Beach, California, vividly recalled being bested by a lion in a gladiatorial contest in ancient Rome. Far from being perturbed by the sight of his mauled body lying in the dust, he was proud of his own fearlessness—a quality he has carried over into the present life. He will always know that no matter what dangers he may encounter, win or lose, the essential part of himself will endure.

The impression that emerges from many hundreds of regression sessions is that in bygone times people used to die far more gracefully than they do today. Perhaps in those rugged eras there was less will to cling to an outworn body, for rarely is there an account of anyone struggling against the final passing. More typical is the description given by a man who clearly remembered an incarnation as a priest in the Peruvian highlands. When it was his time to die, he sat down for his usual early morning meditation and invited the cold to enter his body. Gradually he became colder and more numb until finally he rose painlessly up out of the top of his head and was free.

One of the many reasons why it is essential for humanity to know that death is not a catastrophe is the possibility that in the near future people will be exterminated by the millions. The present insane proliferation of populations guarantees major conflicts of interest, while psychically sensitive seers are virtually unanimous in envisioning cataclysms involving earthquakes, tidal waves, and land changes. Already, individuals with foresight are seeking to establish themselves in remote mountain retreats which may serve as sanctuaries in times of crisis.

But what of those who will not survive? Should not some thought also be given to their welfare? The thought of the congestion that might ensue on the astral plane following the violent demise of millions of confused, terrified, unprepared victims of a natural disaster is appalling. It is, however, exceedingly difficult to persuade skeptics that someone who has passed through the gates of death still exists in a realm beyond the physical. At this stage there seems to be a far greater chance of convincing the public that someone now living once died, and that this has happened to all of us repeatedly.

In some universities the field of psychology has already been enlarged to include *thanatology*—the study of death. This is divided into theoretical and applied branches. Theoretical thanatology encourages a scientific study of the evidence for survival, whereas applied thanatology teaches the art of correct dying. Because death is a part of life, thanatology should include such life-embracing disciplines as hypersentience, yoga, and astrology.

UNDERSTANDING THE KARMIC LAW

Above all else, the practice of hypersentience is a supremely effective way of demonstrating the *modus operandi* of the law of laws known as *karma*. Karma is the principle of cause and effect as it operates on a mental and moral plane. Hence the karmic law decrees that for every action there is a corresponding reaction, so that in the end we all receive exactly what we have solicited.

A widespread grasp of the nature of karma could change the world. If people could really accept the truth of the injunction, "As ye sow, so shall ye reap," they would be far less inclined to exploit their fellow dwellers on this planet. The exhortations to love thy neighbor and to turn the other cheek would be regarded as practical rules of the road rather than as remote spiritual ideals. It would then be known that in the final tally there is nothing we can take with us beyond the grave except that which we have given away.

A single incarnation may not show the manner in which an individual receives what he has given, but an overall view of successive lifetimes is bound to make it clear that karma is also the law of fair play. One woman went back to an existence as a haughty Roman lady who arrogantly mistreated her servants. After this episode she scanned two lives during which she had been a mistreated serving girl, dying each time by the age of twenty. On returning to her normal consciousness she commented, "Now I see that I had to go through those awful experiences because of the way I exploited those who were dependent on me." However, she did learn her lessons, for in this lifetime she is a totally giving person who is lovely to everyone whether in a high or low station.

Often the positive side of the karmic equation is seen. A man who struggled to salvage the best that the Atlantean civilization had to offer is now in a position where he has sufficient wealth and influence to perform this service again. A woman who was once a dancer returns to pick up the thread of her endeavor with a naturally lithe body. One who was a troubadour in the Middle Ages has come into a family which can provide a good musical education.

Even a lifetime of antisocial behavior may bear worthwhile fruit. An outstanding physician who is a pioneer in his field admitted that one of his former personalities had been a successful bank robber. In that existence he had caused several deaths; hence he is now using his medical skill to save lives. However, the main lesson acquired from his experience as an outlaw is a disregard for the "establishment." Today, as he forges ahead, miles beyond his conservative colleagues, his ability to stick to his guns regardless of what others may think is standing him in good stead.

Not everyone who suffers has necessarily deserved his tribulations. There may be karmic credits which accrue to the victims of unjust oppression so that they do indeed receive their "crown in heaven." It appears that there are some seraphic beings who come to Earth in a sacrificial spirit in order to transfuse their radiance into the turgid pits of darkness that have for eons tainted the life of this "star of suffering." These children of the light are persecuted, misunderstood, and crucified in every generation, yet they continue to work in behalf of sorrowing humanity until they are allowed to return to their native habitats.

It is, therefore, dangerous and possibly erroneous to conclude that just because a martyr has been laid low he is thereby suffering for some unremembered sin. The great karmic law which holds the denizens of the spheres to their appointed rounds is more complex than this. Yet it may be assumed that in an ultimate sense there is always a just reason for the events which transpire here on Earth, and that this is reason enough to seek the ways of justice in all endeavors.

PERSONAL INTEGRATION

We have found that the experience of each regression session tends to bring the ego-encapsulated mind into an easier acceptance of the communal relationship between conscious and unconscious processes. As one subject expressed it, "My consciousness was opened so that I got thoughts while in an everyday state of mind that fit into and added to the information received while in the hypersensory state."

In this way an individual may gradually clear the network of psychic veins and arteries through which his vital forces energize the various aspects of his personality. He can maintain a dialog with the subconscious and thereby control his instinctual nature by means of deliberately implanted suggestions. This progressive integration of the formerly fragmented components of his total being makes him a stronger, more disciplined character.

An example of the effects which may ensue when the powers of the unconscious are invoked is given in the following letter received from nineteen-year-old Claudia Barnes of Ventura, California, a month after a hypersensing session during which we had discussed her problem of deciding what she wanted to do in life. Claudia wrote:

> When we got together last month, at the end of the session you asked me to ask my "wise man" if he would give me some insight as to what my life's work would be. I requested that this would happen within the next two weeks.
> Well, within a week I was very restless at night and would lie awake several hours before falling asleep. At this time I was feeling a lot of tension and sorrow because of the loss of my boyfriend. Then, in the middle of the night I had a vision. It was an outstanding dream of dreams and it had a terrific impact on me—like an omen from God.
> I was driving some sort of vehicle down Thompson Boulevard in Ventura. It was night and I was with my old girl friend. We turned south onto

Seaward Avenue and there up in the sky we saw the most eerie, fantastic colors. Then, all of a sudden, I saw up in the sky in huge red letters the word "NUTRITION."

I was shocked and said to my friend, "Do you know what this means?" She didn't, and it obviously didn't have nearly the impact on her that it did on me.

Suddenly my vehicle stopped and spun about so that I could keep my eyes on the sign which was moving. Then down from the heavens a jar of dark jam came floating right into my hand. It was small and on the label was written in big letters NUTRITION. I was utterly speechless and awoke from the dream with tears in my eyes. I was really shook up. What a crazy dream!

Yet this still doesn't really define my life's work. I mean, what can I do in the field of nutrition? I guess only time will tell. But words truly can't describe the effect this dream had on me, just as words can't express the feeling one experiences when united with God.

I am very grateful to you, Marcia, for turning me on to meditation. Thank you very much.

When the unconscious is allowed to send its messages into the light of everyday awareness it can give useful warnings of impending events. A case in point is that of Rosalia who was keeping house with Rupert, a man she believed to be the love of her life. Then, for no apparent reason, she started to have anguished dreams in which she saw the breakup of their romance. This seemed strange because as far as she knew all was placid. For several months she underwent the suffering contingent on the loss of her companion purely on the subconscious level. Then, when unforeseen circumstances wrenched them apart, she was able to let go without tearful recriminations. There was sadness but no shock.

Since Rosalia was not thrown off-balance by this unexpected turn of events she was able to maintain her friendship with Rupert on a high level of mutual admiration and respect, even though it was no longer possible for them to be together. Afterward, she attributed her ability to deal constructively with a potentially scarring situation to the manner in which she had, through the practice of hypersentience, maintained a sufficiently close rapport with the intuitive part of her mind to receive and assimilate the information it chose to impart.

SPIRITUAL INSPIRATION

To be an integrated, well-adjusted human being is an eminently worthy goal. Most people are sufficiently challenged by the necessity to eradicate complexes, stabilize good habits, and function as responsible members of society. If, in addition, they can express themselves creatively, so much the better.

However, some individuals aspire toward nothing less than a total spiritual transformation. There is indeed a world of difference between the force exerted by a strong-minded personality and the dynamic influence of a dedicated server of mankind—a difference comparable to that between the heat of a coal-burning fire and the blazing forth of the power within the atom.

Ultimately, the practice of hypersentience should lead beyond the stage of personal integration to a higher level of harmonious cooperation with the will of the universe. In the beginning, exercises such as the imagining of a high place where the sensor can link up with an inner guide help to show that consciousness can be raised through a simple act of visualization. Then, if a person wishes to continue his efforts, he can make this expanded awareness a pervasive factor in his daily life. Thus he will realize that it is not enough just to see the light; the incandescence of the sun within the heart must shine through an ever-widening sphere of influence.

Most people are soon bored with explorations of prior lifetimes. Once assured that they have existed before, their minds turn naturally to the thought of what they may ultimately become. Knowing that they have been evolving for countless millennia, they are better able to imagine a time when they will attain formerly undreamed of powers. Not only can they now admit the possibility of higher stages of development; they can take steps to hasten their progress upon the Illumined Way.

Much of the incentive to move on stems from the de-egotization produced by the conviction that the undying essence of any human being is far greater than the mortal shell that is so soon left behind. At best, the hypersensory experience is like being transported from a smoggy valley to a mountaintop. There, the air is clearer, the sky more crystalline, and the sunshine more intense. In this lucid atmosphere the dreamlike desires of the egocentric personal self fade into insignificance. The observer then knows that in the past he has adopted many guises, or disguises, and that in eras to come he may be assigned other roles. Yet, like the encompassing round of the heavens, the One Self remains, and in communion with this luminous presence he is again made whole.

THE INWARD WAY OUT

Great ideals must be as deeply rooted in the world of spirit as natural laws are rooted in the world of matter if they are to be of any real worth to humanity. They must spring from pure cognition, not from fantasy, frustration, or desultory desire. Until we can gain a truer knowledge of the workings of the cosmos we cannot avoid embracing the distorted values which have brought the world to the brink of chaos.

All our vaunted systems of science, religion, philosophy, and government have not prevented men from despoiling the planet and abusing their own kind. Clearly, there has to be another way out, a more direct means of knowing what the Mind that programmed the universe intends for us. It is my hope that the technique of hypersentience will enable thoughtful people everywhere to turn again to the source of their own being and to cooperate more willingly with the guiding intelligence that lights our pathway through the stars.

2

THE BASIC TECHNIQUE

The technique of hypersentience is, in and of itself, supremely simple. Yet there are a few "tricks of the trade" which can only be acquired through experience. I have tried to impart all that I know in the following pages. Nevertheless, other workers in the field are sure to have much to add, and I still expect to learn much from them.

Normally, the procedure encompasses the eight stages listed below.

1. PRELIMINARY CONVERSATION

It is important to allow time for the people who plan to share this intimate human experience to become acquainted. Usually we try to give the candidate a brief description of our methods, making it clear that he will be in control of all his faculties. *There is no imposition of one will upon another.* Rather, the sensor's own volition will be strengthened in accordance with his deepest desires. He will do nothing he does not wish to do, nor say anything he would rather not reveal.

If possible, the facilitator should gain some understanding of the sensor's basic problems, desires, and aspirations as he endeavors to ascertain what should be accomplished in the hour ahead. The sensor should feel that he can let down his defenses without surrendering his own autonomy and that there is no need to be ashamed of whatever repressed material may come to light.

It is advisable to explain that in hypersensing sessions people often weep, sometimes for no discernible reason. Tears should be allowed to flow freely. There is no need to wipe them away, but a box of tissues should be available for anyone who needs to blow his nose. Contact lenses and false eyelashes are best removed ahead of time.

Since it can be disconcerting to have to answer a call of nature in the midst of a retrotrip, the subject should be encouraged to visit the bathroom before he lies down. Occasionally, when a knotty problem arises, the unconscious mind will try to evade the issue by making the body itch or twitch, or by putting pressure on the bladder. This may be no more than a trick played by the childish part of the psyche but it is wise to take precautions.

Check your tape recorder if you are using one. The easiest kind of tape machines to use are those equipped with a hand-held microphone with an on-off button. The microphone can then be held close to the sensor's mouth if he is speaking in a low voice. Also, the recording apparatus can easily be stopped during repetitious counting or long pauses, thereby saving tape.

Normally it is advisable to have a pen and paper handy in order to jot down subjective reactions and to keep track of significant body movements such as shaking, crying, or smiling. Even when the session is being recorded I generally take notes in order to have the information available for handy reference.

2. RELAXATION

Make the subject comfortable on a bed, mat, or reclining chair. Although it is permissible for him to remain in a seated posture we prefer to have him lie on his back.

Usually the facilitator chooses to sit near the head of the bed, just out of the range of vision. He should be close enough to hear what is being said, even when the words are barely audible.

If the room is too bright, a scarf laid over the sensor's eyes may induce a sleeplike mood. It may be helpful to work in a slightly darkened room without covering the sensor's face in order to observe the rapid eye movements (REM) which occur when images are being perceived. Most people feel cozier with a light blanket drawn up to the chin.

Letting the Body Go

Begin the hypersensing session by instructing the various parts of the body to relax. Proceed from the toes upward so that at the end, consciousness will be centered in the head. Do not fear repetition. A gentle flow of oft-reiterated words can serve as a soothing verbal massage. Although each facilitator will have his own approach, suggestions can be phrased more or less as follows:

> Let yourself sink into a sleepytime mood, just as when you go to bed at night. Remember how busy you have been and how good it feels to lay the body down for a refreshing rest. For a little while there is nothing you need do or think about. You can let everything go and float away in a warm golden pool of light. This inner radiance heals and purifies every fiber of your being.
>
> Now your toes are relaxing—all ten of them. You don't have to make them do it. Just speak to them gently but firmly as though they were small children and they will obey. Tell them to let go, and see how easily they comply.
>
> Next your arches relax . . . and your heels. Say to them, "Heels, relax!" Don't just take my word for it but speak to them directly as though addressing them by name. "Ankles, that's right, you too relax and be at ease."
>
> There is a magic in names which enables each part of the body to respond when you address it properly. That is, you can say, "Calf Muscles and

Shins, just relax and be quiet ... and now the knees. Please, Knees, take it easy and have a holiday. We know how hard you have been working and this is your chance to rest."

Now your upper legs are relaxing ... and the hips ... thighs ... stomach ... and lower back. The entire pelvic area, inside and out, is utterly serene, peaceful, relaxed, and still. From the waist down your body is sinking into an ever-deepening state of repose.

Your chest is relaxing, as are your ribs ... heart ... and lungs. "Dear Heart, you have done a wonderful job and I appreciate it, but it is time for you to beat very quietly and rhythmically so that the body can rest." Now this soothing sensation is sweeping up your back, vertebra by vertebra, right on up to your shoulder blades. Let all the cares and burdens of the day slip and slide away off your shoulders until they feel altogether quiet and composed.

A delicious feeling of relaxation is moving down your arms ... down to the elbows ... forearms ... wrists ... palms ... and fingers. The last little bit of nervous energy runs right out of your fingertips so that your arms are resting lightly at your sides.

Your neck is now exceedingly peaceful and relaxed ... and your chin ... jaw ... cheeks ... forehead ... and the back of your head. They are all so tranquil and still. Your eyelids are very very heavy. You know you could open them if you wished but it just doesn't seem worth the effort. Let them remain tightly sealed.

Your face is like a marble mask—serene, beautiful, and still. Erase your face. Erase all lines of expression upon it as you draw your vital energies up toward the crown of your head.

Your whole head and body are now exceedingly relaxed. You are falling into a state of pure, profound repose, sinking ever deeper into the life-giving center of your being.

After the first session this process of physical relaxation can be shortened but it should never be completely abandoned. The body, like a child, wants to hear the same comforting bedtime story in the same words each night. It finds reassurance in this familiar routine even after it has learned to fall asleep on command.

Resting in the Light

After it has been relaxed the body can be blessed and left to its own devices. Usually we allow a few extra minutes to lift out of the corporeal consciousness by suggesting that the sensor is being bathed in a shoreless sea of radiant golden light, that he is basking in the warm glow of an inward sun, or simply that he is feeling very bright, glowing, and free.

Like a driver shifting the gears of a car, the essential self can shift the gears of awareness out of its earthbound vehicle and into an ethereal body of light. From there, the indweller is at liberty to move at will through higher dimensions of being. This moment of meditative realignment should remind the sensor that in all he aspires to accomplish he will endeavor to work in the light of the high self and of the Divine Presence in all creation.

In order to maintain this illumined state the subject can be given a phrase, such as the following, upon which to reflect.

At the center of all light I am, and naught can touch me here. Let the living light illuminate all who seek its steadfast glow.

This potent seed thought can be deliberately implanted in the subconscious mind where it can continue to grow and bear fruit. Then, when life seems dark and dreary and the walls are closing in, it will be possible to repeat these magical words and to remember how it felt to open up to that sustaining radiance.

Eventually this kind of conditioning should enable an individual to open up his own private pipeline to a universal reservoir of light and love and power. The regenerative energies are always there; the recipient needs only to create an unobstructed channel through which they can flow.

Opening Invocation

In some instances the facilitator may find it helpful to repeat an invocation such as the one below.

OPENING INVOCATION

Now let the clear light
    of the all-seeing Self shine through
    to dissolve the shadows of ancient errors
    and reveal the primal essence
    of our true identity.

May we be guided
    by the spirit of truth,
    by pure intelligence,
      and all-encompassing love

As we endeavor to discern
    who we are,
    where we are going,
    and what we are meant to be.

Grant us the vision and the insight
    to serve as conscious cooperators
    with the Divine Plan
    which shall raise and redeem
    the earth and its creatures.

May all beings be blessed!

The Mesmeric Pass

Occasionally it is feasible to induce a deepened state of consciousness by using a mesmeric pass. This gesture, which was first popularized by Franz

Anton Mesmer in the eighteenth century, is performed by sweeping the right hand slowly through the air over the sensor's body, moving from toes to head and then back again to the toes. The process takes about half a minute in all. The hand is held palm down about a foot from the reclining figure.

As the facilitator's fingers move upward from feet to head the suggestion is given that the sensor will feel a slumberous sense of relaxation flowing up the legs and spine to the top of the skull. Then as the fingers move down toward the toes, the sensor is told that his eyes will be sealed and that he will fall into a state of profound repose.

This passing of the hand over the body can be envisioned as a blessing and a protection. We also speak of it as "sealing the aura." Many subjects say they can feel the gliding motion of the hand even though there is no actual physical touch. Although the mesmeric pass can be powerfully suggestive, it is not essential to the hypersensing process and should be used only by those who feel comfortable with this special effect.

The use of the hands to induce relaxation can be extremely helpful in work with the deaf. A person with poor hearing can, by a touch, be given a signal to open his eyes and read a written command. It should be possible for him to respond to prearranged stimuli even while deeply immersed in the hypersensory reverie.

3. COUNTING IN

In order to produce a totally relaxed condition we usually rely on some form of counting. The number of counts necessary will vary according to the extent to which the sensor can switch to a dreamlike form of consciousness. Thus we might say:

> I am going to count from one to ten, and by the count of ten you will be even more deeply relaxed. Your body will be in a sleeplike condition, but your mind will be clear, lucid, and in touch with my mind.
> Even though you are in a state of such supreme quietude you will be able to hear my voice and answer my questions. There will be enough energy flowing to your throat, mouth, lips, and tongue to enable you to speak easily and tell me how you feel.
> One, two, three ... with each count you are going deeper and deeper— deeper than sleep. Four, five, six, seven ... you are sinking ever deeper ... eight, nine, ten. You are now in a state of profound repose. You can hear the sound of my voice but nothing else will distract you. And still you are going deeper ... into the source and center of your own being.

With the passage of time I have placed less emphasis on the word "sleep" and often do not use it at all. In virtually every case the countdown is just as effective when I merely tell the sensor that he is feeling serene and tranquil and that he is sinking into a state of introspective repose in which he will transcend his normal bodily awareness.

An argument against insisting that the subject fall asleep is that even though he may be in a trancelike state he probably won't *feel* as though he were sleeping because he will remain conscious of all that transpires. He may, therefore, think, "But I'm not really asleep at all," and this negative response will counteract the efforts of the facilitator. Hence, we speak not of falling asleep or of going into a trance but rather of adopting a meditative attitude of mind.

As the facilitator gains self-confidence, he learns to inspire similar confidence in others. He will find, then, that he can usually create as profound a state of repose as is needed without having to pound his suggestions home through wearisome repetition. He operates less and less through verbal virtuosity and more and more by placing himself en rapport with the person with whom he is working. Then, merely telling the sensor that by the count of ten he will be deeply relaxed will suffice.

4. THE HALFWAY STAGE

Some people are such accomplished intro-spectators that as soon as they close their eyes they can conjure visions of former lives, or of whatever they choose to feel out with their psychic antennae. This ability to induce a hypersensory reverie usually develops with practice. If we are likely to continue working with an individual we will often suggest while he is in the meditative posture that henceforth he will find it easy to proceed from where we left off.

At first, however, it is advisable to allay the sensor's fear of failure by experimenting with various methods of creative visualization. These exercises accustom him to the idea of being a passive observer of the images which flicker across the movie screen of his mind and to carrying on a conversation about what he sees. Soon he learns to let the scenes shift of their own accord so that they start to tell a story. The impressions received may be predominantly abstract, like dimly recollected memories, or they may reconstruct a series of events with all the sound, color, and sentiment of an extraordinarily vivid dream. The following are examples of some of the introductory games that may be used to "put the show on the road."

Recapitulating Childhood Memories
It is often helpful to begin by asking the sensor to recollect a scene from early childhood. Thus we might say:

> Go back to a time when you were very young . . . right to the edge of memory. Try to see yourself as you appeared then . . . feel the way you used to feel . . . be as you were in those days. Tell me now, what comes to you out of your own past experiences?

As the sensor starts to delve into memories of former times he may remain a detached sightseer or he may mimic the child he once was, speaking as though reliving the time to which he has returned. If the recollections were sad he may weep. Joyous events may provoke spasms of laughter. Usually he can envision some long-forgotten occasion. He may, for example, describe his fifth birthday party or his first day in school in graphic detail.

The facilitator should remain alert to the fact that the memories brought back from early years will often symbolize the sensor's state of mind or indicate a problem that needs to be scrutinized. Apparently random images that come to mind may provide valuable clues which should not be overlooked.

The advantage of starting with the known past is that everyone can recollect a childhood incident unless there is, for some reason, a reluctance to cooperate. In the rare instances where nothing is recalled, it can be assumed that there is a mental block. In such cases we seldom press the issue. At this stage we are opening the caverns of memory in order to show what can be done, not to arouse ghosts of the past.

When we ask people to go back into childhood, they often explain that they aren't actually watching the pictures they describe but are only remembering them. This provides an opportunity to explain that it is all right to use the imagination to prime the pump. Most people do—at least at the start. Once the sensor ceases to fear that he may be fantasizing, the images usually flow more freely.

Often a person who has psychological inhibitions about infantile experiences can break through the time barrier into another existence in which he has well-nigh total recall. I have worked with many subjects who had great difficulty seeing themselves as they were a few years back but who, once they plunged below the surface of conscious memories, were able to peer into the remote past with remarkable clarity.

QUESTIONS

As the sensor starts to relinquish his ego defenses it may be helpful to tell him that he will be asked a question to which he should give the first reply that enters his head. That is, he should take note of whatever thoughts rise spontaneously to the top of his mind. The question we most commonly ask is, "What do you want? What do you really want?"

Usually the answer consists of an abstract word or phrase such as "peace," "freedom," "enlightenment," "love," or "to know who I am." A few people are utterly unable to say what they want and this too provides a clue to their state of mind. If a reply seems too prolix or facile, it may indicate that the sensor is still operating on a superficial level of awareness.

This and other queries such as "What do you hope to achieve?" or "What qualities do you most admire in people?" can sometimes help the sensor to penetrate the layers of social conditioning which conceal his deeper desires.

Sometimes tears will come to his eyes as he asks, "What indeed do I truly want to be . . . to have . . . and to accomplish in this brief span of existence and in my lives to come?"

In propounding these questions we are trying to point the way to greater self-fulfillment. Clearly it is necessary to have some idea of what an individual wants in order to enable him to find the path he should take.

In dealing with personal problems we are usually as direct as possible. First we ask the sensor to speculate on the reasons for his difficulties. It is harder to be self-deceptive in the deep state than when operating on the surface of consciousness. Hence it may now be possible to pinpoint previously unrecognized trouble spots. Even when the sensor thinks he is merely rambling on, there is usually some important symbolic truth in his narrative. In general, it is the conscious, not the unconscious, which is the great dissimulator.

VISUALIZATION EXERCISES

As the sensor learns to carry on a conversation while in the deep state, he usually acquires greater facility in calling pictures to mind. The practice of guided visualization helps him realize that he is a self-aware participant in the hypersensory process and not merely a recorder of the cinemascopic images that flash upon the eye of his interior vision. This active involvement may be enhanced by the practice of one of the following exercises. In most cases it is best to use simple phraseology, leaving it up to the sensor to embellish what he sees.

THE IMAGINARY ROOM

Imagine a room where you would like to be. All resources are at your command so that you can create exactly the kind of place that pleases you most. The room can be any size, shape, or color you wish. That is to say, it should be *your* ideal retreat—a sanctuary to which you can always return.

Describe this room. How is it furnished? Is there a comfortable spot where you can rest. What do you especially enjoy about it?

Finally, make a mental note that you will remember how satisfying it is to have this inviolable sanctuary where the storms and stresses of the world cannot pound you down. Know that you can come here again and again, whenever you have need of a place where you can be undisturbed. This is your own private retreat where you can call upon the strength and wisdom of your inmost being.

When the sensor has imagined the room we encourage him to put himself in it.

THE IDEAL SELF

When you find your resting place try to see yourself as you would like to be. This is your ideal self—the flower of which your small ego-bound personality is the seed—the essence of what you may one day become. Feel the difference in the quality of your attitudes and aspirations when you transpose yourself into this new mode of being.

Now, your ideal self has a message for the little self that you are in your daily life. There is something he (she) wishes to communicate. Listen, pay attention, and repeat what it is that you should know.

Our next visualization is usually one which accustoms the sensor to the idea of stepping beyond the present time and place, and of entering a distinctly different state of consciousness. The following exercise has proven so helpful in producing a sleeplike condition that we often recommend it as a means of overcoming insomnia. The more often it is used the more effective it becomes.

WALKING DOWN STAIRS

You are walking down a long flight of steps which lead to an underground cavern. I will count to twenty-five and as I count you will descend step by step. You are starting down now, taking one step for every count.

One, two, three . . . you are going deeper and deeper, deeper with every step. Four, five, six, seven . . . still going down . . . eight, nine, ten . . . already you are very far under . . . [The counting proceeds to twenty-five, or whatever number has been designated.]

Now that you have arrived at the bottom of the stairs you find that you are in a vast underground cavern. Just ahead of you there is a doorway. You can open this door and walk on through. Lift the latch. Let the door swing open and pass through to the other side. That's right. Now, look around and tell me what you see.

Occasionally there is a surprise on the other side of the door. One insomniac trudged obediently down all fifty steps, growing sleepier with each count. But when he opened the door at the bottom a big jazz band was blaring so noisily that it woke him with a start.

One person will imagine cold stone steps like a dungeon while another will construct an elegant circular marble staircase with a finely wrought handrail and a pool at the bottom reflecting the stars. There are wide variations in the ways in which subjects direct their powers of visualization. These idiosyncrasies often give the facilitator clues as to how he should proceed.

Frequently subjects will spontaneously enter a previous lifetime after passing through the doorway, especially if it is known that this is the purpose of the hypersensing session.

ASCENDING TO A HIGH PLACE

You are trudging up a narrow mountain path. The journey has been arduous but now you are about to emerge into a high and beautiful place—a place where you can lay down your burdens and rest. But still there is a little way farther that you must go.

As you continue on upward I will count from one to twenty. By the count of twenty the path will open out. There you will find a pleasant spot where you can stop and enjoy the view.

One, two, three . . . you are climbing upward . . . four, five, six, seven . . . moving on up, step by step . . . eight, nine, ten. . . . [The count proceeds to twenty.]

Now you have come to the top of the path and have arrived at the delightful place that was the goal of your journey. The air is clear, the sky is blue, the wind sings in your ears, and the golden sunshine is all around you, very warm and bright. Look about, take note of your surroundings, and tell me what you perceive.

This exercise can be varied by asking the sensor to imagine that he is ascending a flight of broad marble steps. At the end of the counting he arrives at the top of the staircase, walks forward into a new place, and describes what he finds there.

Occasionally the sensor is so primed with the idea of what he wants to do that on his arrival at the top of the path or steps he has already slipped into a previous incarnation. When this happens we encourage him to follow the course he has set. Otherwise we may go on to the next visualization exercise.

THE SPIRITUAL GUIDE

Now that you have arrived at your high and beautiful place I want you to think of a very wise person. See if there is someone kind and compassionate who will come to meet you and who can guide you on your journey into the past. This may be a personage you have known or never known, someone living or dead, contemporary or historical, imaginary or real. Whoever it is will be your special friend. Now look around and try to see who is here waiting for you.

If at this point the sensor sees no one he will simply say so. Should he succeed in invoking a guide we continue along these lines.

Describe your spiritual guide. Does he [she] make some gesture to show an awareness of your presence? Has the guide a message to convey? If so, what is the message?

Now let us ask the guide for permission to investigate some episode in your soul's history. Is there a way in which he shows his approval?

In virtually every case the guide does give some token of consent. We then proceed to take the sensor back into the past.

More than half the people with whom we have worked have been able to envision a spiritual guide. While skeptics may find the idea inadmissible, we have made it a practice to pay homage to the unseen companions who operate on the "inner planes" of consciousness. These real or hypothetical helpers may be called figments of the imagination, thought forms, or projections of the sensor's high self. As far as we are concerned the explanations given to account for their presence matter little, although people's propensity to assume that the guides *have* to be projections of their own subconscious personalities does seem to betray a subtle form of conceit.

We are, however, open to the possibility that assistance may come from communicators whose reality is as objective as our own. Some of these may be entities who are carrying on their work on the "other side," some may be what people think of as angels, some may be "inner-dimensionals" from another evolutionary scheme, and some may be members of a hierarchy of illumined souls who have transcended the human kingdom.

No one needs to accept these speculations in order to apply the techniques herein given. Nevertheless we can at least consider the idea that there may be great and compassionate beings who will gladly supplement our puny efforts if we invoke their help. It is, therefore, wise to be prepared for tokens of their concern and to know that they extend their recognition like an accolade.

THE SYMBOL

Now we are going to search for a symbol which will have some special meaning for you. It may come from your spiritual guide, from your high self, or from the mind of the universe, but it will be your own personal emblem.

Make believe that you are looking at a television set. All at once your symbol will appear upon it. Concentrate on this form and resolve to remember what you see. If you will meditate upon this symbol it may help you to focus your mind. Little by little its significance will be revealed to you.

Everyone who has given a child's party knows that if the occasion is to be a success no youngster should be allowed to leave without a favor. In the same way a message or symbol may serve as a mental memento. We encourage the sensor to contemplate his symbol and, if he finds it thought-provoking, to use it as a stepping-stone to higher consciousness. The symbols most commonly encountered may be classified as follows:

1. *An eye*—This leads the popularity list. The eye is often bathed in blue or violet light.

2. *Astronomical signs*—Suns, moons, and stars frequently appear, and also glyphs for the zodiacal signs and planets. Thus a subject may say, "I see a purple moon," or "I see the sign for Gemini made like a cross."

3. *Numerical signs*—Here we come to figures such as "a green five," or "two threes back to back."

4. *Geometrical signs*—examples of geometrical forms are a pyramid with wings, hearts, triangles, spirals, and circular motifs.

5. *Hieroglyphics*—Many of these glyphs resemble letters of forgotten alphabets.

6. *Mythological objects*—Dragons, unicorns, and winged horses are still alive and well in many people's imaginations.

7. *Floral objects*—Many types of flowers appear including lotuses, chrysanthemums, and the fleur-de-lis.

8. *Natural objects*—Gems, crystals, trees, mountains, pools, and the like fall into this category.

9. *Man-made objects*—Here we encounter artifacts such as lamps, rings, doorways, staircases, and headdresses.

10. *Auditory*—A few people hear their symbol. This may be a tone, a mantram, the Sanskrit syllable AUM, or a word such as "try."

11. *Abstract shapes and colors*—These come in diverse forms.

WHEN THE SENSOR BLOCKS

If, for some reason, the sensor balks at these mind games and insists that nothing comes to him, there is one last query that will often give a clue to whatever problem he may have. We then ask him, "What is the last thing in the world that you would ever normally think about?" At this juncture he may hem and haw or giggle self-consciously and make some evasive remark such as "Aw, I don't know."

"Go ahead," we insist. "Just say any absurd thing that comes into your head as long as it is something you'd never ordinarily consider."

Eventually, even if only to placate the facilitator, he will toss out some supposedly far-fetched image. In virtually every case this will symbolize a pressing issue in his life.

For example, one young woman who was instructed to evoke a random mental image replied, "An enormous mammoth in Siberia. Like one of those big elephants that was frozen in the Ice Age. In fact I once read that some of them were frozen so quickly that when they were opened up fresh buttercups were found in their stomachs."

As it happened, this woman was being figuratively "frozen" by an unhappy marriage. What she did not know at the time the question was propounded was that she was having a miscarriage. The baby inside her had already died and the fetus was expelled a couple of days later.

A mother of three small boys seemed ill at ease with the hypersensory technique despite her desire to cooperate. On being asked what she would never ordinarily think about she paused for about three minutes. Finally, as the pressure to reply became more intense, she said, "My children," and burst into sobs.

This reaction seemed illogical because her main preoccupation was with her family. As it turned out, however, she was resonating to the emotion generated in a previous lifetime in which she had been a Polish woman who, prior to World War II, was killed in an unsuccessful attempt to protect her children from the Gestapo. She needed to confront this experience because she was unwittingly identifying her present husband with the Nazis who strangled her, and because her oldest child in the present lifetime was tuning in on the same situation through recurrent nightmares. With this insight into her problem she was in a position to take remedial measures.

5. COUNTING BACK

In the first interview it usually requires about fifteen minutes to relax the sensor, pick up some childhood memories, and practice one or two visualization exercises. Then, once the subject has gained some facility in conjuring images and describing what comes to mind it is usually possible to take him back into the past.

By now the facilitator should have some inkling of how successful the regression session is likely to be. Still, he can never be quite sure. People who can evoke vivid images while playing the preliminary mind games practically always succeed in recapturing prior lives. Occasionally, however, even those who have thus far drawn a blank have finally become sufficiently relaxed to allow the next countdown to sweep them over the ego barrier into a reverie of remembrances. The following are some of the means whereby the sensor can become a time traveler.

The Time Tunnel

The sensor is asked to imagine a tunnel stretching into antiquity. He is then told that as we count from one to fifteen he will enter the tunnel and journey into a bygone era. By the final count he will find himself in another time and another place. He will then be able to step out of the tunnel, look around, and describe what he sees.

The actual number of counts is arbitrary but is usually between fifteen and twenty-five. During the counting the suggestion is repeated that the sensor is going back, far back, to a time before he came into his present body. We may end by saying, "Eleven, twelve . . . there is a light at the end of the tunnel. You are starting to emerge. Thirteen, fourteen, fifteen . . . you are stepping out of the tunnel and have now arrived back in this other time, this other place. Look about and tell me what you perceive."

At first we may substitute the word *perceive* for *see*, because not everyone can immediately register clearcut pictures. Often it is a matter of apprehending vague impressions. Hence, the sensor may feel more comfortable with the word *perceive*.

The facilitator should not become discouraged if it takes a while for the psychic slide show to begin. Normally a person's eyes require a few minutes to adapt to a darkened room after being in the midday sunshine. Similarly, a period of adjustment may be needed before the eye of the inner vision learns to focus.

Since the tunnel is symbolic of the birth canal, many people find this a psychologically apt way to enter the light of a new day. The metaphor is also reminiscent of a subway tunnel, suggesting an underground passage through the labyrinth of the subconscious. Occasionally, however, we encounter subjects who become claustrophobic in tunnels. Therefore, we may select an alternate means of transport.

The Rainbow Bridge

Some people prefer to go up over a bridge and drop down into a former lifetime rather than to burrow through from underneath. In using the image of the rainbow bridge we usually start from the "high and beautiful place" where the sensor has endeavored to contact his spiritual guide.

The subject is informed that from his elevated position he can see a rainbow bridge arching into a mass of pearly white clouds. He is instructed to walk along this bridge for fifteen counts, first going up over the top and then descending through the swirling mists. When he steps off the bridge he will find himself in another lifetime.

This has proven to be one of our most successful methods. However, just as some people hesitate to enter a long dark tunnel, others feel insecure on the bridge. They complain that it feels squishy or that they are afraid of falling off. Eventually, the facilitator develops an instinct that tells him which way an individual would rather go. Pragmatists are apt to feel more at ease in the tunnel, while idealists prefer the skyway.

The Ferryboat

The system of rowing the sensor to another lifetime was devised by my friend Akeva. Since Akeva is a powerfully built man, most people, especially women, feel relaxed and secure as the vessel glides through the violent twilight to an unknown destination. The sensor rests back, trailing a finger in the water, while the boatman handles the oars.

When the boat reaches its destination the passenger alights on the far shore and the ferryman returns alone, disappearing into the hazy glow in the center of the stream. The voyager then sets forth to explore the new territory, describing what comes to view.

Water is the symbol of the psychic world. Moreover, the entrance to the afterdeath state has long been likened to a stream. Most people have heard of the legendary rivers Lethe (from whence derives our word *lethal)* and Styx (giving rise to the word *stygian).* It seems appropriate, therefore, to navigate the ever-flowing torrent of time in a boat. This method often appeals to psychically sensitive people.

Doorway to the Self

Nowadays most people are familiar with the theory that there is a sensitive spot akin to a "third eye" located in the center of the forehead. On a dollar bill this organ of spiritual vision is symbolized by the all-seeing eye at the top of a pyramid, the two base points of which correspond to the physical eyes. In the terminology of yoga this focal point of subtle energies is known as the *ajna chakra*, or brow center, and is designated as a bifurcated lotus of ninety-six petals. With the development of the clairvoyant faculties, these streams of radiating power extend to the right and left, covering the upper part of the face with two winglike formations.

Intuitive people often respond favorably to the suggestion to direct their attention to this third eye, as though observing a doorway covered by two velvet curtains. Gradually, the curtains part to reveal images from previous lifetimes. As the scenes become more sharply defined, they follow one another like images on a television screen. Then, if the spectator wishes, he can walk through the door into that former existence.

Other Modes of Transport

When possible, the facilitator should take advantage of images that spontaneously arise. For example, a subject who has been asked to imagine being in a beautiful place may happen to mention sitting by a pool. He can then be asked to look in the water and see pictures from the past forming on the water's mirrorlike surface.

Another simple but effective method is to have the sensor imagine himself walking along a path and observe where it takes him.

One young man, without prompting, found himself in a desert. In the distance was a tent. He walked up to the tent and opened the flap. Inside was an Arab who had been waiting for him. The Arab lit a candle and indicated that the youth should stare directly into it. Then, gazing into the flame, the youth started to envision incidents from former incarnations.

6. THE HYPERSENTIENT STATE

As soon as the sensor discerns a picture it should be brought into focus. If, for example, he glimpses a cobblestone street he should be told to follow the street, describing the houses on either side, the people he encounters, or whatever captures his attention. Although he should linger long enough for scenes to develop it is best to keep the chronolog moving from one situation to the next.

Usually we wait until impressions are flowing freely before asking the sensor to describe himself. Purely abstract questions such as "Who are you? What is your name? Are you male or female?" may be too remote from the image-making mind to produce the desired results. If, on the other hand, we ask, "What are you wearing?," an answer is usually forthcoming. One can obtain a remarkable amount of information simply by knowing whether a person is a knight in armor, a dhoti-clad East Indian, an elegantly garbed lady, or a ragged waif. Even then, care must be taken. One man told us, "I am wearing a long gown." Thereupon we assumed he must be a woman. A few minutes later it came out that he was a merchant of Tyre in classical times when men wore long robes.

It is also relatively easy to elicit information about hairstyles. If, for example, a woman happens to mention that she has a black beard, we assume she is speaking of a time when her soul tenanted a male body. In the early years there may be some sexual ambiguity but by adolescence the situation becomes clarified.

Most sensors can give the names by which they were known, though it may take a while to elicit this information. Once we have obtained the name it is used repeatedly. If at present the sensor is called Ann, and in her regressed state she gives her name as Ivan, then it is important to address her (him) as Ivan. In fact, Ivan may become extremely irked if some nosy stranger insists on calling him Ann!

It should be borne in mind that the regressed subject probably won't remember anything beyond the mental range of his former personality. Since, in bygone eras, most people were isolated and illiterate, political events, dates, and the names of ruling monarchs mattered little to them. One man who went back to an existence as an impoverished farmer in an Asian land described how a band of soldiers killed his wife and children, stole his animals, and burned his hut as he watched helplessly from the underbrush. When asked who the marauders were and what war they were fighting, he was unable to say. All he knew was that an army had swept across the land and laid waste to his property.

REFLECTIVE QUESTIONING

As the impressions begin to flow, the facilitator can keep the story moving by performing a mirroring function. That is, every time the sensor makes a statement the facilitator repeats what he says and leads on with a question. For example, the conversation might go like this:

> You have now stepped out of the time tunnel. Look about and tell me what you see.
> (Pause.) I see something that looks like a circle.
> You see a circle. What else?
> Well, it looks like a dial, and there seems to be more than one of them.
> What do these dials remind you of?
> An instrument panel. Yes, that's it. I feel as though I were in the cockpit of an airplane looking at the instrument panel.
> You are looking at an instrument panel. What are you doing in this aircraft?
> It's a bomber and I am the pilot.
> You are the pilot. What are you wearing?
> Something brown. It looks like a World War I outfit. There seems to be a war going on.
> There is a war on and you are in it. Which side are you on?

I think I'm English. I feel English. And there's a sense of danger.

What danger?

They're coming at me. I'm being shot at. I think the plane is about to crash.

All right, we'll return to this scene later. But first I want you to relax and look at some of the circumstances which preceded your being in the plane. Are you relaxed now?

Yes, I feel better.

Very good. I'm going to count to five and on the fifth count you will be the same personality but younger. You will be sixteen years old. One, two, three, four, five. Hello. What are you doing now?

I'm walking up some steps.

What steps are these?

They lead to a house. I guess it's my house.

That's fine. Continue on up the steps. Now you are walking through the front door. What do you see?

There is an entrance hall with a big umbrella stand, and a parlor to the right. Toward the left is a dining room and then a kitchen.

Do you feel like going into one of these rooms?

The kitchen is where I like to be. I go there the first thing.

What is in the kitchen?

Brown wood cabinets and a big old-fashioned stove and a sink. There is a table where people can sit and eat.

Who else is there?

My mother. She's making pies. She's putting them out on the table to cool.

What is your mother wearing?

A long dress . . . blue . . . with a white ruffle at the neck. And a flowered apron. Her hair is pulled back at the nape of her neck and she is smiling.

Your mother is looking up as you come in. Now she is addressing you by name. What name does she call you?

She calls me Ronald. She's asking where I've been.

Very well, Ronald, tell me something about your father. What does he do?

He seems to be away a lot. I guess he travels. I think he's in India now. I respect him but we don't see him very often.

As the conversation proceeds the sensor comes to the point where he can carry on a dialog or even a monolog. At first, however, some reflective feedback may be required in order to establish a flow of visual imagery.

TIME TRAVEL

When it becomes desirable to take the sensor forward or backward through time, we usually tell him that we will count from one to three (the number of counts is arbitrary) and that by the third count he will be the designated age.

Suppose, for example, the subject has picked up a former life in which he is a ten-year-old boy named Joachim. We have gathered as much information as we need about this lad's circumstances and now wish to advance to the age of twenty. Therefore we say: "Now, Joachim, I am going to count to three and by the third count you will be twenty years old. You will then be able to tell me where you are and what you are doing. One . . . two . . . three. You are twenty years old. Hello there, Joachim. Where are you now?"

Then when we wish him to move on again we may tell him: "That was very good. Let us go forward now and see what happens next. As I count you will move forward year by year. Twenty-one . . . twenty-two . . . twenty-three . . . twenty-four . . . twenty-five. You are now twenty-five years old. Tell me, Joachim, what is going on in your life these days?"

Ordinarily we take the sensor progressively forward to the time of his death. If it happened that this personality did not survive to a designated age, he will either draw a blank or will simply state that he did not live that long. At this point we may ask outright, "How old were you when you died?" Or we may instruct him to go forward to the time of his passing and describe his situation.

When the sensor comes to the end of a particular incarnation, or immediately after he has left his body, he can be requested to survey his life as a whole. The facilitator can then ask questions such as: "What was the most significant thing that happened to you in this lifetime?" or "What lesson did you learn from these experiences?" or "Is there someone you knew then whom you know now in a new form?"

Usually an answer will be forthcoming. Thus, looking back on an embodiment as a warrior, the sensor may say, "I had to learn fearlessness." A woman who has reenacted a career as a hardworking housewife may report, "I found out how to be patient and loving." A former miser will admit, "It was shown to me that my greed brought more pain than pleasure."

It appears that there are few wasted lives since even those which turned out badly demonstrated the futility of selfishness, laziness, avarice, or whatever shortcoming was exemplified.

THE DEATH EXPERIENCE

Although we do not dwell unduly upon the inevitable shedding of the body, neither do we ignore this significant event in the life of the soul. Ordinarily, we try to ascertain the cause of death by taking the sensor forward to his last illness, or even to the moment of his departure. Seldom is the process of dying registered as a painful event. Usually the indweller breathes a sigh of relief when he realizes that he has passed over. Since most lives are fraught with difficulties and pain, he is as glad to be done with the body as he would be to shed an outfit of mud-spattered clothes and lie down for a refreshing nap.

After the sensor has made the transition, we ask him where he is and what he is doing. Usually he makes a reply such as, "I am in the light," "Floating," or "I am up among the stars."

It is important not to assume that consciousness terminates with death.

Most sensors are able to describe the reactions of the friends or family left behind, though there is seldom much interest in the discarded physical form. Rarely does the soul linger around its former habitat. Occasionally, however, people will wait for their loved ones to join them. By the same token, some speak of being greeted by companions who have passed on before.

To date, I have not encountered anyone who went to Hell, but this may be because I have worked with so few Fundamentalist Christians. Although we make it a point to ask, "Where did you go next?," there is usually a break in consciousness after the body has been set aside. The next thing we pick up is either another lifetime or the interval prior to descending into the present incarnation.

A few individuals have some inkling of where they were between lifetimes. Often they describe learning experiences in templelike heavenly schoolrooms or libraries. For some, Paradise seems to resemble a park or garden. Others migrate to more remote realms which they do not identify with this planet.

Those who demonstrate continuity of consciousness in the afterdeath state are usually spiritually aware people who have more than average control of their faculties. Some say they were trained in the art of separating soul from body in the mystery schools of ancient times. Thus it appears that one of the benefits of learning to transcend the world of matter during the span of earthly existence is the ability to continue to progress even after the body has served its purpose.

PRIMING THE PUMP

Once the sensor picks up a series of specific images success is virtually assured. Even when the first impression is one of swirling mists, colored lights, or abstract patterns, more clearly defined impressions usually follow. As soon as a picture appears it is best to focus attention upon it until it gives way to another, and then another, sequential scene.

If it takes awhile to get started we will sometimes instruct the sensor to look for a path. Then, before he has had time to worry whether the impressions that come to mind are real or imaginary, we ask questions such as, "Is this a dirt or a paved road? Does it appear to be straight or winding? What sort of countryside does it pass through?"

As the sensor gains facility in describing what he sees, he may be told that the scenes will change by themselves, like the pictures in a slide show. Gradually, he becomes so engrossed in the story that unfolds that he will move from one episode to the next of his own accord.

Should the sensor remain blocked, we may ask him to think of a congenial episode in history and imagine himself there. Thus he might say, "Well, I've always been interested in the Civil War."

"All right, then, make believe you are involved in the events of this period.

Where would you see yourself?"

"I can think of myself in a white house with columns. I'd have a bedroom upstairs . . . on the right side of the landing. But somehow I don't seem to enjoy this room."

"Why not?"

"It's because I'm not well; I seem to be some sort of invalid."

"Are you confined to bed?"

"Yes, part of the time. I don't seem to be able to walk."

"Why can't you walk?"

"Oh, now I know. I fell off a horse."

By this time the retrotrip has turned into something more than a guided fantasy as the chronolog of how this person was crippled and what came after spontaneously unfolds.

Often the sensor will slip out of the contrived situation and into one that seems more authentic. One girl dutifully started to spin a tale set in eighteenth-century America and then suddenly jumped into a far more vivid experience shortly before the French Revolution. As so often happens, she needed only to prime the pump to cause a stream of memories to spurt forth.

Normally we use this deliberate make-believe only as a last resort. Our aim is not just to produce symbolic material, useful though this may be, but to determine the truth. Since there are a number of fundamental differences between the ordinary storytelling propensities of the mind and the emotion-fraught narratives that come to light in hypersensing sessions, it is fairly easy for a trained observer to distinguish which is which. For example, the appearance of actual images is often, though not always, signaled by rapid eye movements. There are changes in voice and skin tone that could hardly be mimicked. The sensor is usually astonished by what he sees, and there is a richness of detail that can seldom be duplicated in the normal state.

If our subjects were merely fantasizing they would surely be able to imagine something more dramatic than the dreary lifetimes that are more the rule than the exception. Many bluntly express their dislike for their former personalities. We know for sure that the tears shed, the grimaces, tensed muscles, and convulsive spasms that accompany particularly painful experiences are not make-believe. Moreover, the aftereffects are indisputably real. An individual who has taken a genuine retrotrip is never again quite the same.

Above all, there is an ineffable sense of veracity about most of the material people bring forth. A perceptive observer can spot an insincere person or one who is habitually self-deceived. Similarly, the facilitator can become sensitive to the subtle differences between real and fabricated stories. Often it seems more fantastic to assume that the sensor made up the events of which he speaks than to assume that he is describing actual happenings.

When the sensor feels that he is only imagining things, the deliberate use of free association may still produce significant information. What counts is that the hypersensing session should not be structured as a success-failure situation. Even if the interview turns into a guided fantasy or merely provides an opportunity for the subject to talk about himself, it can still be a valuable experience.

Occasionally we will deliberately stage a situation designed to facilitate the retrieval of information. If, for example, the sensor is unable to describe what he is wearing we might say, "You are walking down the road after a heavy rain. Now you are coming to a puddle of clear water. As you bend over and gaze in the puddle you see your own reflection. How do you look?"

Sometimes a counting method will overcome a block. Thus the subject may say, "I can see a book but I don't know what is written in it." Thereupon we reply, "I will count from one to three and then you will be able to read this material." Or we might tell him that at the third count he will know telepathically what is in the book.

Once in a while we will ascertain a date by asking the character that the sensor has become to compose a letter, starting with the day, month, and year. Although this gimmick may work in the case of a literate person, one who was illiterate will be helpless to comply. Similarly an unlettered person will be unable to read a newspaper headline, nor will a teetotaler enter a saloon.

In most cases the sensor will cater to our various memory-prodding tactics. However, he cannot be moved through a make-believe world like a pawn in a chess game. If too much is asked, he simply balks. On the whole, people are remarkably definite about what they can and cannot do, especially if they know they are expected to tell the truth.

COPING WITH PAINFUL MEMORIES

When a woman arrives for a regression session with her eyes fortified with mascara, eye shadow, and false lashes, we often sigh inwardly, knowing that in an hour all that meticulously applied makeup may be black and smeary. Even in the midst of some agonizing recollection, however, she may remark, "I guess I'd better remove my false eyelashes." We then lay the lashes carefully on a piece of paper as she returns to her weeping. All this is, perhaps, symbolic of the fact that it is extremely difficult to maintain any kind of mask while in the hypersensory state.

If a situation seems too painful to bear the simplest recourse is to ask if this line of probing should be continued. Usually the answer is yes. One reason the technique of hypersentience works so well, even for amateurs, is because most of the guidance comes directly from the subject.

If the sensor starts to cry, it is best to encourage an emotional release. On the other hand, he obviously should not be allowed to sob for an hour. When he has confronted the unhappy memory, the suggestion can be given that he is now feeling very peaceful. Once he has quieted down, he can move on to a less turbulent series of recollections. If one session does not suffice to alleviate whatever hangups may have been caused by the pain-laden material, then it is possible to go back over the same area at a later date and allow him to cry it out.

An anxious or fearful person should not be allowed to dwell morbidly upon the rigors of a long-gone past. If the subject has recapitulated one or more wretched experiences, it may then be wise to vary the procedure by having him look back upon some happy times. Even those whose souls' histories have been turbulent have enjoyed respites. It may be important for these storm-tossed ones to realize that joy can be as instructive as pain.

A surgeon will use all his skill to excise a tumor as quickly as possible. Similarly, the facilitator should strive to exorcise a malignant obstruction to the normal flow of positive feelings with the least possible emotional wear and tear. The crucial operation is the removal of psychologically debilitating material from the murky depths of the subconscious. Then, after the regression session is over, the sensor can continue to resolve—or dissolve—the problem in the light of his higher intuition.

TERMINATING THE INTERVIEW

Normally we allow an hour for a hypersensing session. In cases where the sensor plunges immediately into a trancelike state, half an hour may be enough. If and when he feels weary, he may say so. Nevertheless, the facilitator should be sensitive enough to know when to ask, "Is this as much ground as you wish to cover today or would you care to continue?" Choosing the correct time to terminate the proceedings requires the same consideration as that which impels a guest at a party to make his exit, even though he may still be enjoying himself.

If the sensor is completely motionless, it is wise to tell him to stretch after the first thirty minutes lest he wake up feeling unnecessarily sore.

As the hypersensing session draws to a close we usually ask, "Is there anything else you would like to look into before we bring you back to your normal state?" Remaining items on his mental agenda can be dealt with briefly. Otherwise the suggestion can be given that this ground will be covered at a future date.

If the sensor wants to explore former lives by himself or in conjunction with another person, we may pick up one or two incidents of an incarnation not hitherto touched upon and imprint them on his memory. We then tell him that the next time he takes a retrotrip he will find it easy to recapture these incidents and develop them further. Thus he is encouraged to continue, even without our assistance.

When the sensor is accompanied by a friend with whom he wishes to carry on his hypersensory research, it can be suggested that the two of them will be able to work together. At this point the friend may wish to take over in order to reinforce the idea personally and bring his companion out. In this way they both gain confidence in their ability to carry on.

If at the start we have contacted a spiritual guide, we customarily reinvoke this personage before signing off. There may be some parting message or word of cheer from one or more unseen helpers. We, for our part, may thank the guide for his assistance. Otherwise we simply allow the sensor to rest briefly in the light before returning to the everyday world.

Should it happen that there is some deleterious habit such as smoking, drinking, or overeating which a person genuinely wishes to eradiate, this is the propitious moment for remedial action. Our method is not to preach but rather to induce the sensor to compose his own pep talk. Usually he visualizes his ideal self as the embodiment of the qualities he wishes to incorporate. The personified projection of his high self then informs the "little self" that it is high time to shape up and shuck off the childish compulsions that hold him in thrall. Seldom is it necessary to belabor this point. If the command is clearly given, it need not be oft repeated. When the sensor's consciousness is raised to a more elevated plateau, the habit will fall away of its own accord.

We may also use this final interlude to convey suggestions of health, wholesomeness, and strength to the organism as a whole, as well as to any ailing part. Vital force can be directed to a sluggish glandular system, an infection may be soothed, or a sore spot induced to mend. Hands knotted by arthritis can be cajoled to unclutch, while a strained heart may be courteously requested to maintain a more peaceable rhythm. Now, as the body awareness is about to be reestablished, an energy implant can be given.

Our final admonitions pertain to the extent to which the sensor will recollect what has transpired. If he has just passed through a miserable lifetime, we may allow a measure of forgetfulness to supervene. Normally, however, enough valuable insights have been obtained to warrant the command that images brought to mind will be remembered and their significance be made increasingly clear.

Even though the sensor may have recounted a series of intensely emotional incidents embellished with a wealth of details, this whole dramatic panoply may fade like last night's dream. Often when we chance to meet someone with whom we have worked and refer to the memories drawn forth we are met with a blank stare. That which has been forgotten once can be forgotten again unless a mental fixative is applied.

If the facilitator fails to give the command to remember and the sensor wakes as from a dreamless sleep, the memories can be reinstated by putting him back under and then making the appropriate suggestion. Once while I was working with the renowned clairvoyant Gayle Eaton at a workshop in Los Angeles, she spoke fluently for forty minutes, pouring forth a stream of information concerning her personal past and the destiny of humanity.

Afterward, when we complimented her on her virtuoso performance, she stared at us incredulously. Immediately I relaxed her again, using a mesmeric pass, and told her she would recall everything she had said. When she reemerged, her recollections were intact. The process of restoring her memory had taken about half a minute.

7. COUNTING OUT

Since the sensor is usually fully self-aware during his voyage through the uncharted seas of inner space, there may be a temptation to overlook the necessity of anchoring him back on terra firma. Yet it can be as important to restore him to normal functioning as to bring a ship smoothly into port.

Should it happen, however, that he is obliged to return without assistance he is unlikely to suffer any ill effects. Like a spectator emerging from a movie theater, he may blink and seem preoccupied as he gradually readjusts to the outer world. Even people who have been in a deep hypnotic trance will awaken naturally if left to their own devices.

We usually terminate the interview by counting backward from ten to one, telling the sensor that by the count of one he will be wide awake and alert, but at the same time peaceful and mentally refreshed. When we are teaching a person to regress himself we may ask him to count inaudibly and then to open his eyes when he is back. In this way he becomes accustomed to the idea of proceeding on his own.

The subject may be in such a pleasantly relaxed state at the end of a session that he would rather not return for a while. In these instances we allow him to rest for as long as he wishes. This is most feasible if he is in a private room where we can exit silently and close the door.

Sometimes I repeat a final invocation in addition to, or in place of, the counting. Whether the facilitator prefers to use a series of poetic phrases or a simple counting method depends largely upon the spiritual orientation of the sensor, the attitude of the people present, and the mood of the moment. The following is an example of the kind of nondenominational invocation that can be used.

INVOCATION TO THE LIGHT

O Thou, to Whom all things are known,

We long for the living light
    of Thy compassionate understanding.
Purge us of our ancient woes,
May our past transgressions be forgiven,
Help us to err no more.

Direct our steps upon the path which leads
　from ignorance to wisdom,
　from hatred to love,
　from strife to peace,
　from pain to bliss,
　from death to life eternal.

May we be restored
　to perfect health and wholesomeness
And may the dark places of Earth
　be illumined and redeemed
By the glory of Thy transforming presence.

Be with us now
　and all the days of our lives.

Even though the sensor may assume that he is entirely back to normal after the final count from ten to one, he should rest quietly for a while longer. People sometimes say that they feel "freaked out" by what has happened or experience a continuing flow of visual imagery. Many times we have watched an overeager person jump up from the couch and then fall back with a look of surprise as his legs wobble beneath him. We assure him that he is perfectly fine but, like a diver surfacing, he must allow a reasonable period of adjustment as he passes from one level to another. Usually we offer him a cup of herb tea and some cookies in case he needs a boost to get the body going again.

8. CONCLUDING CONVERSATION

When possible it is wise to allow some time after the termination of the session to discuss what has occurred. If a tape machine has been used, it should be left on since comments made afterward may clarify many obscurities, especially if the sensor has been speaking in a low voice.

A person often discovers that in delving into the subterranean wellsprings of the psyche he has released a continuing gush of insights into his own character and motivation. While this fount of inspiration is still flowing, he should be encouraged to clarify his thinking. Much that could not be said before may now be explained.

The facilitator should be alert to the possibility that even after the interview has been concluded there may be subjective reactions which can be elicited only by remaining open to communication in a follow-up letter or conversation. Often we encourage those with whom we work to keep a journal in which to record additional impressions. We also recommend relevant literature and suggest where it can be obtained.

The sensor may be instructed to watch his dreams, since messages from the unconscious frequently slip through in unguarded moments of sleep. The door to a new region of the psyche, which he has unlocked, is one which he should be able to open and shut at will. This door can be locked again if he chooses, but at least the key is in his hands.

The day may come when highly efficient, accredited facilitators will conduct hypersensing sessions in series of fifty-minute hours one on top of another, but something will have been lost. In my work, the many occasions when we have sat on a rug around a tray of refreshments and discussed the strange and wonderful revelations conjured out of our minds have been the most stimulating of learning experiences. Academic training is, of course, of immense value in this or any therapeutic discipline. Nevertheless, when it comes to the expression of love (the ultimate healing agent), amateurs may be as good as professionals. To us, the people with whom we work are not cases but friends and should be treated as such.

We try to help these cooperators to feel that they are participating in an exciting new movement which can expand man's capacity to achieve a higher level of happiness and self-fulfillment. If the technique of hypersentience is to promote the benefits that we believe can be achieved it will be largely because this has been a grass-roots endeavor to which any sincerely interested person can make a significant contribution.

THE BASIC TECHNIQUE

Summary

1. PRELIMINARY CONVERSATION

2. RELAXATION

> Relaxing the Body
> Resting in the Light
> Opening Invocation
> The Mesmeric Pass

3. COUNTING IN

4. THE HALFWAY STATE

> Early Childhood Memories
> Questions
> Visualization Exercises
>   The Imaginary Room
>   The Ideal Self
>   Walking Down Stairs
>   Ascending to a High Place
>   The Spiritual Guide
>   The Symbol
> When the Sensor Blocks

3

GROUP DYNAMICS

When a strike of electrical workers brought a four-day power failure to Southern California, many people suffered severe inconvenience, even to the point where lives were threatened. However, the most widespread lamentations came from those who complained, "What can you do in the evenings? There's no radio or TV; candles are too dim for reading; there's just no way to pass the time."

A hapless victim of economic crises, energy failures, and pollution problems has been the recreation industry. Gas is too costly for pleasure jaunts, fish no longer abound in streams, parks and beaches are unreachable. With urban decay and suburban sprawl, even walking and bicycling are often difficult. Rising inflation and taxation curtail vacation plans. Should present trends continue, people en masse may have to face the possibility that, for a while at least, *the only way out . . . is in.*

Ideally an individual should investigate hypersentience because he wishes to know more about himself and the universe which brought him forth. If, however, he decides to take a retrotrip to add novelty to a dull weekend or because his friends are doing it, this should not be held against him. There is no reason why consciousness-expanding techniques should not be entertaining as well as edifying.

While we do not wish to relegate hypersentience to the category of fun and games, it does provide a fascinating way to vary a monotonous routine. Moreover, many significant advances in psychic research have begun with the recreational use of Ouija boards, table tipping, and automatic writing. Obviously care should be taken in such attempts at paranormal development. Anyone who fears being "taken over" by irrational forces should immediately cease all efforts to probe the psychic world. At this time, however, there is a large and accessible body of literature on parapsychology through which any open-minded investigator can learn about the pros and cons of various occult practices.

A person who takes a camping trip is sure to encounter some dangers. He may smash his car, drown, or fall off a horse or a mountain. Such accidents run into the thousands every year, yet no one denigrates camping on that account. Certainly hypersensing is nowhere near as perilous as football, skiing, or surfing, not to mention fighting bulls, parachuting from planes, or speeding in racing cars. Even in terms of consciousness-altering techniques, it is less hazardous than pill popping, drinking, or prolonged fasting. It behooves us, therefore, to realize that much of the criticism which this practice is bound to receive is based less on objective evidence of negative effects than on fear of the unknown, religious bias, and the taboo against the investigation of afterdeath conditions.

The main issue is one of motivation. If a person sincerely desires to expand his higher faculties and to help others, he will be protected. If his motives are impure, then whatever he does will turn out badly. The chances are, however, that the insight which retrocognition gives into the operation of the karmic law will provide an increasing incentive to work for the highest good.

It is with these thoughts in mind that the following information is offered to those who wish to come together in groups in order to learn more about hypersensing—and themselves.

WORKSHOPS

I have introduced many people to hypersentience through workshops organized on an informal basis by friends and interested people. Usually these gatherings are held in homes or some convenient meeting place and are attended by acquaintances of the host or hostess.

Normally about fifteen people are present. Although some groups have been larger, anything over fifteen seems like a crowd, while twenty is the maximum that can be effectively handled. It is important that there should be enough space for everyone to stretch out flat at the same time. Each participant should bring a blanket and pillow and be comfortably dressed. Usually we sit on the floor. The use of tape recorders is encouraged.

Most of my workshops begin promptly at ten in the morning and end about five in the afternoon. Each participant is asked to contribute an item of food such as a salad, casserole, fruit, cheese, nuts, or beverage toward a potluck vegetarian luncheon. Sometimes it is more convenient for people to bring individual picnics, but, when circumstances permit, the sharing of food contributes to the congeniality of the occasion.

Although I have worked successfully with open-minded skeptics, the prejudices of carping critics can spoil the atmosphere for everyone. It is important, therefore, to ensure that everyone present is in harmony with the purpose of the gathering. People should realize that the issue is not one of naive belief but of impartial investigation. No one is trying to prove anything to anybody. There can be nothing to judge or criticize. One individual's experience is, in this endeavor, as legitimate as that of another.

No one thinks it strange that a camera film must be developed in a darkroom under controlled conditions. Similarly, it is justifiable to insist that the development of psychic images projected from the depths of the subconscious should proceed in an atmosphere conducive to the work being accomplished. Moreover, it is a matter of simple courtesy not to expose one's friends to ridicule.

Undoubtedly, the supportive attitude of those who have attended my various workshops has contributed immeasurably to the success of these experimental gatherings. When most of those present were students of yoga, astrology, or meditation, a high level of accomplishment would invariably be reached.

Normally the schedule of activities for a hypersensing workshop will proceed more or less as follows:

10:00–10:30 INTRODUCTIONS

The facilitator is introduced. He thanks the sponsor of the day's session, then gives a brief summary of the proposed program. This provides an opportunity to make people comfortable and for latecomers to find their places. A pencil and paper may be passed around to obtain a list of the names and addresses of everyone in attendance.

The members of the group then introduce themselves and say a few words about their backgrounds and reasons for being present. It is often helpful to know how the participants happened to hear of this work, what books they have read on the subject, and what they hope to accomplish. Have they already some knowledge of their own prior lives, and if so, how was this information gained? People who have practiced meditation, studied mind control, or been hypnotized often prove to be particularly good subjects. At this point the facilitator may make mental notes as to which candidates he will regress later in the day.

10:30–11:30 DISCUSSION

During this period the facilitator may explain the basic purposes of hypersentience in general and of this workshop in particular, drawing upon his own experience to illustrate salient points. The material covered will probably be similar to that which provides the background for the chapter Hypersentience, What It Can Do. Time should be allowed for questions and general conversation.

11:30–11:45 BREAK

At the end of the question period it normally requires about fifteen minutes for people to stretch, take a break, and spread their blankets and pillows on the floor. After an hour and a half of concentrated attention this much of a change of pace is needed.

11:45–12:15 GROUP HYPERSENSING SESSION

Since it is easier to show than to explain how a state of deepened awareness can be induced, we ask everyone to lie down while we demonstrate the procedure. Since an entire group is involved the technique is not quite the same as that used for individuals. The lack of conversational give and take means that if there is too protracted a silence subjects may lose their train of thought or fall asleep. Hence we do not pause very long until after the final stage of going through the time tunnel. At the same time, quiet intervals must be allowed while the sensors try to capture the images which rise before the eye of their inner vision.

Normally it takes about ten minutes for people to become thoroughly relaxed. A variation of the introductory technique given in the previous chapter is this exercise in creative visualization.

> Lie flat on your back with your arms resting at your sides. With eyes closed, breathe slowly and deeply in and out . . . in . . . out . . . in . . . out. . . .
>
> Imagine that you are floating in a tropical sea. The warm water soothes your toes and bathes them in rippling waves of relaxation. Each toe relaxes, as do the arches, heels, and ankles. Let them rest and vibrate in perfect harmony with the life-giving current that buoys you up. . . . Next your shins, calf muscles, knees, upper legs, and thigh muscles relax. Abandon them; let them go.
>
> Now relax your abdomen. If there is any tension there, release it and set it free. Your stomach moves gently up and down with the rise and fall of your breath as though the entire universe is breathing through you. Let all your cares and anxieties wash away.
>
> Your chest area is also feeling very light and open. Be aware of the shield of ribs protecting your lungs, of your heart, and of the great arteries and the veins that are carrying blood throughout the body. Your vital forces are flowing freely in and out from this radiating center of your being. Feel how peaceful it is to be rocked by the gentle rhythm that springs from the heart of all creation. There is no sense of separation between you and this surrounding sea of pulsating streams of light. Let go, and let it flow.
>
> Your arms are lying limp and loose at your sides. They too are channels for the luminous currents that follow the measured beat of your breath. All the way down to the wrists, hands, fingers, and fingertips you are floating free. Now forget them, let them go.
>
> Your neck, face, and brow are utterly smooth, serene, and tranquil as your whole head relaxes. Let your thoughts dissolve into a pool of pure awareness. The glow behind your eyes is very bright, as though you were gazing inward upon a shimmering nighttime sky. This starry ocean of space surrounds, supports, and sustains you, body, mind, and soul.
>
> Now let everything go and flow fluidly into this ever-shining Light.

After this initial relaxation the facilitator may count from one to ten, giving the suggestion that by the final count everyone will be in a profoundly relaxed and peaceful mood.

MIND GAMES

The group members are now asked to practice the art of guided recollection by going back to an incident in childhood and trying to see it clearly. A minute or two of silence passes as each endeavors to capture a half-forgotten memory. Occasionally someone will start to weep at this point but most people find the exercise pleasant and easy to accomplish.

The next stage requires a more challenging effort of the imagination. Each participant is requested to try to visualize a beautiful place in a natural setting. All resources are at his command; hence this retreat can be just as he wishes it to be. It may be a place he has known or never known but he is to think of it as his spiritual sanctuary.

Most people can carry out this suggestion without difficulty. Those who cannot think of any place at all are seldom able to be regressed without a considerable amount of preparatory work. They may eventually succeed but first must release their imaginations from a restraining load of inhibitions. It is not necessary to literally *see* the retreat but it should be at least as vivid as a memory.

After a pause the subjects are asked to step into their retreats. There they should picture themselves as they would like to be, vital, happy, and free. As they visualize and identify with this ideal self, they should try to sense the resultant heightening of the quality of their awareness.

Following another pause the facilitator suggests that the ideal self has a message to convey to the small personal self that is caught up in the exigencies of daily living. Each member of the group should formulate his message as succinctly as possible and resolve that it will be remembered.

The sensors are then asked to gaze out over the landscape and take note of the view. Then, when they turn around and look back at the place where they have been, they will see a symbol. This form should appear spontaneously and with the least possible deliberate thought about what it should be. It may provide a seed for future meditations or a key to the door to the unconscious. There is no limitation with regard to what the symbol may portray.

THE TIME TUNNEL

The final phase of the group hypersensing session is given over to the effort to pick up some threads of memory leading back to former existences. Participants are told that as the facilitator counts slowly from one to twenty they will feel as though they are journeying back into the past through a time tunnel. When they arrive at the end of the tunnel, they will emerge in another time and another place and in the body of a different personality. They will then be able to look about, observe their surroundings, and remember what they perceive.

During the counting the suggestion is reinforced that the time traveler is passing through the tunnel and then stepping out to the other side. At the end of the count approximately five minutes of silence should be observed. At this stage it is often possible to tell which individuals have established a train of mental images by observing the flickering of their eyes.

RETURN TO NORMAL CONSCIOUSNESS

The journey back to the here and now can be accomplished simply by counting from ten to one. The sensors are told that by the count of one they will feel wide awake, cheerful, and refreshed, and will remember everything that has transpired.

12:15–1:00 DISCUSSION

It usually takes a few minutes for people to stretch, sit up, and reestablish their rapport with the group. When they are ready to proceed the facilitator should ask them to relate their experiences. This exchange allows everyone to make a contribution and to compare his responses with those of others.

As each person describes his impressions he may touch on:

a. The glimpse into childhood
b. The beautiful place
c. The ideal self
d. The message
e. The view
f. The symbol
g. Experiences at the end of the tunnel

Some people will, of course, have much more to say than others. By the time everyone has spoken, the facilitator should have selected several candidates for the afternoon demonstration period.

Now that the onlookers have been through the basic procedure, they should have a greater appreciation of the sensor's situation when the work continues on an individual basis. This should enable them to empathize with him, even to the point where they may be able to go along on his mind trip.

Since the opening of the unconscious memory bank can involve an intensely personal revelation of feelings, we discourage the presence of nonparticipating spectators. Everyone in the room should feel attuned to the others and each should give something of himself to the group as a whole.

1:00–2:00 LUNCH BREAK

An hour should provide ample time for everyone to eat, converse, and enjoy a change of pace. This will prove to be an important day in many people's lives. Hence we try to make it a festive occasion with good food, pleasant surroundings, and congenial companionship.

2:00–5:00 INDIVIDUAL HYPERSENSING SESSIONS

In working on a one-to-one basis it is best to allow considerable leeway since there is no way of knowing what sort of experiences will be brought up out of the past. Basically, the procedure is that which has been described in the previous chapter. Normally we work with from three to five individuals in the course of an afternoon. When more than one facilitator is present and there are extra rooms we may divide the group so that more than one regression session can be carried on simultaneously. During this part of the day participants can learn how a dialog is carried on, become familiar with the methods which can be used to stimulate the flow of images, and observe what is done to meet the various contingencies which may arise.

ONGOING GROUPS

It frequently happens that those who have attended our workshops wish to continue meeting on a regular basis. This has made it possible to experiment with a variety of mind games, as well as to work in greater depth with individuals. The following exercises of the imagination include some that have been part of our repertoire and also a number which our colleague Billie Hobart of Kentfield, California, has been using with her group. Several of these visualizations are so archetypal that they have been developed by many different teachers; hence it is not possible to give due credit to their originators.

VISUALIZING EXERCISES

•   Give yourself the beginning of a story. Then allow your imagination to take over and just go along with whatever happens.
•   Experience being born again.
•   Stand in front of a house. Observe it carefully, then enter, look around, and remember what you see.
•   All at once you have become very tiny. Enter your own body at any place you like and explore your cellular self.

• You are standing in front of a cave. Over the entrance a word is carved in rock. Read it, and then enter the cave and experience something which will clarify the meaning of this word for you.
• Walk through a hall of mirrors and explore yourself in them.
• You are standing at a crossroad. Read all the signs, choose one direction, follow it and see where it leads you.
• Using whatever equipment you need, dive down through the ocean depths to an undersea kingdom. Look about and describe what is there.
• Construct a garden spot where all the members of your group can come together. Wait until everyone is present and then join hands and pledge to assist one another in the work which all of you are endeavoring to accomplish.
• Imagine yourself being bathed by different colors which are showering down from the top of your head to your feet. Starting with red, continue on through orange, yellow, green, blue, indigo, and violet, ending with a cleansing stream of pure white light. (In this exercise it is helpful to have one person name the colors in order.)
• Inhale as though you were breathing in a warm golden light. Then as you exhale, let it fill the space around you with shimmering radiance. Sitting silently within this luminous sphere, visualize the members of the group. Take each spiritual companion into your glowing aura and then pour light out upon the group as a whole.

MULTIPLE REGRESSION SESSIONS

We are often asked if it is possible to regress more than one subject at a time. The answer is that it seems to depend a great deal on what one is trying to accomplish. The first person I knew to conduct simultaneous hypersensing sessions was nineteen-year-old Claudia Barnes. The following letter from Claudia dated 31 March 1974 gives a picture of some of the advantages and liabilities of this method.

Late Sunday afternoon Doug Scotland, Johnny Strobal, John Richardson, and I decided to try a group regression. I had the three young men lie down together and gave them blankets and pillows for comfort. Each of them had been meditating for quite some time so it wasn't hard for them to relax, though I did go through the routine of talking to each part of the body, suggesting relaxation.

I wasn't sure how to go about working with three people but they were very cooperative and I think we were all pleased with the results, though we decided that a "one-to-one" regression would be easier and more fulfilling. The rest of this report should clarify this belief.

I asked them not to get hung up on whether they personally believed in reincarnation—to keep their minds open to whatever ideas or visions came. Whether imaginary or not they mean something, so just watch and accept what happens. I told them to try to grasp one of the images that came and concentrate on it. Concentration is a funny thing—you can't force it, yet it takes a lot of effort. The rewards of concentration can be spiritually uplifting.

I asked them to visualize their sanctuary as a beautiful place that vibrates with love and peace, the place you can always go and be YOU and feel really good about it.

John saw Kings' Canyon with green grass and a river. He was camping there with Doug. It was very beautiful.

Doug used his imagination and saw ferns and green trees. He saw himself walking.

Johnny saw a grassy meadow with pine trees. He could hear birds and feel the wind, even smell it, but couldn't see himself.

I then asked them to think of something in the past, to go far back and dig up some experience they hadn't thought of in a long time—anything meaningful, sad, funny, or ordinary.

John saw himself sitting on his mother's lap in their living room. She was reading the story of Raggedy Ann. He was wearing a brown and white striped T-shirt. He liked the story.

Johnny remembered when he and his sister Heidi stole some food from their neighbor's just for fun. They went into the house and ate chocolate cake and bananas. His parents found out and they got a spanking and no candy. He also remembered when he went to kindergarten and didn't like it at all. The first day he stayed home and cried. He couldn't remember why he was so unhappy.

By the time I got to Doug he had gone through a sackful of memories and at the moment wasn't working with one in particular. That was the major problem of working with more than one person. Going from one to another can easily leave a track of lost thoughts.

Next we walked down ten steps of a spiral staircase. At the bottom was a door with each person's symbol over it. John saw a mountain with the sun rising over it. He then saw an intricate design like an animal, possibly a dragon.

Doug saw something golden and bright, like a four-pointed star with a circle around it. When he grabbed it, it melted into a puddle. He didn't feel good about it. It pulsated and had no temperature.

Johnny saw half of a white umbrellalike object. He couldn't touch it.

We then went through a tunnel to the count of twenty to someplace in the past—another time, another place, never seen or thought of before.

John saw himself as a young man in England outside of an old, large house. He talked to someone riding by on a horse and also to a young woman. He was carrying a bucket of fish. Possibly he worked at the house (a small castle). He zoomed into one of the windows and was able to talk about the furniture.

Johnny saw an older man dressed in robes in a marketplace. He had the feeling of an Arabian or Hebrew atmosphere. He was a sheepherder and had a son. Possibly he lost his wife and was a lonely man. After a while Johnny began to feel that he might have been that man.

Doug saw a man in a dirty white suit with big black buttons leaning against a building. He was watching some people dancing in the street. It was like a fiesta. He was a white man with black hair who came from a different country. He had a white cap on and might have been in the French foreign legion. He felt that he was drunk as he watched the musicians and the people dancing.

Then we returned to John in England where he was a serf or peasant. The girl he talked to was a servant. They were just friends. Somebody in high office drove up in a large coach and there were trumpets to announce the coming.

Going back to Johnny—his man had a goat with him and a very young son. He was a skinny man with dark hair. He felt lonely.

More than an hour had gone by and Johnny was complaining of a sore butt. I asked them if there was anything else they wanted to do and they said no, so I counted them down from ten to one.

In concluding, I would like to say that it was fun and we all hope to continue our explorations into the wonderland of hypersentience.

On a few occasions I have inadvertently regressed more than one person at a time. That is, while working with a subect I would suddenly notice that someone else in the room was taking a mind trip. This occurred once when a young woman named Jane came for a private session along with her boyfriend Eddie. The understanding was that I would work with Jane while Eddie observed and then, if time allowed, I might get around to him.

The first thing that happened was that Jane entered an extremely peaceful headspace and simply wanted to remain there basking in the light. Glancing at Eddie I could see that he was equally far under. Consequently, I let Jane have her quiet time and took Eddie back to a prior lifetime. This existence turned out to include some incidents that he wanted to mull over, so periodically I would allow him to digest what was happening while I returned to work with Jane. In the end, time and energy were saved and both subjects were grateful not to be hurried. Usually it is feasible to give the suggestion that one individual will not be disturbed by what is being said to another. If people are friends and time is limited this can be a helpful way to proceed, despite its obvious drawbacks.

Occasionally I have worked with people who have known each other in previous lifetimes and who were able to tune in simultaneously on the same circumstances. These instances in which two sets of memories mesh to produce a single story can be remarkably convincing, especially when they happen in workshops where I have not realized that these individuals were connected.

A LIVING MANDALA

My first deliberate attempt to regress several people to the same place involved four young people who were living in the same house. The group consisted of two girls and two men, including Jack Kerollis, an account of whose experiences is given in the chapter on Inner-dimensionals. The four participants lay on the living room rug in the shape of a cross with their heads at the center, thereby forming a human mandala. (A mandala is a circle with reference points commonly used for meditation.)

Since Jack and I had worked together several times previously, it seemed natural to take him to his special retreat on a remote plateau in the Peruvian highlands. As he traversed this mountainous landscape, the others accompanied him in their imaginations, giving corroborating descriptions of the terrain. Together they mounted the steps of a large stone house inhabited by a band of mysterious beings and tried to make contact with these guides.

Although all four sensors felt that they were in the same space, it was hard for me, being outside that charmed circle, to ascertain what was really happening. Certainly they appeared to be tapping some potent energies. As they spontaneously reached out to hold hands, their breathing became labored and the girls shook uncontrollably. The session ended with the group chanting some of the familiar Sanskrit invocations which they had been accustomed to using in meditations, including the sacred Sanskrit syllable AUM. Everyone remained in an exalted mood for some time after.

Since this introductory experience, considerably more work has been done along the line of inducing altered states of consciousness in groups of congenial people. We have found that it appears to be possible to harness and direct potent psychological energies by constructing various types of human mandalas. These circular formations comprise from four to seven friends who share the same philosophic outlook on life and who have some common point of interest. The participants lie on the floor with their heads at the center, hands clasped, and feet raying out like the spokes of a wheel. Those who have practiced meditation, hypersentience, or some form of mind control usually find that they can, to some extent, enter the same headspace and reinforce one another's efforts at creative visualization.

Our groups have also experimented with methods of spiritual healing involving the construction of what we call "human batteries." In one of these batterylike patterns either three, five, or seven people lie side by side with their heads pointing in alternate directions. Each one clasps his neighbor's ankles, except for the two at the end who have one free hand apiece. Two more would-be channels of healing currents kneel at the head and feet of the person in the center to whom they transmit their power. Generally, the people in the battery can feel the force flowing through them. In any event, the exercise helps them to think of the body as a dynamo of circulating energies, and to realize that this electrical potential can be aroused by the consciously focused mind.

One of the most gratifying aspects of my work in hypersentience has been the tendency for the groups to whom I have imparted a few simple techniques to continue to develop on their own. Some have specialized in historical research, some in psychic diagnosis and healing, some in communicating with spiritual guides, and some in karmic astrology (correlating horoscopic indicants with the circumstances of former lives). To date, their enthusiasm and effectiveness have provided convincing evidence that the widespread promulgation of hypersentience can make a significant contribution to the evolution of human thought.

4

THE NEED FOR CAUTION

A decade ago, after the conclusion of a yoga class which I was teaching at the Lexington School of the Dance one of my students came up to me and said, "I have a son who is in the seventh grade. Now he and his friends are regressing each other to previous lifetimes. Is this safe?"

Since I could see no harm in the practice, I tried to set her mind at rest. Why shouldn't the children be free to know who or what they were? Can any real harm come from believing oneself to be immortal? For what reason should they be forbidden to extend their mental horizons?

Needless to say, the youngsters came to no bad end. They had merely grown bored with the constant din of violence on TV and thought it would be a novelty to look into their own prenatal histories. The exploration of these previous lives and deaths was at least as exciting as the dramas they watched nightly on the screen. Yet, like the actors they admired, here they were still functioning and playing new roles.

When I completed the first draft of this book a well-meaning friend exclaimed, "For goodness' sake, take out the story about the schoolchildren! Otherwise people might think that anyone at all can use this technique." Several other critics, none of whom had any firsthand experience with the subject, insisted that more emphasis should be laid upon the potential dangers of dredging up memories of former lifetimes.

It must be admitted that my promulgation of the technique of hypersentience has elicited some negative reactions. However, the problems which have arisen have been caused not by those who have experimented with the methods presented in this book but rather by uninformed critics who rarely wish to know the real facts about the subject they condemn.

When I look back upon the personal troubles caused by the unreasoning antagonism of those who dwell upon the supposed dangers of recollecting the past and who resent the use of altered states of consciousness to violate the "taboo against knowing who you are," I console myself by thinking of what the knowledge of immortality might do for human beings who otherwise would die in fear and ignorance. At one time I had the idea that it would be a good thing if a group of volunteers could be recruited who would sit by the bedsides of dying people who had no one else to see them through the great transition. I even went so far as to persuade a friend who is a nurse to smuggle me into a hospital where, on the night shift, there was only one attendant to look after sixty patients, many of whom were terminally ill.

As a result of this experience I found out how truly horrible are the conditions under which multitudes of sufferers in hospitals and nursing homes depart from this life. The saddest part of the situation is that much of this misery is unnecessary. People are capable of learning from an early age that death need not be dealt with solely in terms of disease; it can also be considered an entry into a more vital state of health and well-being. They can be taught to release the soul from the body with dignity, efficiency, and a joyous anticipation of self-renewal. But first, they must have some vision of the plan and purpose of their own lives. At this point, the best way I know to impart this much-needed faith is to make the precepts of reincarnation a matter of easily available firsthand experience.

For my own part, I finally abandoned my project of sitting by the bedsides of the dying because I knew that if the authorities discovered what I was up to the nurse who admitted me to the wards at night might lose her job. Later I read of a new organization whose members might remain with terminally ill patients for a fee of six dollars an hour. Our society being what it is, the exchange of money makes this a permissible activity. As of this writing, however, it is difficult for a person like myself to go and offer a helping hand to a fellow soul who may be old, lonely, and dying in bodily pain and spiritual anguish.

I believe that hypersentience can be practiced by any interested individual regardless of age, status, or educational background. Not all will be able to pick up past lifetimes but anyone who wishes can at least practice some helpful visualizing exercises. To date, people who are mentally unstable or who might be upset by the revelation of who or what they once were have avoided any contact with the technique—and they are well advised to stay away. Of our many built-in safety mechanisms, the most effective is the propensity of fearful or unbalanced individuals to remove themselves from our sphere of influence. Those who might be hurt simply don't seek us out.

Since, however, there is so much at stake in this issue it does seem important to make some answer to the objections which have been raised by opponents of our work.

PROS AND CONS

The practice of hypersentience, insofar as it pertains to retrocognition, has been denigrated by critics who stress the uselessness of dwelling upon the past or of desiring to know what happens after death. As one skeptic haughtily announced, "I'm not interested in regression; my concern is with progression."

Indeed, we all wish to progress. But it is demonstrably true that those who fail to learn from past mistakes are bound to repeat them. We might also reply that if the study of the soul's history is pointless, then why do we remember what happened yesterday and why are we compelled to plan for the morrow? If it is futile to look back upon the way we have come, then schools might as well discard all of history and most of art, psychology, and the humanities. Literally, man's humanity rests on his ability to function as a time-binding creature who can attain an overview of past, present, and future.

It has also been common for detractors of hypersentience to say, "Well, it depends on what a person wants to remember *for.*" The implication here is that mere curiosity is not enough; some practical benefit should also be forthcoming.

When people question the motives of those who wish to gain information about past lives, I sometimes point out that when Columbus set forth to discover the New World or the astronauts to walk on the moon, they were not primarily concerned with the ways in which their adventures might translate into material gain. For most great explorers the simple desire to know what is out there has been reason enough for their endeavors. First come the pioneers, then the profiteers; first pure research, then technology. It is my belief that human curiosity is a divine attribute which needs no further justification. The desire to discern the pattern of many lives arises from as noble a stirring of pure intelligence as the desire to grasp the laws of physics which govern matter, or the laws of justice which govern society.

In the days when I used to teach Hatha Yoga, people sometimes came to classes because they wished to diminish the size of their hips or to improve their sex life. Some of my colleagues looked askance at these "unenlightened" ones who apparently had not yet realized that yoga is a "spiritual" discipline. For my own part, however, I accepted them gladly, assuming that by practicing the postures they would be plunging into a stream whose current would naturally carry them on to deeper realizations. "I'm coming here because I need the exercise," one of my male students once confided to another. "But if she starts in on that meditation jazz I've had it." Three years later this man was teaching a successful meditation class.

Any reason at all is good enough for practicing yoga. By the same token, any reason for wanting to be regressed should elicit a willing response. People's motivation is their own business. If they have the desire to probe the past this shows them to be questioning, questing human beings. What is surprising is that so many people have no interest at all in finding out who they were, not that some do seek this additional insight into the wellsprings of their preconditioned responses.

The antagonism which the practitioner of hypersentience can expect to encounter may come from a variety of sources, including the following:

1. Religious fundamentalists who oppose occultism in general and who see

the work of Satan in any proposition which fails to support their literal interpretations of the Bible. Many of these adversaries automatically assume that any knowledge of human survival of death (however scientifically acquired) falls within the province of religion and is, therefore, an infringement on their ideological territory. Consequently, some theologians regard the theory of reincarnation as a threat, since their belief system holds that souls may be eternally damned, that the dead must sleep until Judgment Day, or that only the few who make it to heaven will survive.

I have had my share of hate mail from religious fanatics and some of it has been vicious. The best policy seems to be to avoid evangelical enthusiasts entirely since most of them are impervious to reason. Anyone so bold as to try to counter their objections should first make it clear that hypersentience has slight connection with church dogma. It is not a religious issue but a psychological technique. Twentieth-century theologians may deny the rapidly accumulating evidence for survival just as their sixteenth-century counterparts denied that the sun is in the center of the solar system, but this will hardly change the existing reality.

2. Opposition may also arise from conservative members of the medical profession. This could come from practitioners who are skeptical of paranormal healing in general and who resent the use of therapeutic techniques by unqualified intruders—namely those who do not possess the requisite academic degrees.

The problem is that many physicians, even in the rare instances in which they are interested in medical hypnosis or hypersentience, are too busy to take the time required to relax the subject and put him at ease. I have found that to obtain the best results it is necessary to devote about two hours to an individual during the first session and at least an hour for subsequent interviews. Hardly one in twenty of the friends with whom I have worked could have afforded to pay the fees which a doctor would have to charge in order to render similar assistance.

Moreover, hypersentience is a pursuit which does not have a great deal to do with the practice of medicine. Owing to their conservative training, which includes a thorough grounding in the tenets of Freudian psychology, many psychiatrists may be less qualified to deal with the idea of immortality than the intelligent layman who has taken the trouble to stay on top of current developments in the ever-broadening stream of parapsychological studies.

For decades most psychologists have refused to consider the evidence that many of the hangups with which they deal may stem from the experiences of former lifetimes. However, once these professionals jump on the bandwagon they are likely to start trying to push everyone else off. We feel it essential, therefore, that before the resistance starts to harden, enough competent laymen should be familiar with the technique to enable anyone who sincerely wishes to explore his soul's history to be able to do so. Even though some novices may be relatively unskilled, on the whole less harm will be done by the popular dissemination of these methods than by allowing humanity to labor under the cruel delusion that death is the ultimate end and that there is little justice in the workings of fate and fortune.

Fortunately, some highly ethical physicians are now working to devise methods for the training of qualified laymen. We are hopeful that these courageous forerunners will eventually demonstrate the obvious benefits of making this new push into the unknown a joint endeavor.

3. Still more immediate problems may arise from so-called experts who have vested interests in gaining monopolies over the high-priced programs now being offered to the public via weekend seminars and quickie training courses. Many of these exponents of quasi-hypnotic techniques which involve the reexperiencing of former incarnations have not imparted their "secrets" in books because once the cat is out of the bag people will find out how simple the methods really are. Not only will the regressors lose some of their mystical panache, they may also find themselves deprived of a lucrative source of business.

On the other hand, the human problems to which the technique of hypersentience may be applied are sufficiently complex so that people possessing expertise will always be needed. Even though the basic knowledge has been disseminated there will always be students who want to continue in a group situation with a qualified teacher, and who will pay a fair fee for services rendered. The whole subject may then be raised to a higher level. There will always be room for legitimate authorities in this field, and as the interest in reincarnation spreads they should find themselves ever more in demand.

4. To date, the most blind and unthinking opposition I have encountered has come from old-line occultists who give credence to the idea that esoteric knowledge should be restricted to an exclusive circle of "initiates." Since they too are believers in reincarnation we are all of the same family—and family feuds can be the most bitter. Having over the years achieved a measure of respectability, these eminently good and idealistic individuals can be defensively prickly with regard to allies who may, they fear, give them a bad name by misusing the tenets of their faith. In general, they would rather spin out attenuated metaphysical complexities than cope with the grubby problems people bring over from the past.

It is sad but true that parapsychologists tend to denigrate astrologers, theosophists, and spiritualists, while the various schools of occultists bicker endlessly among themselves. By stressing the hypothetical "dangers" of the recapitulation of past lives, these esotericists can persuade themselves that theirs is an exceedingly difficult and demanding discipline which the layman should not presume to emulate.

What they do not realize is that the times have changed. The level of public comprehension has risen and people en masse are ready to take the next step forward. That which was esoteric knowledge in the past must now be made available to all. The universe still has plenty of secrets which can be made known only to those who have achieved the requisite state of consciousness, but the fact of reincarnation is no longer one of them.

As early as 1919, the Tibetan Master, Djwhal Khul, writing in collaboration with Alice A. Bailey, gave a detailed description of the esoteric schools due to appear throughout the world toward the latter part of the twentieth century. In his book *Letters on Occult Meditation* he describes the qualifications of those who will teach in these schools, saying:

> Exercises in telepathy, causal communication, reminiscence of work undertaken during the hours of sleep, and the recovering of the memory of past lives through certain mental processes will be taught by them—themselves proficient in these arts.[1]

One argument of the conservative wing of the occult establishment against recapturing the memories of former incarnations by the means outlined in this book is that at a certain stage of evolution these powers unfold naturally. Any premature awakening is, they maintain, dangerous.

My reply is that human progress has not come about all that "naturally." Rather, people and institutions have a propensity to sink into inertia, to crystallize, and to preserve the status quo. Mankind has moved forward only because in its vanguard there have always been individuals who were willing to fight and die for their vision of the truth.

The same principle applies to individuals. Seldom do the higher senses stretch, yawn, and awaken by themselves. A person must work diligently to arouse them through meditation, study, and service. It is well known, of course, that the opening of the psychic centers can be accelerated by unnatural practices and that these can be perilous. However, inasmuch as it is natural to strive for enlightenment, even against opposition, the "meditative posture" adopted in hypersentience is a safe, sane way to progress toward self-realization.

Since we have been able to speed up our physical movements by means of cars and jet planes, should we not experiment with comparable psychological measures in order to hasten our inner development? Cannot our modern expertise be used for spiritual as well as material gain? Indeed, we may be obliged to apply our hard-won scientific ingenuity to the broadening of our capacity to comprehend the meaning of life on Earth if the evolution of human minds is to keep pace with the technological progress occurring today.

Apart from the outright critics of hypersentience, there are many people

---

[1] Alice A. Bailey, *Letters on Occult Meditation* (New York: Lucis Publishing Co., 1922).

who would like to experiment with the technique but who fear a loss of self-control. I have sought to allay some of their trepidations in chapter 6 which compares hypersentience and hypnosis. There are, however, a few questions which can be answered here.

Is there any danger of not being able to wake up after a hypersensing session?

To date, I have had no difficulty waking subjects up, nor have I heard of anyone who encountered this problem. Nevertheless it is always wise to anchor the sensor securely in his body at the end of the regression session by giving the command that he will be wide awake and in control of all his faculties.

Sometimes I instruct the sensor to bring himself back by counting from ten to one. This helps to give him the confidence to proceed on his own. Even when a subject is so much in charge of the situation that he doesn't need this final count, he is encouraged to follow the routine anyway.

Once a group of us who had been experimenting with hypersentience on a weekly basis were having a meeting at the home of our friend and co-worker Isabel Buell in Thousand Oaks, California. At a quarter after eleven Isabel put some corn on to steam for luncheon. The corn was supposed to cook for one hour. Immediately after tending to this task Isabel lay down on the rug, went into a deep trance, and began to describe the details of life on the now-vanished continent of Muraya four million years ago. Suddenly she interrupted her flow of recollections to say, "It's time to turn off the corn." Glancing at my watch I saw that Isabel had made this request at precisely 12:14. She then brought herself back to normal consciousness and served a delightful luncheon.

Seldom is an individual so dissociated from his daily affairs that he would have any trouble coming to his senses, even if the facilitator were to walk off in the middle of a regression session. Knowing this, I will occasionally allow the sensor extra time to relax quietly and reflect upon that which has been experienced. On one occasion I was working with Margaret Granger at the home of the popular author Jess Stearn in Malibu, California. As it happened, we were using the same room in which Taylor Caldwell had been regressed when Jess was writing his book about her past-life experiences. After half an hour Margaret was in such a beatific state that she didn't want to move, but I had to leave. While departing I said to Jess, who had just come in, "Oh Jess, there is a strange woman in your bed; I hope you don't mind. If she has any problem waking up you can count her back."

"It's all right," he said nonchalantly—and indeed it was. When Margaret was ready she simply arose and went on her way with no ado. Needless to say, however, I would not leave a person this way unless some trusted friend was around to check up.

Only once did a sensor's dissociated state cause me some concern. At this time I was working with a friend who has the ability to fall into a deep hypnotic trance at will. This lady was suffering from a condition of extreme fatigue, aggravated by a mysterious allergy. While she was regressed I contacted a spirit physician named Dr. Cunningham who astutely diagnosed the cause of the allergy and offered advice as to how it could be remedied. (That is, my friend would relay the doctor's instructions to me and I would talk back to him through her.) After our consultation I did not bring her back immediately but gave the instruction that she should sleep a while longer in order to allow time for Dr. Cunningham's suggestions to be assimilated.

An hour later my friend wandered out of her bedroom and into the living room. One glance was enough to see that she looked just like Little Orphan Annie with big empty circles for eyes. Immediately I counted her out and she was her normal self again. Even though this was an exceptional case, it shows that one must take care to ground the sensor before sending him on his way.

Is it possible that a regressed subject may reveal secrets that should remain confidential?

In both individual and group sessions it may be necessary to relieve the sensor of the fear that if he flings open the door to the unconscious, pent-up skeletons will come rattling and clanking out of the past. Reassurance can be given that nothing will be said that a person would not normally wish to reveal. Anyone who wants to keep a secret will have no trouble doing so.

One prim southern lady came out of the time tunnel and found herself in the guise of a small black boy in the jungle. This thought was so shocking that she turned and scuttled back into the tunnel, ending the retrotrip right then and there. "Nothing to it!" she muttered as she departed, not even taking the time to stay for lunch.

Normally, however, people accept what comes with good grace and a saving sense of humor. If a woman had been purely virtuous or a man strictly honorable in every existence, there would be no need to reincarnate. Moreover, concepts of virtue and honor vary with the period of history and the evolutionary status of the individual. Earth is a school for souls in which the lessons of sloth, greed, incontinence, and all the sins to which the flesh is heir are an integral part of the curriculum.

An attractive young woman found herself retracing the career of a black servant named Jack who lived in Virginia and drove a carriage for a middle-aged couple named Lloyd. Jack was fond of Mr. Lloyd but complained that Mrs. Lloyd was a bitch. Eventually his desire for independence took him to New York City where he eked out a living doing odd jobs. "Jack, what do you do for recreation?" I asked. Immediately a raffish tone came into his voice as he (she) retorted, "I'm not saying!"

A youth was taken back to an existence in which he was a wealthy stockbroker who was apparently engaged in some shady transactions. On being asked how much money he made, he hedged and became suspicious.

After returning to the present he acknowledged that he hadn't been strictly truthful. He did not care for his previous personality but admitted that there were elements in his present character that were reminiscent of this former embodiment.

A friend who is a medical hypnotist was regressing a patient to the prenatal period when he suddenly found himself dealing with a tough, taciturn Boer farmer in late-nineteenth-century Africa. For a while the hypnotist had difficulty eliciting information because the farmer mistrusted the stranger who kept asking impertinent questions. To overcome this resentment the farmer was told that he was talking to his mother. This ploy was only partially successful, because there were many details of his life that this surly individual wasn't about to confide to his mother. Thereupon the hypnotist took the part of the farmer's best friend. This was only slightly more effective because the farmer, thinking he was conversing with his longtime confidant, kept saying, "But you know these things already. Why do you ask?"

The sensor is seldom in so deep a state that he is not aware of his present personality and circumstances. Like a spectator at a movie, he may be engrossed in the story and still know who he is and that his neighbor is munching popcorn. He can also act as a censor, shutting his eyes to that which he would rather not confront.

On the whole, the aplomb with which most people accept the contents of their unconscious memories has enhanced our respect for human nature. One highly intellectual gentleman, a writer by profession, acknowledged with great good humor that in the life prior to the present one he had been a six-foot-tall black woman who worked as a cook on a southern plantation. In no other way, he admitted, could he have learned so valuable a lesson in humility.

Some secrets are not meant to be revealed. An oath taken three thousand years ago may be as binding now as it was then. An ethereally beautiful woman at one of our workshops described her life on the planet Venus. On being asked her Venusian name she said, "I'm not supposed to tell."

Occasionally there are repressed elements in the psyche which are not yet ready to bubble up to the surface. When it is apparent that an individual is evading an unpleasant truth we do not force the issue. Our method is to treat people as responsible adults who are doing their best, not as delinquents to be coerced into confessing some misdeed. If a sensor chooses not to impart certain information, even to himself, then we may assume he has some adequate reason for holding back.

It may seem as though an individual who needs to work out a pain-producing complex is doing himself a disservice by refusing to dig down to the roots of his problem. If, however, one believes that all destinies will eventually be fulfilled in accordance with the Divine Plan, then there is no need to push those who are unready to relinquish their pet neuroses. Most people who practice hypersentience assume that ultimately the laws of evolution ensure that every individual is guided upon the way he must travel. The facilitator may extend a helping hand but in the end each one must walk his own path.

Above all else, the facilitator should never place himself in the judgment seat. The word "sinner" has no place in his vocabulary. In the rare instances where a person is appalled by misdeeds committed in a former existence, we remind him that this was a different personality acting under an entirely different constellation of circumstances.

A college student who came to a hypersensing workshop to gather material for a thesis on hypnotic regression was dismayed when he exhumed the memories of having been a thief and murderer in India who was finally hanged by the British. "I wish I had known better," he sighed. On the other hand, he was cheered by the thought of how far he had progressed in terms of moral development. It seemed a token of how much farther he might go in lives to come.

To date, there has been small reason for anyone to be upset by secrets divulged while in the deep state. Some of this equanimity may rest on the fact that there probably isn't anything that can be dredged out of the subconscious that we would find shocking. Our business lies not in dragging out ghosts of the past, but rather in laying them decently to rest.

It should be added that the material with which we deal is seldom embarrassing anyway. As far as we are concerned people can leave their bathroom doors shut—although it doesn't disturb us if they don't. Septic tanks and sewer systems can remain underground where they belong. Our aim is to probe far deeper than that—all the way down to the living wellsprings of man's pristine sanity.

A thoughtful person does not go barging about clumsily in someone else's unconscious mind, nor does he push in where he is not invited. In dealing with people in the regressed state we endeavor to use the same delicacy and discernment that governs our conduct in any intimate conversation.

Are people sometimes oppressed by memories of past lives?

It may be that fearful persons should not be encouraged to dwell upon the rigors of a long-gone past. In my work the problem does not arise, largely because the kind of people who are likely to suffer morbid reactions do not seek me out. A medical hypnotist who habitually deals with disturbed patients might have to give this issue more consideration.

Occasionally the recollection of a painful demise will leave a psychic repercussion. Thus we have the instance of a sensor who, after having been stoned to death, still felt battered after his return to normal consciousness. From cases such as this we have learned that it is often advisable to implant the suggestion that a particularly distressing memory will leave no negative aftereffects.

On the whole, human nature is far more resilient than many people think.

A friend once lent me a book by Anya Seton called *Green Darkness*. This offbeat historical novel recounts the woes which befell a young woman as she started to recover the memories of a previous life in which her husband (then her lover) was the inadvertent cause of her suffering a nasty death. In the story, the shock of finding out what had happened several hundred years ago was so horrendous that the husband went raving mad, beat up his wife, and would, but for the intercession of a friend, have murdered his kindly old nanny who had nothing to do with the affair. Meanwhile, the wife lingered near death in a cataleptic trance.

While a succession of hysterical reactions on the part of a rich, spoiled, and vapid couple and their hangers-on may make a bizarre twist for a Gothic novel, in real life people are surprisingly nonchalant. Curiously, the woman who gave me the novel had a far worse experience with *her* husband's previous personality from which she emerged fresh and smiling. In one of her regression sessions she recapitulated an experience as an Egyptian temple maiden who was being wrapped as a mummy while still alive. The one doing the wrapping was an implacable priest whom she identified with her present spouse.

As it turned out, the Egyptian girl's soul managed to rise like a bird out of the body before the wrapping was completed, thereby escaping her oppressors. Being converted into a living mummy was an undeniably disagreeable experience, even in retrospect. Yet her main reaction was a sense of relief in the discovery that she had eluded the machinations of the priests and was floating peacefully in the light.

The interesting part of this real life-and-death story is that she held no grudge against her present husband for what happened those thousands of years ago. (She did, however, discreetly refrain from telling him what she found out about their mutual past.) They have long been a happily married pair who have raised several fine children and created a beautiful home together. She feels that subconsciously, by being a generous provider, he may be trying to make up to her for what he did in Egypt.

On the negative side, the husband tends to be intensely possessive, as though wrapping her in the strands of his determination that she belong entirely to him. Her reaction to this smothering concern is a longing to escape into a larger sphere of freedom. These are problems which they are still working out together, but at least she can deal with his attitudes in the light of her understanding of the karmic antecedents of the present situation.

How can you tell if a sensor should not be regressed?

Normally, a person who has reservations about being taken back to a former lifetime will simply blank out. He may think he wants to know what happened but the subconscious has decreed otherwise. There is little anyone can do to contravene the decree of this final authority.

Occasionally a spirit guide will inform us that it is inadvisable to explore the past. Once at a workshop a young man relived a series of distressing episodes in which he was a bootlegger who was gunned to death by mobsters in the 1920s. These recollections included his own funeral at which he was incredulous to see himself lying in a coffin with his grief-stricken mother in attendance.

Unknown to me, his present-day mother, who was also his mother in the former incarnation, was sitting beside him at the workshop. When I started to work with her individually, the first thing I did was to contact a spirit guide and ask if it was permissible to look into her soul's history. To my surprise the guide shook his head and said no. In obedience to this command I made no effort to regress her. Later, when I became aware of the delicacy of the relationship between this woman and her son, and of the pain she had suffered in tuning in on his memories, which were also her own, I was grateful not to have proceeded further. Under that particular set of circumstances it would have been too much.

A report from Rita Brite, a facilitator working in Niles, Illinois, shows how helpful this cautionary technique can be. In a letter dated 15 June 1975 Rita wrote:

> I had a girl recently who could not get beyond the darkness. We contacted a spiritual guide who said, "It is not advisable at this time." She was very disappointed so I asked the guide what the purpose was for her present incarnation. He said, "To learn humility and service."
> She is very sensitive spiritually and was surprised to hear the word "humility." It was a very helpful retrotrip after all. Her husband was following along and he said that when I asked what was at the end of the time tunnel a loud crash came to his ears, as though an iron gate had closed at the end of the tunnel.

For the most part our business is the opening of doors, but when a gate clangs shut it is contingent upon us to respect the power that knows enough to say, "Go no further. Beyond this point thou shalt not pass."

How important is the personal character of the facilitator?
As I made clear at the start of this chapter, the technique of hypersentience is so simple that it can be used by an untrained seventh grader. Undeniably, however, it works better for some people than for others. One reason why a particular facilitator may be notably successful in inducing memories of former lives is that the method is so direct that the force of any given personality is magnified. That is, the quality of voice, inner poise, purity of intent, and the desire to be of genuine service—all come through "loud and clear." If, on the other hand, the facilitator is on a money or power trip, or has ulterior motives, this deviousness will also be conveyed.

It is advisable to remember that the sensor is often telepathic and can tune in on the sentiments of the person with whom he has established a rapport. The facilitator may also tap the consciousness of the sensor and anticipate his replies. In the book *Many Lifetimes* by Denys Kelsey and Joan Grant, descriptions are given of the manner in which this husband-wife team would blend their psychiatric and psychic talents. While Dr. Kelsey was regressing a patient to a previous incarnation, Joan Grant would be so attuned to what was happening that she could advise him how to proceed. She might, for example, dissuade him from pursuing a certain line of questioning because she could see clairvoyantly that the patient was not yet ready to cope with the memories this would bring to light.

If the facilitator is not pure in heart he can be as harmful as a surgeon who operates with a dirty knife. A mind polluter can besmirch any close human relationship, but in hypersentience the benign or malevolent influence of a given personality may be greatly magnified.

It is said that a higher quality of silver must be used for a plain silver bowl than for one which is ornately decorated. That is because the smooth surface will show every scratch or imperfection while the elaborate design will distract the eye from flaws in the basic material. Similarly, there is so little that the facilitator must *do* that the lucidity of his inner being becomes a supremely important factor. To a large extent he serves as a mirror, reflecting the sensor's self-image with minimal distortion. The function of a mirror is simply to reflect, yet without this unpresuming implement a person cannot see his own face.

The facilitator can afford to be mirrorlike in his nonjudgmental attitude because he puts his faith in the sensor's own high self. Hence, there is no need for mind-molding manipulations or anything more than minimal guidance. Without a belief in the divine nature of man, however, hypersentience may be worse than useless. Inasmuch as a poor reflector will present a distorted picture, the technique may even produce negative results. Consequently, it seems unlikely that orthodox psychologists, whose training has been of the mechanistic school of behavioral psychotherapy, will be as successful as the students of yoga, zen, astrology, and metaphysics who to date have been pioneers in the field. In this work purity of character means more than academic degrees, useful though the latter may be.

THE FEAR FACTOR

In the days when I used to travel about the country giving yoga demonstrations it often happened that some frail person would come up to the platform and say, "I always wanted to practice these postures but never dared begin because I was afraid of getting hurt."

The tragic part of this attitude, so prevalent in our fear-ridden culture, is that the effort to move their bodies in a reasonably careful manner could hardly have proven as harmful as the timidity which prevented these unhealthy people from simply doing the best they could. Certainly the results of this timidity were far more disastrous than the effects of any mishap likely to occur while exercising.

Many people are so out of touch with their own instincts that they can no longer rely on common sense when it comes to knowing when and what to eat, how to exercise, relax, or meditate. Consequently, they demand an authority who can relieve them of the burden of ministering to their own needs. They scarcely realize that in the last analysis self-realization has to be a do-it-yourself affair. The main thing they need to understand is that yoga, hypersentience, and related spiritual disciplines have built-in safety factors which require only minimal common sense to make them foolproof. If the beginner will take the first step; the next stage will be revealed.

I have long been suspicious of the current trend toward specialization. It is true that in many professions such as law, finance, or physics, advanced study is necessary. But the belief that only highly paid experts can tell us how to handle our bodies and how to remember former lifetimes has escalated to monstrous proportions, especially in view of the obvious failings of the system which produces these authorities. Needless to say, incompetent people can be found in any field and should be screened out. However, the would-be sensor who has a modicum of intelligence can easily discover the guidelines which will enable him to distinguish the true from the false guide. It is not quite as simple as selecting a melon at the fruit stand, but in this, as in any marketplace, discrimination is required.

Most of the supposed dangers pertaining to the recovery of former incarnations simply do not exist. It is true that a person who is in a suggestible state should be treated carefully. Unfortunately the formulators of television programs and advertising campaigns, as well as parents, teachers, consultants, and advisors, often fail to take responsibility for their power to affect others for good or ill. In this respect hypersentience is not a special case. It is merely one of many sensitive areas in which an individual may be helped or hurt by someone he trusts. Since the facilitator is alerted to the fact that the sensor is in a delicate situation, the chances are that he will take special precautions to avoid any possible pitfalls.

The few people who, for obscure psychological reasons, are bound to go to foolish extremes will find some way to vent their self-destructive impulses. They should not be allowed to give the systems they abuse a bad name. It has been said that an aspirant to higher wisdom does not deserve to find a real guru until he has developed the powers of discernment to recognize him, even in the midst of a host of pretenders. This much we must do for ourselves.

For my own part, I can only say that in all the years during which I have endeavored to transmit the knowledge which has passed through me I have had enough faith in human nature to believe that the recipients would make intelligent use of what they were learning and give it forth again to others. To date, this faith has been abundantly justified.

5

HYPERSENTIENCE AND PSYCHOLOGICAL SUGGESTION

As the guide, I felt shaken. There is a holiness about each individual life and something in me trembled lest I violate it. One should be ordained and consecrated for such a task. The guide should pray and fast. Then, both the guide and the subject should be cleansed in a pool at the heart of the temple. They should receive the high priest's blessing there, and then go to a simple cell made of shining white stone. Nearby there should be a flautist playing music in tune with the subject's highest vibrations. And then the guide should begin.

—Kathleen Jenks

The art of hypersentience is far from new. Occultists claim it to be a legacy from Atlantis, ancient Egypt, Peru, and Central Asia. We know that as early as 1000 B.C. a similar technique was being used in the temples of Asculapius in Greece. There, a group of specially trained physician-priests employed a form of sleep therapy to minister to the sick people who came to them for healing.

In his somnambulistic state the patient was instructed to ask the gods to grant him a vision. During the reverie which followed, he might both diagnose his own ailment and prescribe a remedy. The entire process was regarded as a sacred communion with the guiding spirits of the universe. Essentially it was a sacrament in which the restoration of health was a natural outcome of the opening of channels through which energy might flow from the beneficent source of all life into the ailing body.

Throughout the centuries shamans, medicine men, yogis, and mediums have deliberately induced altered states of consciousness in order to ascertain the causes of illnesses and to banish disease entities. In modern times, the best-known exemplar of extrasensory diagnosis and prescription has been the saintly seer Edgar Cayce (1877–1945), a man who could at will become trance-formed into "the sleeping prophet." A notable feature of Cayce's contribution to the annals of psychic healing was his insistence that what he did others could also do. He believed, and our research has borne out, that the same ability he so superlatively demonstrated is possessed by many ordinary people and can be cultivated like any other talent.

The specific technique which I have called hypersentience had its immediate genesis in the method used in hypnotic age-regression. For practical purposes, however, it has been necessary to draw a distinction between hypersentience and the sheep in wolf's clothing known as hypnosis. Hence it has proven expedient to adopt a whole new vocabulary.

This emphasis on terminology is no mere hairsplitting diversion. In many places laymen can encounter serious legal difficulties if accused of practicing hypnosis or of healing without a license. Also, an inordinate amount of energy can be wasted in trying to counteract the criticism of negative-thinking individuals who regard hypnosis as a dark and dangerous enslavement of the mind. Informed people are aware of the constructive potential of this therapeutic tool, but nevertheless we have found it easier to start with an unsullied new name.

VOLUNTARY ACTION

In hypersentience there is not imposition of one will upon another. A conventional hypnotist may tell his subject that he cannot open his eyes, unclench his fist, or lower his arm. This I never do. It is made explicitly clear that the sensor has perfect command over all his faculties and can function precisely as he pleases. Indeed, the sensor may even give instructions as to how to proceed and when to terminate the session.

Once I regressed a girl named Jean who was so much in control that she turned the tables altogether. Jean was one of the half-dozen or so people with whom I have worked who could not only explore her own past lives but could also tune in one other people's incarnations. At the start she would do this by entering the great hall where the akashic records are kept and looking through one of the Books of Life in which each page is an incarnation. Later she was able to tune in directly to the history of a particular soul.

On this occasion Jean was describing one of my existences in the Middle Ages during which I had been a young woman confined in a dungeon. This was, we both felt, a source of my abnormal dislike of the cold. Suddenly she said, "But you could do this as well as I. Now I want you to tell me how it is in that dungeon."

For the next ten minutes Jean played the role of regressor while I endeavored, with middling success, to recollect that dreadful period of suffering from chill and exposure during which I finally died alone on the dungeon floor. Since Jean was still entranced she could use her clairvoyant vision to direct my fumbling recollections. When we came to the moment when I finally roseabove the body and saw my inner Guide waiting to usher me into the Clear Light, our minds were in such rapport that I could feel her strength of will supporting mine.

Even when the sensor wants to draw upon the facilitator's mental energy in order to suppress an addiction, I try to reinforce his own willpower rather than condone his dependence on outside assistance. A hypnotist may discourage a client from smoking by implanting a posthypnotic suggestion that cigarets will have a repulsive taste—like rancid cat food and rotten onions. This strategy may work for a day or two, but then when the suggestion wears off the client drifts back to his old indulgences.

Our method of eradicating unwanted habits is somewhat different. While in the hypersensory state the subject—who must already have evinced a genuine desire to quit smoking—is instructed to visualize his ideal self. This pure and perfect being admonishes the small personal self to set aside the childish nonsense of sucking upon a cigaret. No longer will the victim of the habit take pleasure in polluting his body, or in pouring filth into the atmosphere which others must breathe. He simply isn't the kind of person who can find enjoyment in callously contaminating the God-given breath of life. The sensor repeats this exhortation and allows a few moments for it to sink in. Thus, he is not merely a passive listener but an instigator of his own reform.

The results of this type of suggestion may not be immediate. The process is so simple and speedy that the sensor may even forget that he has made the affirmation and continue smoking for another day or two before the resolution percolates down into his everyday consciousness. If, however, there is a real wish to kick the habit, this method will prove effective.

While minor bad habits such as nail-biting, swearing, or procrastination may be overcome in a single session, major problems such as alcoholism and obesity will almost certainly require a comprehensive psychoanalytic approach which endeavors to remove root causes rather than to obliterate symptoms. However, it is always helpful to invoke the sensor's better self and to strengthen his determination to be his own master.

EMPHASIS ON CONSCIOUS AWARENESS

It is not necessary for the sensor to go into a trancelike state, though this does occasionally happen. As much as possible the work proceeds on a conscious as well as on an unconscious level, since the aim is to fortify the network of communications between the ego and the deeper psyche. Critics have claimed that hypnosis tends to produce dissociation which weakens the will. But we work to develop the ability to make associations, a process which involves the art of remembering. This account by Maria Comfort of Santa Barbara, California, describes some of the effects of opening these portals of memory.

HOW IT FEELS TO BE REGRESSED

Although I had been able to hypnotize myself, no one have ever guided me through a regression. Finally, one of my astrology students made the offer and I accepted. Mostly, I was curious about how it would feel to be regressed. Would the sensation be different from self-hypnosis?

Lauren began counting me down, using the same procedure that I had taught her and in no time I felt perfectly comfortable. It is like daydreaming. You are consciously there, but still in your own far-off place.

As we went back I had the feeling that I already knew the things that came to me about my earlier years since they were part of my memory. But that is what regression is—the opening of memory. My recollections became more and more vivid as we went along and finally she brought me to the time of birth. I could actually feel the experience of not wanting to leave the warmth and comfort of the womb. When she brought me to the point where my soul entered my body prior to being born.

"Wow," I said, "what an experience! Whoom! It feels just like that—whoom!" Then I started to laugh with glee. "No wonder they call it that!"

Lauren was puzzled. "Call it what?" she asked.

"Womb. It's because that's what happens—whoom!"

Even though I was in a supersensed state my sense of humor and consciousness were at a peak. I found that I was simply tapping my memory. For example, if someone asks you what you did last Friday you would say, "Let me see, hmmm, well, I went to see the dentist, and then I worked on the yard . . . " You are consciously aware of what you are doing and saying, and at the same time you are tapping your memory.

That is what regression is like. You are sufficiently sensitive to the person guiding you to know what kind of rapport you have and whether he can be trusted. It is a sort of ESP in which you increase your awareness of those around you.

After Lauren counted me out I felt refreshed as though I had had a two hour nap.

If the experiences recollected during a regression session have been traumatic, we may simply ask the sensor if he wishes to bring these unpleasant memories into the light of his conscious awareness. Virtually always, he says yes. Even after recapitulating an apparently agonizing episode, the sensor may feel purged and exhilarated. Like a sleeper who has had a bad dream, he will still awaken refreshed.

In rare instances the material brought forth is so distressing that the sensor prefers to rebury it. A twenty-year-old girl started to pick up a lifetime in which a passing stranger brutally assaulted her in an old barn. The incident was so painful that we agreed that it would be better to relegate it to the scrapheap of the unconscious. With her permission she was told to forget the entire experience—which she promptly did. On awakening she could not understand why her knees wobbled.

That night a few defused momories did come through in dreams. Through these spontaneous flashes her psyche was able to reduce the negative impact of what she needed to know. As it happened, this was a propitious time for her to confront her deep-seated mistrust of sex because she soon became engaged to a young man who romantically insisted that she be a virgin on her wedding night. (Until then the greatest liberty permitted her boyfriends had been a chaste good-night kiss.) In view of what we discovered about her unconscious fear of sex, I was able to warn her that if the honeymoon was less than ideal she should not hold it against the bridegroom. Thus, even without remembering the details of the assault she was able to profit by what she had learned.

Even when a person is told to forget an event he remains free to reverse the decision. Once when I was regressing the palmist Ethel Brown who runs a metaphysical bookstore in Anaheim, California, she went back to a life during the Inquisition in which she had been condemned as a witch. As Ethel described being bound and hauled off to the place of execution in a straw-filled oxcart I thought, "Oh dear, this trip is going to be a bummer! Better take special care."

Suddenly Ethel gasped and shuddered convulsively.

"What happened?" I asked.

"They burned me to death right there in the oxcart."

"All right, you are out of that body now. It is all over and you are feeling very happy and peaceful . . . back in the light. Are you in the light?"

"Yes, I feel fine now."

"Do you wish to forget this incident?"

"Yes, I'd really rather not think of it."

Thereupon I gave a strong suggestion that all memories of this incarnation would be blotted from her mind, and we went on to the next stage of the hypersensing session.

Later that day Ethel chanced to remark, "You know, I wasn't supposed to have been burned in that oxcart. It happened that way because a soldier became impatient and flung a lighted torch into the straw."

"Hey, I thought you were going to forget that scene."

"Well, I decided I'd rather remember it after all."

Because Ethel genuinely wanted to know as much as possible of her own soul's history, her higher mind overruled both her immediate impulse and our command. There were no adverse effects from this confrontation. Rather, she gained renewed confidence in her ability to face up to even the most unpleasant of earthly realities.

In another instance I was approached by a physician, Dr. L., who having recently earned a degree in hypnosis, wished to add our technique to his repertoire. I had no difficulty taking him back through several incarnations. Afterward Dr. L. mentioned that his original teacher had given him the posthypnotic command that no one else would be able to hypnotize him— something this teacher did routinely with his students. Nevertheless, Dr. L. was easily able to override these instructions.

A person is no more obliged to follow a posthypnotic suggestion than he is to purchase a product he has seen advertised. The suggestion may have some immediate effect but most people remain quite capable of running their own show. Normally, when we make such suggestions it is more for the sake of inducing the sensor to *dehypnotize* himself from the illusions produced by social conditioning than to induce him to follow our orders.

It has been said that hypnosis makes people passive and dependent. However, hypersentience requires active visualization and a positive effort of the will. We do not pour information into the brain as though it were a vessel to be filled. Rather, we help the subject to draw the information needed out of himself. Thus he can attune his mind to realities which can add depth and significance to his everyday life.

Unfortunately there are still some professional hypnotists who prefer to keep their subjects in the dark about who and what they may have been. An example of this attitude can be found in the popular musical *On a Clear Day You Can See Forever*, in which the heroine doesn't even know she has been regressed until she accidentally learns the truth. The implication is that she is too stupid to know how to deal with the material in her own subconscious, and hence the clever hypnotist deliberately keeps her in the dark. My experience in trying to help people who have been subjected to this type of inhibition is that it has an extremely negative effect upon the subject and betrays a well-nigh unforgivable arrogance on the part of the hypnotist.

In Jess Stearn's best-selling book *The Search for a Soul*, the novelist Taylor Caldwell never held on to the memories of the lifetimes to which she was regressed. Everyone is entitled to his modus operandi, including the hypnotist who worked with Taylor Caldwell. Nevertheless, I would not have encouraged or even allowed this evasion on the part of a woman who is quite intelligent enough to deal with the material in her own psyche. In view of the enormous difference it could make to humanity to know that death is only the gateway to a larger sphere of experience, a great opportunity was lost. It is regrettable that Taylor Caldwell had to undergo all those awful lives, but certainly she has no monopoly on suffering. It is to be hoped that she will speak up for what she knows to be true before she passes from the scene.

A few hypnotists actually crave control over their subjects. Being in a position to say, "I know a secret about your past that you don't know," can swell this type of ego. Acknowledging that such people exist need not discourage the many dedicated professionals who adhere to the highest ethical standards. It is just that the sort of character who is on a power trip is apt to be the very one who wants to be a hypnotist.

DISTINGUISHING REAL FROM IMAGINARY EVENTS

A significant difference between hypersentience and hypnosis is illustrated by an incident which occurred during a regression session conducted by a prominent medical hypnotist. The entranced subject had reverted to a lifetime as a soldier. In the midst of a fierce battle he suddenly realized that he was about to be run through by a lance.

"Hey, get me out of this!" he yelled as the vision of his imminent demise flashed before him.

"It's all right," the hypnotist reassured him soothingly. "You have a strong shield which is deflecting your enemy's weapon. Now you have escaped and are enjoying a victory celebration. Nothing happened to hurt you."

To us, the unwillingness to give credence to the impressions welling up from the unconscious is tantamount to encouraging the subject to be a liar. To encourage a deliberate act of deceit is, in our opinion, never justified, even if the dupe is only oneself. In many ways the subconscious mind is like a small child who, in his desire to please, may tell tall tales, but who can also be trained to distinguish truth from falsehood. Hence, the facilitator strives to hold the sensor to the realities of his own immediate experience.

Before taking off on a retrotrip, the sensor is primed with the idea that he will be able to pass through the deaths of his former personalities without excessive strain. Knowing what to expect, he is seldom dismayed. His recapitulation of the universal human experience of passing in and out of a physical body strengthens his conviction that repeated births and deaths are but transitory incidents in the larger life of the soul. Having already endured the worst, he can look forward fearlessly to the time when it becomes necessary to relinquish his present vehicle because it can no longer take him where he wants to go.

Under hypnosis a subject can be made to believe a fabricated story. Stage performers have for years titillated audiences by inducing volunteers to mimic bullfrogs, drunks, or Hottentots, thereby generating a few belly laughs at someone else's expense. On the positive side, experiments have been conducted in which people of mediocre talent have been hypnotized and told that they were great artists. As a result they were induced to perform far above their normal optimum.

In hypersensing, by contrast, the sensor learns to distinguish between the products of his superficial imagination and the flashes which arise spontaneously from the deeper levels of his image-making psyche. Even when it is necessary to play games in order to exercise the faculty of creative visualization, as for example by pretending to be Picasso or Leonard Bernstein or the president of the United States, it is still made clear that the ultimate purpose of the game is to sharpen the mind to the point where it can more easily discern the truth.

PROS AND CONS OF CONCENTRATING ON THE PRESENT LIFETIME

Some people have been discouraged from consulting a regular medical hypnotist because they lacked the time and money to undergo hours of psychoanalytically oriented probing of their early years. By the same token, a well-known hypnoanalyst affirmed that he would not grant a patient's request to be regressed to a former lifetime until after at least a dozen preliminary sessions.

I feel that by going directly back into one or more previous incarnations the sensor may be so impressed by the power of his own mind that he thereby gains the incentive to take a new look at what he has done, is doing, and hopes to accomplish in his present existence. Consequently, we are apt to begin with the remote past and then work up to the point where we can regard the events of the current life in the light of this startling new knowledge.

It seems to me that to pin the responsibility for all neurotic quirks entirely on parental and environmental deficiencies can be like saying that clouds are the cause of rain, without taking account of the more fundamental factors that create climatic conditions. Sometimes, however, the establishment of a simple cause and effect relationship with regard to the incidents immediately preceding a situation will alleviate a specific hangup. If all that a person cares about is staying dry, then it may be enough merely to know that clouds are harbingers of rain.

A case of this sort, in which it did not seem necessary to delve into prenatal memories, was that of Mrs. Q., an elderly lady who sought me out in the hope that I would implant a suggestion in her subconscious that would enable her to control her gagging reflex. For several years she had been obliged to function with no teeth because every time her dentist tried to reach inside her mouth in order to fit her for dentures she would choke spasmodically. At one time Mrs. Q. paid forty dollars, which she could ill afford, to a hypnotist in the hope that he could help her, but a fruitless session with this specialist left her all the more discouraged.

During the course of our hour together I encouraged Mrs. Q. to drift into a guided reverie until it finally came out that the root of her trouble lay in an incident some years previously when she had suffered a nervous breakdown. Because of her refusal to eat she had been force-fed through a tube inserted in her nose. This violation of her sensibilities was so horrifying that allowing any foreign object to enter her mouth produced an unbearable choking sensation. Once I understood the immediate cause of the problem, I was able to take specific measures to help this woman, even without probing her more remote past.

A case in which knowledge of both past and present lifetimes was needed to cast light upon a long-standing affliction was that of a psychically sensitive young woman whom I shall call Janet. As the younger child of a large, ill-tended brood, Janet had ample reason to develop a variety of physical and psychological problems, including migraine headaches. (This person has come back into my life and it seems advisable to go easy on her and not to do anything to upset her frail psyche.)

Whenever, as a tiny child, Janet suffered from her convulsive headaches, her mother and stepfather would lock her in a bedroom, letting her weep and thrash until she collapsed in exhaustion. In view of the traumas endured during those vulnerable years it hardly seemed necessary to search further for the source of her troubles. However, when Janet was asked to trace the deeper causes of her headaches she went back to an existence several hundred years ago during which she was afflicted by a form of epilepsy connected with the unsupervised development of her clairvoyant faculties. Because of her terrifying fits, which were often accompanied by visions and revelations, she was obliged to live as a solitary outcast. Ultimately, the seizures became so severe that she died alone and untended.

A still earlier cause of Janet's problems was traced to a lifetime in India when, as a member of the cobra cult, she misused her psychic gifts. There, motivated by jealousy, she had used the hypnotic power of her mind to destroy her sister, taking advantage of this sister's blind and unquestioning trust. Having betrayed the faith of one who loved her, she became fearful of what others might do to her if she invested the same kind of faith in them.

For our purposes, the important issue was the discovery that Janet's shattering headaches were a hangover from her former epileptic condition and might, therefore, be at least partially dealt with on a physical level. While the issue of learning to trust others by proving to be trustworthy herself would have to be resolved over a period of time, she could at least be advised to have an electroencephalogram and to find out if any of the medicines normally prescribed for epilepsy would be useful in her case. Without some knowledge of the manner in which former lives led to the disabilities manifested in childhood, it would have been difficult to discover this particular source of her problems.

HYPNOSIS, HYPERSENTIENCE, AND PSYCHOANALYSIS

It is extremely helpful for the practitioner of hypersentience to understand the tenets of the major schools of psychology. He should be prepared to cope with the phenomena of transference and countertransference, and should understand the basic premises of classical psychoanalysis. The hypnotist, by contrast, can often function effectively without any special psychological insight.

The only instance in my experience in which negative results accrued from a series of regression sessions showed the extent to which the facilitator can, like a psychoanalyst, become a target for repressed fears and frustrations that have long been buried in the subconscious.

The subject, a young woman I shall call Barbara, had been woefully mistreated in childhood. In the beginning, Barbara saw the facilitator as the embodiment of the "good mother"—the all-protecting, nurturing, maternal parent she had always wanted but never possessed. This feeling was so powerfully projected that an element of countertransference entered the situation. That is, the facilitator began to behave in a motherly way toward

Barbara, voluntarily taking on many of the duties that a mother would perform for her child. The emotional nature of this tie was intensified by several sessions which were spent exploring a lifetime in which there actually had been a mother-daughter relationship between these two women.

Then when the newfound mother figure began to devote her attention to someone else she suddenly became transformed into the "bad mother" in the eyes of the jealous child. The anger that swamped Barbara's normally rational intellect was not aroused by the regression sessions per se, but rather was an outcome of the psychoanalytic process. Indeed, no ordinary insult (and none was given) could account for the steely cold rage which caused Barbara to lash out in fury, spreading a miasmic smog of slander and innuendo, and causing irreparable damage to several innocent people who had the misfortune to be caught up in her whirlwind of vengeance.

It required only one incident of this nature to convince us that the facilitator should tread cautiously when working with disturbed people, and should when necessary call upon the assistance of a psychiatrist. Fortunately there is now a growing band of specially trained medical hypnotists whose proficiency in regression therapy is such that they can deal with just about any problem that may arise.

Even in ordinary cases, however, the facilitator should take due precautions against the negative reactions with which every psychotherapist is familiar, especially if he intends to cope with long-standing complexes. It should be possible for him to maintain an attitude of professional impersonality, refusing to become an object of either positive or negative transference, and maintaining an attitude of spiritual detachment. Somehow he must continue to be warm, friendly, and interested without being sucked into the subject's inner conflicts.

PSYCHOSYNTHESIS

The ultimate aim of hypersentience goes far beyond the initial stage of recovering unconscious memories. A person must crouch down in order to jump up, or draw back his fist in order to thrust it forward. Similarly, it may be necessary for him to descend to the lower depths of the psyche before he can reascend into the radiant presence of the high self. First he must clear the snakepits of the mind; then let the sun shine in. Otherwise the searchlight of his inwardly focused attention may merely intensify the shadows which lurk in the dank caverns of his unregenerated instinctual nature.

To a large extent this cleansing of the subconscious has been a function of orthodox psychoanalysis. Now, the necessity to reintegrate the diverse elements of the self on a higher level of health and wholesomeness has become the province of the group of humanistic, experiential, value-seeking, and transpersonal psychologies which have gathered under the standard of psychosynthesis. We might say, therefore, that what hypnotism is to psychoanalysis, hypersentience is to psychosynthesis—an enormously potent therapeutic instrument.

The founder of psychosynthesis was the Italian psychiatrist Roberto Assagioli (1888-1974). His basic textbooks *Psychosynthesis: A Manual of Principles and Techniques* [1] and *The Act of Will* [2] should be required reading for all who aspire to work in the field of hypersentience. Now that Dr. Assagioli has passed on, it can be revealed that the source of his inspiration was the same Tibetan guru who dictated a series of esoteric books through Alice A. Bailey between the years 1919 and 1949. Letters written from "the Tibetan" to Dr. Assagioli are among those published in Alice Bailey's book *Discipleship in the New Age, Volume I.* [3]

The popularized version of Freudian psychology has given many people the idea that the subconscious contains an inchoate mass of animalistic biological urges. According to the teachings of psychosynthesis, however, the instinctual realm of libidinal drives is part of nature's storehouse, providing the raw materials needed to lead a richly satisfying life. After all, do not the precious metals and gems which we so extravagantly admire come from under the ground!

Hence, the practitioner of hypersentience aims to do more than release the pent-up frustrations which steam beneath the surface of people's polite facades. He also endeavors to draw upon the magnificent wealth that glitters in the hidden caverns of human nature. By calling upon the power of the high self he works to transform these psychological resources into the treasures with which to create a society of true abundance.

Hopefully, the emphasis placed upon the superior aspects of the constitution of man will help people to realize that the recapitulation of past lives is neither a difficult nor a dangerous process when accompanied by a reasonable degree of common sense. Hypersentience bears about the same relationship to old-fashioned hypnotism as a jet plane does to an automobile. It is possible to take an interesting trip in either vehicle, but in hypersentience the subject strives to rise to a level of awareness which can make his experience more personally satisfying and relevant to his spiritual aspirations.

THE NEW BREED OF MEDICAL HYPNOTISTS

Now that hypersentience is developing into a popular movement, it is to be hoped that lay practitioners will work in increasingly close cooperation with

---

[1] Roberto Assagioli, *Psychosynthesis: A Manual of Principles and Techniques* (New York: Hobbs, Dorman and Co., Inc., 1965).
[2] Roberto Assagioli, *The Act of Will* (New York: The Viking Press, Inc., 1973).
[3] Alice A. Bailey, *Discipleship in the New Age, Volume I* (New York: Lucis Publishing Co., 1944).

the rapidly growing band of medically and psychiatrically trained hypnotists who are experimenting with past-life regression therapy. Exchanges of ideas and techniques may prove particularly valuable because these two groups attract distinctly different types of people.

Thus far, most of the investigators who have become interested in hypersentience have been those who operate within a broad context of metaphysical assumptions that include the acceptance of reincarnation, karma, and the higher spiritual evolution of man. For the average psychotherapist the situation is more complex. He may have to spend many hours on the preliminaries of adjusting the patient to the idea of digging into prenatal memories before he can even begin to make the connections between this person's immediate problems and his former lives.

The issue became particularly apparent to me during a discussion with Dr. Richard Willard, the founder and director of the Institute of Medical Hypnosis in Fort Wayne, Indiana. Dr. Willard is at this time America's foremost medically trained authority on the therapeutic benefits of hypnotically induced recollections of former lifetimes, and he has persuaded many of his fellow physicians to experiment along these lines. In the course of our conversation Dr. Willard described how he would sometimes run afoul of the prejudices of his patients when he regressed them to a previous incarnation. After passing through the death experience, he would move on to the point where the patient was about to be reborn.

"But doctor," the patient would argue, "now that I've died I'm supposed to stay in heaven. Why should I come back when I don't even believe in reincarnation?" This was one dispute which the doctor could always win since it was evident that, like it or not, this soul had returned to complete its unfinished business in a new body. Nevertheless, special handling was required to ease the patient's dismay at the discrepancy between his personal experiences and his religious beliefs.

The position of the medical hypnotist is also complicated by the fact that patients come to him because they are burdened with serious psychological problems for which they hope to find a solution. In the practice of hypersentience, on the other hand, the facilitator usually works with normal well-adjusted people who simply want to understand themselves better or who are seeking to accelerate their spiritual development. If, therefore, the medical hypnotist charges a fee consonant with his training and with what he is expected to accomplish, while the facilitator may request only a voluntary donation for his services, this is as it should be, since they are working in two different areas and for different purposes.

It would be a pity if ill will should ever arise between these two groups, as could happen if a movement were launched to make hypersentience a medical monopoly. In actuality, what the lay practitioners are doing is not to undercut the professionals but rather to educate the public to the point where distressed people will know enough to seek out those who can provide the most effective kind of regression therapy. Ideally, the amateurs in the field will send their problem cases to qualified physicians or psychologists while the latter will in turn profit by the research being carried on by those who have the leisure and the interest to broaden the base of understanding of what hypersentience is and can do.

The experiences of two outstanding medical hypnotists are illustrated in the following reports. The first account comes from Lloyd Koelling, M.D., founder and director of the Institute of Medical Hypnosis in Scottsdale, Arizona.

This is a case history of a fifty-six-year-old white male physician specializing in medical hypnosis, hypnoanalysis, and hypnotherapy. His problem was a fear of failure in his newly established practice of hypnoanalysis.

He had been in general practice for twenty-five years with two years of psychiatry and extensive background work in the field of human sexuality. He became interested in hypnoanalysis when he discovered that sexual disorders as well as other psychosomatic diseases can be remedied more completely and permanently with hypnosis than in any other way. He completed his specialty training but was still haunted by a deep-seated fear of failure.

In November of 1973, he was regressed by Marcia Moore to two previous lives, one in the mid-sixteenth century and the other in the latter part of the nineteenth century. In a later analysis by a colleague these two existences were explored in greater detail.

The first life dated back to 1542, at which time the subject was an English warrior named John Moore. He had been transported to Europe to fight a battle on horseback; hence he was wearing a knight's battle dress, including a metal helmet, gauntlet, gloves, leggings, shield, a long spear, etc. John was leading his troops on horseback down into a valley that was a "bloody mess" with men and horses being slaughtered in hand-to-hand combat.

During a preliminary word-association test the subject had responded to the word "red" with the word "bloody," and had also stated that if he failed in his current practice he would be in a "real horrible mess."

John Moore died after a short hand-to-hand combat when he was knocked off his horse and a spear pierced his heart—another "bloody mess." He was left with a sense of failure that he had not been able to win the battle.

His soul was then transported to the United States of America. Here, in the 1860s, he was a pioneer in Illinois named John Grant. He had a wife, two children, and a small farm. While he was cultivating the land around his cabin his farm was raided by Indians. He managed to get his family safely into the cabin where he and his son held off the Indians until they were rescued by settlers from a nearby area. John Grant died of a lung disorder at the age of 63. The probable diagnosis was consumption and the disease attacked him on the side of the chest where he had received a spear thrust through the heart in his previous existence.

In his current life the subject was confronted in his office one night by a bleeding abortion patient. Here was another "bloody mess." The patient was immediately admitted to the hospital across the street from the office. Nevertheless, she later accused the doctor of attempting the abortion himself. He was indicted but was completely exonerated in the District

Court. But before the case was heard he had lost his local hospital staff privileges and as a result his private practice started to decline. In other words, there was a failure in his professional career at that time because of another "bloody mess."

This physician has had extensive training and experience in his present specialty of medical hypnoanalysis and, after reliving these previous episodes, he was able to see why he had so long suffered from an insidious fear of failure. He felt reassured that he is mastering the lessons that God sent his soul to Earth to learn, that he will succeed in his present specialty of medical hypnotherapy, and that he will thereby achieve his goal of helping his fellowmen to be happy and well.

Our second report is taken from the tape-recorded notes of a lecture given by Richard Willard, M.D., at the 1974 annual convention of the American Institute of Hypnosis in Las Vegas, Nevada. The title of the talk was "Know Thyself by Understanding Past Lives."

> The patient was a physician who came to me with several problems. As these were being worked out he commented, almost as an afterthought, "I am unable to deal effectively with women. I just don't seem to be able to do or say anything which might in any way put down, hurt, or harm a woman."
>
> As a result he was unable to discipline or fire his female office employees, even when he had more than ample cause to take firm action.
>
> In searching for the cause of this particular problem I told him I would regress him to the origin of the difficulty. First, he went back to an incident which occurred at the age of sixteen. He was supposed to pick up his mother downtown, but being preoccupied with trivia and the thrill of driving the car he forgot to meet her. By the time he arrived home she had already walked the distance and, being in poor health, was lying on the couch in great distress. So great was his guilt that he swore he would never allow himself to hurt a woman again if Mom would just be OK.
>
> After removing the guilt from this symptom-producing incident I told him he would go back even farther in time and space—all the way back to the very first time he had made this promise to himself or had the same feeling that he couldn't possibly hurt a woman, no matter what.
>
> As he started describing where he was he said, "I'm on top of a tower."
>
> "Fine, that's good." I replied.
>
> "And there's a moat around the tower."
>
> "Fine."
>
> "It's a beautiful day. I can see the woods, the pasture and the green grass. The sun is shining and it's beautiful here on top of the castle."
>
> I'm not the brightest guy in the world but I immediately knew this was a little unusual, so I turned on my tape recorder. As it happened, he was on the tower of a castle in Wales. He then went on to say:
>
> "I can't tell if I'm alive or if this is afterwards. Yes, it's afterwards. I'm looking down on it. It's a casual day and I'm looking out over the fields. I just screwed a gal, one of the wenches. That's why I don't have any warrior armor on. I just got my . . . it's like cloth. I put my robe on. [Pause.] Jesus! She wouldn't do that! She's just pushed me over. But I grabbed her. We're going down together now . . . headfirst. It's coming . . ."

A word of caution. If you're regressing a patient he may go into a prior life anytime, even during the word association test. Be awake, be aware, be ready for whatever may come.

The only time you have a problem when dealing with a patient under hypnosis is if the therapist panics. I don't care how much the patient panics or how much distress he is in; if the therapist is calm and relaxed he has the situation under control.

If the patient experiences a death in that lifetime you reassure him . . . reassure him that the spirit survives. Regardless of how horrid, how cruel, how terrible it was in this other existence he will suffer no undue harm from it because the spirit goes on forever.

So at this point I reassured the patient—your spirit will be OK. It is safe and secure. You are safe and secure in the knowledge that the essence of you will survive.

He did land on his head and his skull was smashed. Incidentally, this patient had had recurring dreams of falling headfirst. Whenever he had to go to any height above ten feet and look down on anything that resembled rocks he would have a vision of himself having fallen and lying there with his head smashed. This happened in dreams and also in real life when the images would come to him. Then the patient went on to explain:

"I'm lying there and she's on top of me, but she's not dead. I loved her. And in that brief instant when I pulled her down with me I crippled her for life.

She loved me too. She tripped. She hit me accidentally and knocked me over the wall and I mangled her. Oh my God, I can't ever hurt a woman like that again!"

After I removed the guilt from the incident the patient breathed a deep sigh of relief. The girl in the tower was blonde, and this patient has always been very attracted to blondes, but had never been able to bring himself to date one. This particular patient is functioning well now, at times to the despair of some of the office girls he works with. He has no trouble dealing with women.

In concluding this lecture Dr. Willard said:

I do not feel that all problems relate to incidents in prior lives, nor will I try to convince you that prior lives are a reality. Our mission is to help people. If an individual has a problem which keeps him from being well, then we should remove it regardless of our own beliefs. Treat not yourself, treat the patient. If it's in his mind and if he feels it's a problem, help him with it.

One of my professors in medical school used to say, "Never be afraid to include the rare, the unusual, or the exotic diseases in your differential diagnoses, for you will never make the diagnosis if you don't at least think of it."

I don't ask you to accept reincarnation, but like my professor I do ask that you think about it. And if it does exist, if there is this possibility, then what can we learn from it, what can we gain from it, and how can we use it to help others?

6

COMPLEXES

In dealing with psychological complexes from a reincarnationist point of view it appears that the tenets of Freudian psychology do little to illuminate the deeper causes of the pervasive malaise which had turned this planet from a Garden of Eden into something resembling a lunatic asylum. Basically, people's problems do not arise out of misdirected sexual impulses; they stem from the inability to love. Hell is congealed out of the substance of cruelty, avarice, and indifference, and we create it for ourselves whenever we fail to care for others.

Sex is an energy which can be channeled in many directions. When this root force runs amuck we are in trouble, but even then the real difficulty relates to the misuse of the mind which directs the libidinal impulses. Ultimately, the whole murky subject of the origins of neurotic and psychotic dysfunctions can be illumined only by a clearer mental apprehension of the karmic law which decrees that human beings must learn to love—actively and intelligently—if they are to better their lot on Earth.

Nevertheless, most of the cases dealt with in this chapter do bear upon the negative results which can accrue when people mishandle their sex-based drives for security, status, recognition, companionship, and the like. For example, a young man whom I regressed started out by recalling an existence as a nomad in a barren land. The only notable occurrence in what was otherwise a life of unsurpassed dullness was his desertion by an unfaithful wife who ran off with another man, leaving her abandoned husband to bring up their child.

Afterward, I felt apologetic that nothing more spectacular had happened. Later, however, I received the following letter:

19 September, 1973

Dear Marcia,

I want to thank you for our regression session together and a delicious dinner. As you said, many valuable insights came days after the actual session. Among the most important was the discovery that my mother had been my unfaithful wife in my unmotivated life in Arabia. I realized this as I was relating the regression experience to her.

I have had several intensely jealous and resentful periods with her when I was in high school, and particularly when my father left her (me) at the age of seventeen. The new man in her life aroused severe and critical jealousies beyond any reasonable explanation from this lifetime.

Only after I had been married several years did I regenerate these very difficult and painful emotions into a complete love and acceptance of her. When this happened, we both felt that an immense weight had lifted. Since then I have been free from this resentment of women.

We spoke openly and at length about it. I believe the regression session triggered the final end to that particular karmic bondage.

Peace, love,

Peter

GENDER-ENGENDERED COMPLEXES

A celibate priest spends a lifetime praying for continence. Now, in a new embodiment, he is impotent.

In the year 1825 a woman watching her children die of scarlet fever swears that never again will she bring anything to birth. In her present life she is barren.

An isolated farmwife with no children longs for human companionship. A hundred years later she finds herself the mother of sixteen lively youngsters and asks why.

In dealing with cases such as these it sometimes appears that human beings have more free will than they can handle. Certainly some of our toughest problems come from getting what we want.

Even when a person is disenchanted with his situation there is usually some reason why he has chosen to incarnate under a particular set of circumstances. Hence we have instances such as the following:

A man who, two hundred years ago, was the ultimate male chauvinist is now an attractive woman who rejects her own femininity, but who has managed to sublimate these feelings by becoming an avid partisan of the women's liberation movement.

A woman who exploited her husband with vain and unnecessary purchases is now a man who, for no apparent reason, feels compelled to knuckle under to the absurd demands of a spendthrift wife.

As we come to problems relating to sexual identification the issues become more involuted. Since human bodies, regardless of whether they are male or female, are basically similar, it sometimes seems surprising that people should suffer such intransigent torments as a result of their sexual ambiguities. If one were to be born with the head of a cow or the hind end of a chimpanzee, that really would pose a dilemma!

Nevertheless, there clearly is some validity in the Freudian dictum that "anatomy is destiny." Although we cannot claim to have done more than alleviate some of the sex-based quandaries that have come to our attention, it does appear that any increase in understanding of the reasons why a soul happens to be trapped in an uncongenial, exploited, or malfunctioning body can in itself be therapeutic.

When problems are as fundamental as those which confront an individual who feels that he should have been born in a body of the opposite sex, it is not always possible to set his mind at rest by *doing* something about his plight. Often little can be done. Rather he may need to gain a new awareness of the qualities of his essential *being*—qualities that transcend the body and its appetites.

Hypersentience has been especially valuable in cases where ordinary psychoanalytic methods have failed. The aim of the facilitator is not so much to prescribe a course of action as to raise the sensor's eyes to a higher level of consciousness. The solution should lie in a clearer grasp of the plans and purposes of the high self. Only then can remedial measures be taken.

Since virtually every human soul, during its age-long history, has functioned through both male and female bodies, the ascription of homosexuality to a recent change in gender is almost certainly an oversimplification. Most evidence shows that an individual who was once a sexually potent man may subsequently operate with equal elan through the body of an alluring woman, and vice versa. The real homosexuals, as well as those who are merely neuter, have usually inherited their predispositions from a series of prior lives during which they were, for one reason or another, unable to express themselves in a normal manner.

A few confused folk hardly know whether they are, or want to be, boys or girls. These psychological hermaphrodites are so undifferentiated in their sexual identities that they can respond to any strong stimulus that comes their way. In addition there are the out-and-out bisexuals who operate on an alternating frequency. Some may be happy, well-adjusted, creative personalities. Others are ambiguously passive and aggressive, masochistic and sadistic, veering first one way and then another. Even when maladjusted in terms of accepted mores, they rarely evince any desire to lead a more conventional existence.

A particularly sad predicament is that of the hapless soul who feels that for some unfathomable reason he has landed in a body of the wrong sex. Such a one may then endeavor to adjust his psyche to his condition, or to adjust his body to an inwardly conceived self-image through surgery and hormone treatments. Seldom does he achieve contentment with his lot. Perhaps the only ultimate answer is for him to use his God-given faculties of reason and intuition to find out *why* he is the way he is. Then if it turns out that there is something he should or should not do, he can take remedial action.

Among creative individuals women often tend to accentuate the so-called masculine qualities of independence and self-assertiveness, while men are not afraid to demonstrate the so-called feminine traits of tenderness and emotional sensitivity. This harmonious blending of male and female components within a single integrated personality is not to be confused with hermaphroditism or homosexuality. Rather, it is an androgynous condition which is a natural outcome of the ability to accommodate varying roles. The reincarnationist might say that these bipolar people probably have had more opportunities to adjust to both male and female bodies and to realize how slight are the differences between.

Consequently, the "divine androgyne" represents the higher end of a spectrum which stretches from a state of undifferentiated response through various grades of distinctions between masculine and feminine characteristics, and on into a realm where memories of both modes of expression are so thoroughly programmed into an individual's memory bank that transitory sexual differences cease to be of any great moment in the ongoing life of the soul.

The point to bear in mind is that homosexuality, bisexuality, and transsexuality are neither unitary nor simple phenomena. There can be many causes and manifestations of each of these conditions. Eventually, when researchers have amassed thousands of documented cases it may be possible to categorize the various types of sexual deviance with regard to their karmic antecedents. In the meantime I will give some illustrative cases and hope that others will carry on from there.

THE STORY OF A TRANSVESTITE

When Mr. A. walks into his richly appointed office in a building he owns, he is the veritable embodiment of the proverbial solid citizen. Well-to-do in his own right, he has an attractive wife who is wealthier than he. Both come from respected families and are leaders in community affairs. Surely no one would suspect that beneath the expensively tailored suit, which so becomingly sets off the silvery sheen of his clipped gray hair, he is wearing a bra and panties!

Mr. A. is "a galloping transvestite." That is, when the urge to don feminine apparel hits him, it is so powerful that he is compelled to secrete his lacy underwear in some accessible place, just as an alcoholic will keep a bottle in reserve. Although he suffers profoundly from his affliction, he has been unable to do anything about it. Years of psychoanalysis have proven fruitless as have conferences with noted clairvoyants and spiritual counselors. During the depressed periods of his life he has toyed with the idea of suicide. Were it not for his belief in reincarnation he might actually have converted his anger and disgust into overtly self-destructive behavior.

Despite his sexual idiosyncrasies, Mr. A.'s charm and intelligence are such that he could, if he wished, make the woman of his choice happy. Instead, he chose to make two women miserable—namely his wife and his mistress. He originally married because he felt that matrimony would keep his feet on the ground and prove his masculinity. No doubt his wife's impeccable social status also helped. It was, however, three years after the wedding before the marriage was consummated. Even then, their sexual relations were far from normal. Nevertheless, two daughters were born of the union and, to the casual eye, the four of them presented the picture of an ideal family.

Not until Mr. A. had been faithfully but miserably married for nineteen years did the love of his life come into the picture. One day while he was sitting gloomily in the park, a striking-looking girl with long honey-colored hair walked up to him and said, "You look as though you need a friend." As it turned out, she too was in need of friendship for she was raising four small children with little help from her estranged husband.

For several years, during which they saw each other regularly, they remained just that—good friends. Finally, however, the demands of the flesh (especially hers) became insistent and their long-term companionship ignited into a torrid romance. For the first time in his life Mr. A. felt that he was functioning like a real man. Although his girl friend was many years younger than he, and far less educated, she was a natural psychologist who helped him to bring his clothing fetish into the light, even to the point of purchasing his transvestite paraphernalia and encouraging him to flaunt it in front of her.

Being a born psychic she was also able to perceive that Mr. A.'s problem was compounded by the fact that he had a "hitchhiker"—that is, an obsessing entity—clinging to his aura. This entity took the form of a sexy female who would periodically demand her due by being allowed to dress in scanty underthings and strut in front of a mirror. Only when thus placated would this temptress permit Mr. A. to relax and proceed about his normal business.

For a while, Mr. A. was able to maintain a tenuous balance between the demands of wife, inamorata, and hitchhiker. During this period he underwent a series of hypersensing sessions which did much to clarify his long-term devotion to the twin gods of status and security, a preoccupation extending back over many lifetimes and several millennia.

At first it appeared that I would have no luck at all in regressing him, for he was too self-conscious to call any images to mind. Finally, as a last resort, I used my old standby and asked him what he would never ordinarily think about. After a long pause and much insistence on my part he finally managed to stammer, "A . . . a . . . big juicy doughnut. . . . Now that really is silly!"

With this unintentional choice of an archetypal feminine sex symbol, he appeared to become more relaxed. Then, just as I started to think that we might succeed after all, a loud buzz saw started to drone in our next-door neighbor's yard. Without much hope of competing with this nerve-shattering uproar, I told him to concentrate on the buzz of the saw and that this would take him under. Amazingly enough he did sink immediately into an extremely deep state from which it was easy to go back into a prior lifetime.

Our sessions together were painful for Mr. A. because he had neither liking nor respect for most of his previous personalities. Only once did he report having a normal married life and that was during an incarnation as a burly farmer in which he had died as a young man, leaving his wife (who is now his girl friend) with three young children to bring up alone.

At first it seemed natural to assume that Mr. A.'s transvestism would in some way relate to a female incarnation. We did indeed find a life two thousand years ago in which he (as a woman) had been romantically attached to his present girl friend (at that time a man). This is but one of a number of cases in which couples with whom we have worked have previously been lovers in bodies of the opposite sex. Usually the switch contributes to a fuller relationship, since each partner can better understand how the other feels. Evidently souls, as well as bodies, enjoy novelty in their lovemaking.

Interestingly enough, Mr. A's girl friend was able to recollect the same set of circumstances during which she (a handsome young warrior) had been obliged to leave him (a helpless and vulnerable maiden) in order to carry out an important mission in a foreign land. Not long after the girl died, brokenhearted and alone. Having once suffered the pangs of being deserted, this entity decided that henceforth he/she would be the one to do the deserting, and so it turned out. There was little pleasure in this reversal of the situation, however, because in the life as a farmer the last thing the husband wanted was to die and leave his wife bereft.

Merely having lived in a woman's body could hardly account for the torments Mr. A. endured as a result of his sexual aberration. It was, therefore, not surprising to discover that there were also several lifetimes in which he had been a monk, renouncing sex altogether. In one monkish existence he had been responsible for the pregnancy of his girl friend (who was then a nun). Though regretful, he did not own up to it, leaving her to the ignominy of bearing an illegitimate child. Karmically, this act of desertion may have related to the later life as a farmer in which he wanted desperately to help his wife raise their three children but was unable to do so because of his premature demise. There is, however, some question as to how well he learned this lesson because in the present existence he has given his girl friend very little help with her children.

Although Mr. A. had a reincarnational history of instances in which his behavior could hardly be called "manly," his compulsion to dress in woman's garments was directly traceable to an existence during the days of the witch trials in medieval Europe. In this instance, the woman he loved before, and still loves, was languishing in jail after having been accused of being a witch. Actually, she had done little to merit the accusation, being but a pawn in a political game that others were playing. As a prelate of recognized power and prestige he could have saved her, but only at the expense of his cherished reputation.

The unfortunate girl had been assigned to a dark dungeon in which she was guarded by rough soldiers who continually threatened to molest her. In order to ward off their advances she clipped her hair and adopted male garb, even though she had been specifically warned that this was blasphemous behavior. Specifically, she was contravening the statement in the Bible that "the woman shall not wear that which pertaineth unto a man, neither shall a man put on a woman's garment, for all that do so are an abomination unto the Lord thy God."

Since this girl was of such obviously pure character it would, under ordinary circumstances, have been difficult to pass judgment against her. Owing to her unseemly attire, however, she was condemned to be burned at the stake.

When it came to the actual execution, which took place in the town square, Mr. A.'s account and that given independently by his girl friend corroborate each other down to the last detail. As she was being led to the pyre, her attention was caught by the elaborate crisscross design of twigs, sticks, and logs which had been laid in such a manner as to ensure that the fire would be well ventilated.

"How sad," she sighed, "that so much human ingenuity should have been applied to so unworthy a purpose!"

As the guards fastened her hands to the stake, she was praying. The next thing she knew she was being lifted straight up out of her body and was surveying the scene from above. As though gazing through a golden mist she saw the assembled throng, the torch being applied, and the ravening tongue of orange flame licking at the white figure atop the platform in the center of the square. Then there was only a sense of blessed relief as she rose into the light.

For Mr. A., the wrenching forth of the memories of the same incident was far more traumatic. With methodical exactitude he described the layout of the square in terms of a clock.

"The church is at twelve o'clock, a blank wall goes off at two o'clock, I am standing at eight o'clock, and the street goes off at ten o'clock. It is a gray day. . . . Now they are bringing her in from the left. She is wearing white. I don't see her face . . . not because I can't but because I won't look."

As this description was given, his body began to protest by itching and becoming nauseated. Knowing that this was a subconscious resistance to a necessary confrontation, we continued the session.

"I am now as I was then," he continued. "There was a protective layer like lard that I kept about me. What I then used to protect myself from her image now shields me. . . .

"In the sky there is a flock of gray birds, just sitting there waiting. Oh Lord, some of these details never came down in the history books. The birds wait until the flesh grows cold and then pick away at it. . . . It's all just so terrible! I thought it wouldn't really happen."

Mr. A. clenched his fists as tears started to pour down his face. "I didn't know what I was doing; I really didn't. I have the feeling of wanting to run away."

At this point I gave the suggestion that his body would relax and that he would feel calmer. Another set of images pertaining to the witch trial and his own part in it started to come forth and then finally he concluded, "I see a monk's robe with a cowl. I don't like this personality. He was gutless . . . wasn't very good looking, an ascetic. He was capable of feeling love but was held back rigidly.

"It's all those conflicts in this man's brain; it's the same conflicts I've had in this life. It doesn't matter what century I'm in . . . one ought . . . what *ought* one to do? How is it that a man can do his duty and still be wrong? But love transcends duty. That's it, love transcends duty. But still I must suffer to know that this is so."

On hearing of cases like this some people protest that it should not be necessary to exhume so many painful details out of the long-dead past. Why not allow the skeletons of yesteryear to remain decently buried?

In Mr. A.'s case, however, the corpse had never been properly laid to rest, and the resultant stench was poisoning his life at the roots. Superficially, his transvestism could be traced to his cowardice in allowing the woman who was his soulmate to be condemned on the pretext of wearing clothes of the opposite sex. But even this was not the real issue. In the medieval life he had betrayed a supremely important friendship. Now once again he was being torn between love and duty, a conflict exacerbated by the fact that he was also being faced with the opportunity to settle the karmic scores of several other incarnations, as well as to carry out a project that would have been of significant world service.

Curiously, this material was drawn out of his subconscious during a time of crisis when he was being faced with several major decisions in the conduct of his personal affairs. Once again a maze of seemingly arbitrary circumstances had forced him into a position of choosing between love and an exceedingly rigid concept of duty, a duty which, as before, was conveniently compatible with his ingrained craving for status and security. Simultaneously, he was being impelled by his misunderstanding of a situation and by an exaggerated sense of righteousness to betray the confidence of a close friend. The most important choices of his career had to be made, but this time he was given sufficient insight into his soul's history to have some idea of the deeper issues involved. Whatever he did, at least he would not be acting blindly.

As it turned out, Mr. A. failed to live up to the faith that had been invested in him. In the end he lost the respect of wife, mistress, and friend, left his job and went off alone to lick his wounds. No doubt, however, the chance will arise in some future life for him to prove himself worthy of the trust of those who have loved him through the ages. Reincarnation has been called "the doctrine of the second chance." In actuality, the chance is given again and again until the test is passed and the soul progresses to higher dimensions of understanding.

This case is not easy to summarize, partly because the main characters are still weaving the intertwined strands of their destinies, partly because a number of people were involved (souls incarnate in groups), and partly because not just one but a whole conglomerate of psychological conundrums lay behind the apparently trite dilemma of a man being forced to choose between wife and mistress. It demonstrates the complexity of the moral decisions with which people are faced, as well as the impossibility of making valid judgments on the basis of what is usually known about a given situation.

This case also reinforces our conviction that a person is seldom left to grapple with a serious obsession, neurosis, or psychosis for no good reason. Personality weaknesses may stem from past iniquities but the fact that they are carried over shows that there is work to be done in the present.

Karma is not retribution; rather it is a call to take care of unfinished business. A person may probe the past in order to untangle the initial causes of a problem, but the knowledge gained makes it all the more imperative to take some remedial action in the here and now. Indeed, if an individual does not intend to settle the score, it may even be best to allow the skeletons to rest peacefully in their various closets.

SCHIZOPHRENIA

Of all mental dysfunctions, none is more baffling than schizophrenia. Some psychologists claim that this condition is usually traceable to a disturbance in the mother-child relationship and that it frequently has its roots in the Oedipus complex. This complex springs from the positive libidinal feelings that a child develops toward the parent of the opposite sex. That is, a boy tends to fall in love with his mother and a girl with her father. Often these emotions draw forth a corresponding response from the chosen parent. When the forces behind this incestuous attraction are unable to find a creative outlet, they may lead to a personality disorder.

Although standard methods of psychoanalysis have proven inadequate in explaining or treating schizophrenia, most of the cases I have dealt with have featured some karmic involvement with the mother or father. Actually, I have had very poor luck in trying to regress schizoid people, but on a number of occasions I have worked with close relatives who knew them in past lives. Generally speaking, it is hard to discern what the parent may have done in this lifetime to set off the illness since the majority of sufferers have had problems from the time of birth. Moreover, many have normal brothers and sisters who have received essentially the same upbringing. While some factors may relate to early childhood conditioning, it seems extremely doubtful that the schizophrenic condition can be comprehensively diagnosed without reference to moral issues which may extend over many incarnations. The following instances are illustrative of this thesis.

In a former life a man betrayed his country with the connivance of a woman with whom he was infatuated. Now she is the mother and he is her schizophrenic son.

A prosperous East Indian family depended on their only son to carry on both the business and the family name. Instead the boy, Ranjit, ran off with an older companion who had persuaded him that he was much too spiritual to be concerned with such mundane affairs, and that he should become a monk in Tibet. In the course of the journey, Ranjit became so addicted to his practice of meditation that he seriously neglected his own welfare. At this point his companion became concerned and tried to persuade him to return, but it was too late. Ranjit froze to death in the Himalayan snows while endeavoring to learn to free his mind from bodily concerns.

In the next lifetime we find that the companion who lured Ranjit from the path of duty is his English mother. Ranjit is now her mentally deranged son. The other children in this family have all pursued successful careers. Although the mother was advised to have the defective child placed in an institution, she felt so responsible for his well-being that she paid a private nurse to care for him until he was in his mid-forties.

More than once we have observed that the karmic penalty for unjustified suicide or deliberate mistreatment of the body seems to involve the necessity to cope with a malfunctioning physical vehicle. Thus, a monk who scourged himself unmercifully in the Middle Ages is now, in his current incarnation, trying to deal with the chronic ill health that necessitates constant attention to the demands of the flesh.

A possessive mother pursued her young son through the streets and in and out of houses in a vain effort to dissuade him from going to sea. Despite her entreaties he joined the navy, became a successful officer, and eventually married and raised a family of his own.

In her present lifetime this woman wishes desperately that she could be free from the physical, psychological, and financial burdens of coping with the peccadilloes of her grown schizoid daughter. Despite this woman's endeavors to disassociate herself from the situation, the child cannot let go but continually becomes enmeshed in difficulties from which the mother is obliged to extricate her.

The image of pursuing the runaway son through the streets came to this woman when she was asked to scan her former lifetimes in order to find the karmic antecedents of her dilemma.

THE STORY OF A PARANOID SCHIZOPHRENIC

For a woman, the necessity to cope with a mentally disturbed child is surely one of the most heartrending of situations. How much sadder, then, the story becomes when the problem is exacerbated by the assumption that the child's parents must in some way be responsible! Could they have toilet trained him too early, weaned him too late, held him too close or not long enough?

This is the impasse which confronted Mrs. R., a bright, beautiful, and outgoing woman whose first child, born while she was still in her teens, has been diagnosed as a paranoid schizophrenic. Despite the best efforts of both parents the boy, now a mature man, is obliged to remain most of the time in an institution.

One can imagine what it must have been like for this conscientious young mother to schedule an interview with a respected psychologist only to have him declare, "You are sitting with your legs crossed. That means you have a fear of being raped."

But what could the learned specialist say, since the conventional assumptions with which his mind had long been embalmed precluded the possibility of finding anything other than a textbook explanation for the case?

In actuality, this instance does illustrate one central thesis of Freudian psychology since, as the disturbed son grew up, he developed many of the symptoms of the classical Oedipus complex. One would have thought that *he* was the jealous husband rather than the small child of the woman who bore him. When he was an adult and his mother came to visit him in the mental hospital where he was confined, the doctor in charge advised her not to hold his hand since even this casual display of affection caused him to become dangerously overwrought.

There is no need to recount the miseries these inexperienced parents endured as a result of their son's inability to come to grips with the demands of everyday living. The fact that he was handsome and intelligent could only lead them to ask, "What did we do wrong?," as they sought advice from one high-priced psychiatrist after another. In a single year they spent more than ten thousand dollars on his treatment, all to no avail.

Even though there was no apparent reason for the eldest child's disability, the law of the universe holds that nothing happens without some cause. Consequently, we decided to explore the karmic antecedents of the problem in the hope that by bringing the past to light, some measure of illumination would follow.

As it turned out, Mrs. R. was an excellent subject who had no difficulty picking up two former lives. The material given here comes entirely from the first hour-long session. This brevity contrasts sharply with the weeks and sometimes years of treatment required for a conventional psychoanalysis.

In the first interview the suggestion was given that Mrs. R. would explore her karmic relationship with her son. A subsequent session the following day touched upon the incidents of two more lifetimes with snatches of some others. Although it was apparent that these other incarnations had contributed to the enrichment of her present personality, they had less bearing on her immediate problem.

When Mrs. R. emerged out of the imaginary time tunnel which took her back into her soul's history, she saw herself as a young widow named Joanna living in the early seventeen hundreds. Originally, Joanna had come from England to Philadelphia as a bride. Now, with three small sons and two daughters entirely dependent on her for support, she found herself bereft. Although she had inherited some property, she could not read or write. With no husband and no education, she was unable to cope with her situation.

For Joanna, the only escape from her dilemma was to marry a much older suitor whom she neither liked nor respected. The man was arrogant and condescending but he did have financial security and a home in Virginia. She was reluctant to move to the South but knew no other way to turn.

Next we shifted to a scene in which Joanna was standing on a box while attendants dressed her in an elaborate wedding gown. The garment had many petticoats, a big red rose pinned to the back, and was far too ornate for her taste. By background she was a Puritan and had always worn subdued clothes. Her aversion to her husband-to-be was greater than ever as she mentioned that he was a politician, wore lace on his cuffs, and told people what to do.

Again we brought her forward. Now she had been married several months. The union had turned out even more disastrously than anticipated and she was abysmally unhappy. "He manages me," she complained. "We have many servants but I can't trust them. He keeps me away from my children and I miss them. There's nothing I can do about it because I can't read or count. I can't stand this man but I have to stay with him. . . . Oh, I wish he were dead!"

Two years later the situation was still deteriorating. Joanna seldom saw her children and was expected to remain in strict attendance upon her husband. Household tasks and needlework were her only ways of passing the time. "I'd be better off if he were dead," she wailed.

In the next scene the husband had fallen seriously ill. A servant scurried by with a bedpan and Joanna insisted upon looking to see if her husband had passed any blood. To her great pleasure she observed that he had indeed been bleeding internally. Whether she actually poisoned him was a question which, at that point, it did not seem necessary to confront. Clearly she wanted him out of the way and was getting her wish.

Before long the cruel husband died and Joanna and her five children lived happily thereafter. Her sons and daughters learned to read and she lived long enough to see them grown and flourishing. On being asked what lessons she had learned from this life she said, "I learned to be strong and not to trust the wrong people." She also surmised that the unloved husband was the same entity as her mentally disturbed son.

We then went back to an earlier life in England around the year 1600. Mrs. R. saw herself then as a young woman named Beatrice. She was standing in a spacious room with ornate furniture and was wearing an elegant green velvet gown. Again, however, she took little pleasure in her sumptuous wardrobe because she was married to an older man whom she despised. In this marriage too, she had had no choice but to accept an unwanted husband because she was without financial resources and he was a wealthy businessman. He was also corpulent, white-haired, and far from handsome. Although it pleased him to show her off at parties, he gave her no real love or attention. Consequently, all she had to do was to dress and undress herself and wander about the big house fingering the heavy carved furniture and brocaded curtains.

It was hardly surprising, therefore, that this pretty but bored young woman took a lover. All we found out about her paramour was that he was young, penniless, and played the violin. Unhappily, the romance was short-lived. The elderly husband found out about the lover and threw Beatrice out of the house in midwinter with nothing but the clothes on her back.

It was bitterly cold, she coughed a great deal, lived with "awful" people, and died before the age of twenty-five. On being asked what lesson had been derived from this life, she said, not unsurprisingly, that she had learned discretion. Again, she identified the jealous husband with her present son.

An interesting feature of this case is that in both lifetimes Mrs. R. had been distressed by her lack of education. In the afterdeath state, however, she found herself in a realm where it was possible to attend classes and to soak up learning as a flower absorbs sunshine.

These classes were, she explained, very informal. People went only if they wished to attend. The students gathered around teachers in a garden, or in a temple with white pillars which was illuminated from the ceiling. Some of these learning places resembled museums while in others people discussed the experiences of their various incarnations. For Mrs. R., the education by which she set so much store appeared to take place primarily on the inner planes while her earthly lives were useful mainly for character building.

In conclusion, it may be surmised that the schizophrenic son's present suffering can in large measure be traced to at least two lifetimes when he was wantonly cruel to those who depended on his kindness. Now it was his turn to be helpless, vulnerable, and dependent on others. Mrs. R., on the other hand, was basically a gentle and loving person, even in the lifetime in which she wished that her husband would die.

Since it is written in the cosmic law book that "thou shalt not kill," she was obliged to make restitution by providing the entity who became her son with a healthy new body. But apart from the problem with her son, Mrs. R. has enjoyed a rich, full life. She has a charming and successful husband, is cherished by her friends, travels extensively, and has had every opportunity to develop her mind. Even with regard to the disturbed son it appears that the debt is paid since the parents are no longer responsible for the cost of his medical treatment. If, in the future, these two souls meet again it will be simply as friends, for he has lost his negative hold upon her.

Moreover, if this story can help others in similar positions she will have converted a bitter experience into a force for good—which is what all our sufferings are designed to accomplish.

OBESITY

A girl suffering from obesity recollected a prior life during which she existed on a starvation diet and resented it bitterly. To this day she is oppressed by the conviction that she cannot get enough to eat, even though her mirror tells her that she weighs two hundred pounds.

Another girl who remembers dying of starvation in a Nazi concentration camp has a naturally slender figure which enabled her to succeed as a high fashion model. In the former lifetime this second girl had shared even the little that she had, choosing to die prematurely in order to help her friends.

It should be remembered, therefore, that in dealing with physical or psychological problems from a reincarnationist point of view, correspondences between cause and effect depend far more on attitudes than on facts. We shape our destinies by the quality of our reactions to inexorable circumstances. Bound though we may be, the manner in which we deal with the immediate issue of our bondage may hold the key to ultimate freedom.

Many relatively normal people are plagued by a tendency to gain unwanted pounds. The following case history submitted by Lloyd Koelling, M.D., of Scottsdale, Arizona, explores some of the reasons why a fundamentally healthy and attractive young girl should feel compelled to armor herself with excess flesh.

> The patient is a twenty-one-year-old white female with a problem of moderate obesity plus a lack of self-confidence. When she came for analysis she was approximately thirty-five pounds overweight. She had tried special diets, amphetamines, etc., without success.
>
> During the first part of the analysis it was discovered that she came from a very religious family. She lost her father by divorce at the age of seven but led a fairly normal life until she was fifteen. At this time she was forced to give up her closest girl friend because her mother and stepfather suspected that there had been a sexual incident one night when in fact there was not. As a result of losing her girl friend and being restricted from social activities, she started eating for satisfaction.
>
> In the beginning we explored some of the present-life antecedents of her problem. These included an incident when as a small child she had inadvertently caused the death of her beloved pet canary by holding it too tightly in order to keep it warm. At the age of four she was almost smothered by her brother when he wrapped her too tightly in a blanket and

pushed her under a bed. In addition, she barely managed to escape from a sexual assault which could have resulted in her death.

Next she was regressed to a previous life in fifteenth-century England in which she found herself confined in a filthy dungeon. She had been imprisoned for having sold or given away potions to people at a time when the witch-hunting mania was widespread. From the age of twenty-two until her death thirty years later she remained incarcerated in this dismal place.

In a later life she was a beautiful barmaid who sold her charms, much like a prostitute. This activity left her with an enduring sense of guilt and shame.

In her word association test she showed a definite confusion between the concepts of pleasure and death. So many of the pleasures she had known both in her previous lives and in this one resulted in unhappiness or death that for her the life-embracing pursuits of love and sex became inextricably linked with the fear of being punished. Hence, eating became her only available source of enjoyment.

Under hypnosis it was pointed out to her that her real mistake lay in her misinterpretation of the connection between the pleasures of sexual love and the fear of retribution. She was made to understand that she is a child of God with a spirit sent back to Earth in order to learn certain lessons and that she will no longer have the need to burden herself with unnecessary guilt and shame. Then, when God feels that she has mastered the art of living on this earth, she will rest at the right hand of the Heavenly Father. Meanwhile, she can continue to love God, love herself, love her neighbor as herself, and be the happy, beautiful, slender young woman she is meant to be.

She has almost reached her goal of a trim 120 to 125 pounds at five feet seven inches tall, and has a very lovely personality as well as physical appearance.

Fortunately there are now enough qualified medical hypnotists working in the field of regression recall to justify the hope that in a few more years this type of investigation may revolutionize the field of modern psychology.

WHAT DOES IT MEAN?

Souls come to this planet to be born in pain, scratch out a precarious living, and then again die in pain. Why must life be this way? We sense that there may exist brighter and more beautiful vistas of the universe. Surely there must be places where men and women can grow through joy and expansion, even as now they are obliged to shape up through sorrow and restriction. Yet for mysterious reasons people must labor obscurely in order to learn lessons which can be mastered only through the squeeze of earthly experience.

Of all the insights hypersentience has bestowed upon me, the most meaningful has been the conviction that throughout the millennia of this planet's evolution not one iota of anguish was ever wasted. No drop of blood nor human tear was ever shed in vain. The same is true for the lower kingdoms; never was animal, plant, or stone sacrificed without some corresponding spiritual gain. There is no death but only transformation, and with each metamorphosis the quality of our world's consciousness is subtly enhanced.

Ultimately, when enough individuals have learned to understand the deeper purposes of the evolutionary process, it will be known that man's continuing struggles, miseries, complexities, and perplexities really were worthwhile. Through these rending conflicts the unifying qualities of sympathy, caring, and compassion have been developed and transmitted to succeeding generations, gradually becoming shared characteristics of mankind as a whole.

With the dawning of a more comprehensive vision of what the past has meant, we will finally realize how it was that *out of all this suffering the soul of humanity was born.* Only at such excruciating cost could the priceless life-essence be distilled. Let us, therefore, remember the words of the Jewish philosopher Simeon Reubeni of Mantua who said:

> Oh companions of our ancient exile,
> as the rivers go to the sea,
> so do all our tears
> flow into the heart of God.

7

LOST CIVILIZATIONS

Marcia— Where did you begin?

*Michael—*I began as a note. It's a vibration—part of the AUM. But I don't know why it doesn't finish.

Marcia— Are you meant to finish it?

*Michael—*Yes, perhaps . . . I am to sound that note, for that is my function in creation. I am like a sound wave or a beam of light. I am the Watcher. There are many of us.

When people are asked to go as far back into the past as possible they often end up in a realm of kaleidoscopic color and sound. In this crystalline concatenation of pure vibratory impulses, prismatic light beams cross and recross without jarring one another's frequencies. Some sensors associate this luminescent sphere with another planet or with the kingdom of the angels. For others, it is sheer abstraction, devoid of emotional ambiance.

A few individuals regard this vision as the "psi-reality" which constitutes the groundwork of creation. They see it as the matrix out of which all forms have sprung. To them it exists not in the sense of temporal beginnings "a long while ago," but as an eternally self-renewing spiritual potential. Although it is an essentially timeless state of being, it is perceivable here and now.

Seldom indeed do we begin with the archetypal caveman or any of the lower forms of evolution. Nevertheless, some people can regress to exceedingly primitive times. One subject went back to an experience in which he was one of a tribe of people who had no names because they did not speak. Their only means of expressing ideas was by drawing pictures. To obtain food they would surround a small animal, capture it, and cook the flesh over a fire made by rubbing two sticks together. Our colleague Akeva also recapitulated a caveman experience but he was busily making sketches on the cavern walls.

Rarely can these instances be geographically or chronologically pinpointed since the sensor can perceive no more than would be registered by the character with whom he is identifying. Even though we sometimes go back to a time before languages were known, it has proven virtually impossible to find an era when people did not have some means of relaying their feelings to one another. Numerous subjects have surmised that this earliest form of communication was a kind of instinctual telepathy. This is not quite like the mental telepathy we speak of today. Rather, it resembles the rapport which joins herds of animals and flocks of birds.

When hypersentience becomes an accepted mode of exploring human origins, it should one day be possible to rewrite history on the strength of many intermeshing accounts. Conventional archeology will be paralleled by a more subjective archeology of the mind. This study, which we call "psi-history," can in its own way be entirely scientific since it will be based on observations by reliable investigators who have proven their ability to produce valid results in the realm of the paranormal. If these accounts fit together like the pieces of a jigsaw puzzle, then they may be deemed worthy of attention.

Thus far, we have been able to discern the shadowy outlines of two major phases of human development prior to the dawn of recorded history. In addition there have been some maverick descriptions of places we could locate neither in time nor in space and which may not even have been on this Earth. The two vast civilizations of which we have some ken seem to coincide with the mythical lands of Atlantis and Lemuria. Although these mysterious cultures have been the subject of speculation since the time of Plato, much of our material has come from people unacquainted with this mass of legendary lore.

For the most part, our subjects were not so much reconstructing as *reliving* their experiences of the distant past. While a clever actor might have duplicated some of their performances, it is impossible to believe that all our fellow workers could have been so unfailingly imaginative had they not been tuning in on some level of reality. In any event, it is still premature to pass judgment on the validity of this technique. All we can do is present, with minimal editing, samples of our findings. The reader can make of them what he will.

LEMURIA

Lemuria appears to have been located where the Pacific Ocean is now. It was the abode of both primitive and sophisticated people. The more evolved inhabitants of this land developed the tool of language while the less evolved (or earlier) races communed by means of telepathy. This vast continent endured for thousands of years and produced a variety of cultures. Probably there was as much diversity then as there is in the world today. Hence, descriptions of it can be expected to vary.

The names assigned to these semimythic islands usually seem to have an "a" sound and to incorporate the syllable "mu." According to Isabel Buell, there were several successive stages of this civilization. Thus, on August 20, 1974, she gave us the following account:

I am going to speak today about Muraya. This is a continent which existed long before Lemuria. Its origins are lost in antiquity—at least four million years ago.

Muraya was a vast island continent like Australia, a veritable Garden of Eden. It had good people and bad but it wasn't the inhabitants who brought it to destruction. It flourished and declined in the natural course of the planet's evolution. It was primitive physically but evolved spiritually. These were the people who started Lemuria; hence the same sound in the name. Lemuria took the Mu from Muraya.

Most of the continent lay across the equatorial zone with temperatures ranging from seventy-eight to eighty-five degrees. It seemed to run crosswise on the globe rather than longitudinally the way continents do now. In the cataclysm when the planet flipped, the continents changed. Each time the globe flips, the continents shift back and forth; that is part of the balance of the planet. There were very few people in the other parts of the earth and very little land mass relative to the watery parts. There was one other continent but it was mostly inhabited by large animals.

The people on Muraya resembled our South Sea Islanders in color, size, and happiness of heart. They were of the same physical structure and mind. They used the wheel but were not mechanized. They were among the first who understood our brothers from the stars and who knew how to use the cosmic forces. These people seemed to understand their relationship with God.

The people of this time traveled in their astral bodies. They were taught this by the brothers from the stars. [In this manner] they themselves could travel to the stars. The air was extremely pure, as was the food and water. The dress was casual and primitive because of the atmosphere. Their clothes were similar to mumus and sarongs, all very simple. They had no sexual hangups and no overpopulation. People reproduced by the star system.

The waters are of a vivid blue and green. The sky is an indescribable color with clouds in Technicolor. Some clouds are white and others are like rainbows. They have tones of yellow, blue, green, pink, and lavender—but no red. You have a constant feeling of living among rainbows. It is all so rich and vivid that it makes our world seem gray.

The sand is pure white. There is no volcanic action and hence no black sand. Nor is there any red earth. The green of the vegetation is almost blinding. I see plants like enormous philodendrons.

The houses are circular. In this they are similar to those of Atlantis. These huts are also flexible. People sleep very little in them. Mostly they sleep on the ground or wherever they happen to be. There are no dangerous animals or stinging insects, no threatening elements, just tremendous harmony and peace.

The houses seem to be made of strong, flexible, hollow reeds shaped like bamboo. The reeds are a gorgeous shade of dark green that holds its color. They can be bent into many shapes and are practically indestructible. The houses are shaped in rounds and also in pyramids. Doors and windows fall naturally into place. The builders stick one end of the reeds into the ground and bring the other up and inward to the center where they are tied in bows. The reeds act like conductors for the forces of the earth. The energies flow up the outside and then back down from the center. The people were taught this art by the brothers from the stars.

Now I begin to see my own pattern. That's three times I have been concerned with temperature control and energy fields in living structures. . . .

Most of those who have glimpsed civilizations long faded into the mists of antiquity agree that while these ancestral peoples may have lacked our technology they were hardly the primitive ape-men postulated by the Darwinian hypothesis. The earliest races may constitute missing links but the chain they help to form reaches not down into the animal, vegetable, and mineral kingdoms but upward to more subtle spheres of consciousness, or, as Isabel Buell put it, to the "brothers from the stars." Consequently, we have descriptions such as the following, by Margaret Joy Granger:

I was regressed by Marcia Moore in early November 1973 at the home of Jess Stearn in Malibu. Before the regression I already had an idea of what was to come. I had seen a watery land with islands and knew that I was a young girl living there.

During our session together I saw a beautiful chain of many islands and sensed that it was a dying land. It was so alluring—misty and soft.

I was a schoolgirl and the island where I lived was ringed by high stone walls that rose sharply out of the ocean. I was on my way home for a visit. The journey was made in a tiny gray metal submarine that held only one or two passengers. This was the usual mode of conveyance between the islands.

When I arrived on my native island I was greeted by my "pets." They were adorable amphibian creatures with tails like dogs but at home both on the land and in the sea.

My father was a revered judge, a wise man to whom people came for counsel. We could read each other's minds. There was no illness in our country. We were a slim ethereal race—graceful and well proportioned. Our language was like a form of music with sounds like reeds blowing in the wind. These people were of an extraordinarily sensitive vibration. We seemed to be able to float or fly—perhaps it was astral travel?

Just recently I realized that there were beautiful butterflies as large as birds that lit on our shoulders and stayed with us as gentle companions. Their wings shone with every hue of the rainbow.

I knew our land was dying and that it would soon be necessary for me to leave. I felt extremely sad to be departing for a strange and alien territory.

Whether this experience occurred on Earth or on another planet I am not sure.

The name of the land is Mulynia.

Normally we would have followed so interesting a conversation with several more. However, we were obliged to desist because the memories made Margaret so nostalgic that she could hardly bear to think of her lost homeland.

ATLANTIS

As we come to the noble continent of Atlantis the information-gathering process becomes easier. The following profile is a composite of material brought forth by many different subjects.

Virtually everyone agrees that Atlantis was beautiful. It encompassed green hills, majestic mountain ranges, fertile farmlands, beaches, and cities. In the harbors of its teeming seaports, large ships lay at anchor, but most people preferred to fly. Apparently, the latter-day Atlanteans were familiar with various kinds of magneto-powered aircraft. There were small individual planes, bus-type planes, and also spaceships which came from elsewhere in the universe.

At the peak of the Atlantean culture the economy was based on solar energy. The radiance of the sun was transformed by laserlike crystals into heat, light, and motive power. Intellectual pursuits were supported by universities where men and women studied phrenology, alchemy, and astrology as well as the arts and sciences familiar to us today. Women held a relatively high position even though they were not considered the equals of men. There were times and places where the culture was virtually a matriarchy, but in general women's position deteriorated with the rise of technocracy.

The government was a theocracy, with much connivance among those who sought to wield the reins of power. No one disputed the dictates of the priests because they controlled the sources of physical energy. Science and religion were indistinguishably commingled and the results were not always beneficial.

This was an elitist society with priests at the top, then aristocrats, a merchant class, and peasants. There was much arrogance among the privileged and little protest from those at the bottom of the social scale.

At one time the rulers of Atlantis were guided by a group of wise and benevolent teachers who came to the Earth from elsewhere in the universe. It appears that at an early stage of the Atlantean civilization some of the visitors intermarried with the earthlings, making it possible for others of their kind to reincarnate in appropriate bodies. Thus, the first sojourners had to come physically via spaceships but after that they were able to travel spiritually and arrange to be born in bodies of their choice. Several subjects have reported that the original Atlantis existed in another part of the solar system and that its earthly counterpart was a colony set up to receive the inhabitants of a dying planet. Just as New York is named after York, England, similarly the Atlantis of which we speak was an outpost of an even grander civilization. This was the start of the caste system, ancestor worship, hereditary monarchies, and of the idea of the sovereign as "the son of heaven."

Such a visitation may account for the Biblical statement made in the sixth chapter of Genesis where it is written:

That the sons of God saw the daughters of men that they were fair; and
they took them wives of all which they chose. . . .

There were giants in the earth in those days; and also after that, when the
sons of God came in unto the daughters of men, and they bare children to
them, the same became mighty men which were of old, men of renown. . . .

The most important of the early gifts of these sojourners from outer space
was agriculture, including herbal medicine, beekeeping, the growing of wheat
and the baking of bread. It may be that they also imparted the art of cooking
with fire—hence the legend of Prometheus. Astrology, sacred rituals, art
forms, metallurgy, and linguistic skills were also brought in by the brothers
from the stars.

To these beneficent overseers the Earth was like a laboratory where a
daring experiment was being enacted. In order to forward the planet's
evolution, genetic mutations were produced in the human race while certain
quasi-animal types were deliberately phased out. Despite the advantages
conferred by these uplifting endeavors, some negative side effects en-
sued. Any influx of spiritual power tends to produce "power complexes"
among those who are still materialistically motivated. Accordingly in its latter
days, Atlantis exemplified the old adage that "the best corrupted becomes the
worst."

Men took the gifts that were offered but refused the one request that was
asked in return—that they share the abundance made available to them with
one another. Hence, their energies became misdirected. They wanted to
believe that they had free will, but could not see that this much-vaunted
freedom necessarily entails the acceptance of responsibility for each individual's voluntary actions.

Some of the subjects with whom we have worked have speculated that
another mutation is occurring in the latter part of the twentieth century,
hastening the emergence of a new breed of human being. Now, on a higher
turn of the spiral, the forerunners of the Aquarian Age are being obliged to
confront many of the challenges that faced the latter-day Atlanteans.

In Atlantis, temples were used not only for worship but also for instruction
and training in the achievement of higher states of consciousness. There was a
sacred science of sound which included chanting, the playing of musical
instruments, ritualistic dancing, and astrological pageantry. Occult practices
were jealously guarded secrets, transmitted from teacher to pupils within the
confines of the inner sanctum. These included an art of liberation through
dreams which involved astral projection, or "soul travel." Deliberately
induced visions and revelations were used to obtain spiritual guidance and to
predict the future. In some instances these same psychic faculties were
diverted to espionage, a practice which persisted long after the fall of Atlantis.
Hypnotism and mesmerism were employed, positively in the field of
medicine, and negatively by practitioners of the black arts of sorcery,

necromancy, and propaganda. Here again, the awesome power of words became corrupted by human avarice. Much of the fear that hypnotism creates in the minds of people today stems from unconscious memories of the extent to which this great therapeutic art was once perverted.

In the latter days of Atlantis the conflict between dark and light forces deteriorated into open warfare. Gradually the space brothers withdrew, like parents who realize that the time has come for their children to strike out on their own and, if necessary, make their own mistakes. Thus, over the centuries, the wise ones receded into the realm of memory, growing ever dimmer until they dissolved into the mists of myth and fancy.

The final breakup of Atlantis (generally believed to have occurred about 10000 B.C.) occurred in a series of cataclysms. This denouement was precipitated more by human arrogance and greed than by any caprice of nature. The delicate balance of terrestrial forces was upset by man's wanton abuse of the powers with which he had been entrusted. Yet, in a larger sense, it was all part of the great developmental scheme which decrees that spirit must become engrossed in matter (involution) before the original divine spark can reascend to its own high estate (evolution).

The Atlantean priests had been warned of the impending catastrophe. Those who took the cue were able to carry out extensive salvage operations. (Some of our sensors claim that certain people were lifted off the continent by spaceships.) Talismans were buried and sacred images smashed by their custodians lest they be profaned by barbarian races who might chance to come across them in future epochs.

After the deluge, refugees made their way to China, India, and Tibet, as well as to Central and South America. Theocratically oriented civilizations were established in Peru and Egypt long before the advent of the Incas and Pharaohs known to history. The legendary culture of the Nile Valley that predated the Egypt known to historians may have been the source of the Hermetic teachings which constitute one of the mainstreams of the perennial occult tradition.

Samples of the readings from which we have drawn this picture are included in the following transcripts of hypersensing sessions. I begin with an account given by Ward Buell, since he was able to obtain a bird's-eye view of the entire Atlantean civilization. During the actual conversation there was more feedback than is indicated here, since it is my habit to repeat key phrases or make some affirmative comment to let the sensor know that I am listening. In general, however, I have avoided implanting suggestions and tried to play a strictly stenographic role.

HYPERSENSING SESSION WITH WARD BUELL—AUGUST 8, 1974

Ward—I'm back in Egyptian times. Once again I'm inside the pyramid reading the walls.

Marcia—Can you travel from this place back to Atlantis?

Ward—I'm using it as a reference point. Now I feel myself being lifted, revolving backward to scan the history of Atlantis. It's like a movie running in reverse; the cities being taken apart.... I feel very savage. I'm back almost to the time when people lived in caves. There is a quivering starting at the base of my spine.

Marcia—Where are you now?

Ward—This was the time when the brothers of the stars came down to endow the Earth with their knowledge. As one of the Earth dwellers I feel the new ideas and patterns running through my mind. All at onee there is the concept of wanting to grow and develop.

My tribe is around me. We are gazing up at the spaceships hovering overhead. They have set up an "other-dimensional warp." It is as though we can look up at the ships and see into another realm. The air is radiating; it's like staring at heat waves. The whole sky is rippling. These seem to be not so much spaceships as conductors, like channels into another dimension.

In terms of history it all happened practically instantaneously—like an electrical spark coming down, the way lightning descends from the heavens. This knowledge is pervading my inmost being, with an undercurrent of communication. No one teaches us; we just know. This is where telepathy began.

Marcia—What about language?

Ward—Language began as telepathy broke down. That was about ten thousand years before the culmination of Atlantis. Before that there was no need to talk. People around you knew and felt the same thing. Knowledge did not come through our kind of learning; it was *endowed*. This was an experiment by the space brothers to raise the level of consciousness on earth. They stayed with us a few thousand years and then left. For several hundred years they remained in the spaceships. They had to build man up to the point where he could accept their coming down.

In those days people didn't speak because there was knowledge in the silence. The space brothers stood guard like silent sentinels. They wore space suits with helmets. They too had to make many adjustments. You feel puny in their presence. They say not to feel puny but you do.

Three thousand years pass, and they're still trying to help. Man is starting to become more independent. Five thousand years after their arrival they start to leave the earth. Man has grounded their energy in the physical. He now has the ability to slip between the dimensions and grasp that power directly. Craftsmen can take a block of stone that weighs two hundred tons and sculpt it into the desired shape by directing their minds like laser beams. People can use their minds together. More and more individuals now have the knowledge that was brought by the space brothers. As this wisdom goes out it becomes more thinly spread. It is dissipated and the level gets lower. People separate into classes and the lower ones are jealous of those on a higher level.

There is a great growth in technology. As man loses the power of his mind he begins to rely on artificial devices. There is more use of machines. The brothers from the stars have now been relegated to the realm of mythology. People start to worship them as gods because they haven't seen or felt them personally.

It's like watching a film run forward. We are now coming to the time of the destruction of Atlantis. When Atlantis fell, the languages started to multiply. The language wasn't strong enough to contain all the different ways of thought.

The Atlanteans caused destruction through the use of solar energy. When he came forth man was an integral part of the planet. It was known that the earth is alive, just as man is. People don't realize how delicate the balance is between them and the planet. We have more and more technology, fighting and bickering, just as before. And then the earth will have to shake it all off again.

Marcia—Do you think there are a lot of reincarnated Atlanteans in the United States?

Ward—I see Atlantis all over the world. The people who were responsible for technology in those days have been coming back, but so too have those who are more spiritual. They are incarnating to try to save the Earth, just as they did before. They know what is about to happen and they'll know where to go to be safe.

The inner-dimensionals are trying to get through. Their guiding light will be seen again after the cataclysm. I feel much hope for the planet. Once the purification has taken place there will be a lifting of the level. Subconsciously a lot of people remember how it was. They don't want man to fall again. There won't be a Dark Age like the last one. In the so-called Dark Ages the guiding spirits couldn't really function. The higher beings stayed away. People's worst instincts came to the fore. But the time to come will be brighter. I can see the sun over the horizon.

The main breakup should be in the 1990s. In fact it will start before that. Up to that time the low-grade energy will find a place to hide. But the events of the 1990s will wash the darkness away. It will be a great purgation—a purification of the whole planet.

The next few years will be chaotic for those who look at life materialistically. But there are some people who won't be touched. You can make a good reality even in bad times. The spiritual people will be starting to produce. There is always a balancing factor—an energy which keeps everything from going down the drain.

Marcia—Will there be an economic crash?

Ward—Yes, there will be an economic catastrophe but it will happen too quickly to do anything about it. For the next eight years it will be hard for the space brothers to get through. They have to hold back for a reason. Man isn't ready to cope with their force. It's the darkness before the dawn.

The Plan *will* be restored on Earth. I can't see the ultimate future as being bad. I see nothing but good.

The following glimpse into the technology of Atlantis is taken from a letter by Ray Robinson of Cerritos, California.

Our July session was very good and our technique is developing. I have no problems with the subjects.

We took Neva [Ray's wife] back to Atlantis and the life there was the same one she described before. She married the soldier who later became an air corps officer protecting the coast. Foot soldiers guarded the cities but everyone else flew. She was killed when her plane failed and plunged into the ocean. She remembered that it exploded first.

I asked about the crystals and she stated that each ship had a small crystal that operated on a radio wave with giant crystals and that they drew power from the solar system.

On asking her about the era in which she was living she answered that it was 10,000 *monitors*.

Virtually all of our subjects who regress to Atlantean times speak of laserlike crystals which were used to convert solar energy into the power required to sustain that great civilization. In addition to producing heat and light for ordinary living purposes the crystals drove the engines of various types of aircraft. In one of her lifetimes Isabel Buell saw herself as the pilot of one of these crystal-propelled planes. This male personality was an arrogant, self-centered fellow who was married to a woman who taught at the university. He had no children and wanted none, making it clear that there was little emphasis on reproduction among the intelligentsia. However, in a prior incarnation the story had been quite different.

HYPERSENSING SESSION WITH ISABEL BUELL—AUGUST 8, 1974

Marcia—Can you go back to Atlantis?

Isabel—I'm there already.

Marcia—Tell me about your life there.

Isabel—The buildings are round with natural air conditioning and heating. All the power comes from solar energy. Each house has a small box in the center which is used for cooking. I have a cooking pan in my hand. It is made out of a special alloy. I put the pan over the fire and dinner is prepared. The secret is in the metal itself. The cooking is done by a combination of the pan and the solar energy field.

I have dark hair and a slender bone structure. My eyes are almond-shaped but not like Oriental eyes. I seem to be blue-eyed with black lashes. My skin is cream colored. My figure is small-waisted with full hips.

I have four children, two girls and two boys. One girl's name is Elena and the other is Rosetta. I know these sound like modern names. The difference seems to be that there are just so many word vibrations that people in different cultures use for names.

My husband is called Dwania. The boys seem to be away. Why can't I see them? I am missing them so much. . . . I have not been well; my mind is strange. Because of my illness the boys were sent away. I want them to come back home. There was some sort of family fight about this. I don't really want to look at it.

My house is bright and beautiful. The walls breathe; they are very flexible, and the inside is filled with sunlight. There are trees, grass, flowers, and shrubs all inside the house, so that it seems to be built around a garden. Small plants are used for air conditioning. We actually sleep on beds of grass and sweet-smelling herbs. These herbs have healing properties. I was visiting a friend and slept on the wrong herb.

Oh no! [Violent start.] She did that to me intentionally. And that was why my mind became unhinged. Why did she do that to me?

This moss is never wet. It has something to do with the solar energy. That is, the energy and the moss are connected. The herbs are used for healing and sleeping. This was the natural gift of the planet bestowed upon the people.

The floors of the house are made of smooth rock. They're never too hot or too cold. Today we would think that was a housewife's dream. They are not flat like slate but are slightly curved. The walls are soft, of a sunlit yellow texture. I love the house, but not my husband. . . .

The following reading is not quite typical of those we receive, but neither is Anne Greacan the typical housewife one might suppose from her description of herself. Tall, blonde, beautiful, and endowed with a searching intellect, this poised young woman gives the impression of being on genuinely good terms with herself.

As interesting as it is to explore the karmic antecedents of the neuroses that torment so many distressed people, it can be just as fascinating to look into the background of someone like Anne who, despite some low blows from fate, has pulled herself together. After our first session I asked Anne for a transcript of the tape we made, along with some personal comments. This is what she gave me.

HYPERSENSING SESSION WITH ANNE GREACAN AUGUST 17, 1974

A year ago I would not have believed that I would be in the space where I am now. I was a traditional suburban housewife with two children—educated, rational, intellectual, very tied into everyday routine matters, and struggling in an unhappy domestic turmoil. Today I feel strong, aware of the direction of my life, and of the importance of exploring my past lives. I want to learn more about the strengths and weaknesses that make up the totality of a continuing soul. Reincarnation, energy transformation, and inner peace are all concepts that have become central to my being. They have been incredible assets as I start to discover who I am, why my life is as it is at this moment, and how better to cope with the challenges that crop up every day.

By chance, the opportunity arose to work in a session with Marcia Moore. I was to be one of the many whom she led back to uncover past lives. But perhaps I had an advantage over some of the others for I had recently been part of a group regression experience with Billie Hobart. It had taken several sessions then to realize what "letting go" meant and how it felt. The Western mind has been trained to doubt, to censor, and to hold back. It took me awhile to learn to trust and to open my mind to whatever came. I also learned that it was important to tune into one's deep emotions, for the undercurrent of feeling is the key to the reality of it all. Though at times regression and past lives sounded like an elaborate fantasy, the intense emotions I felt as these lives came into focus assured me that I could not be making up these stories.

After being guided through a general body relaxation and count-back, my mind felt alive, fresh, and cleared from its daily trivialities. First I climbed a mountain, walking up twenty steps until I reached a high valley. Here it was suggested that I meet a wise person who would be my guide on the journey into the past.

Ann—I am in the midst of gold and yellow flowers. Straight beyond me is a higher peak covered with snow. This is a narrow valley with high rocky sides. I'm not sure that the tallest peak is reachable. It is capped with snow, very high. I am wearing a filmy white short robe and my hair is falling free.

Marcia—Look around and see if you can find your guide. Is there someone wise and kind and compassionate who can meet you here?

Ann—He's sitting to my right about thirty feet ahead of me on a rock. And he's laughing and saying, "Well, you made it." He's got some flowers, a few mushrooms, and some sage.

Marcia—What is the meaning of the flowers, mushrooms, and sage?

Ann—To totally use the senses to bring oneself into higher knowledge. The smell of the flowers touch that very sweet, gentle place. The mushrooms are beautiful with white spots and intricate insides—very pleasing to the eye.

Marcia—What does your guide look like?

Ann—He too has a white robe. It has a waistband of many colors. He's a very angular strong man about seven or eight feet tall, squarish clean face, green eyes. Very beautiful man.

Marcia—Make it very clear in your mind how he looks. Ask him, does he have any message for you today?

Ann—[At this time I felt an overwhelming depth of searching for knowledge. My whole being was in a whirling turmoil as I searched for words to describe the dimensions my mind was reaching. My body was extremely heavy and physically I felt like a huge fat woman lying with my hands heavy on my tremendous bulk.]

He's telling me I can leave my body. There is no reason to stay with the body. I am there.

Marcia—Let us now look back into your soul's history. Have we his permission to take a journey back through time and see where you came from?

Ann—Yes, he says it's all right.

Marcia—Imagine a rainbow bridge extending out into space. First we will walk up and then drop down through the clouds and swirling mists. We are going to take you a long, long way back into your soul's history, back almost to the beginning. Then you will know something about why you're here and what you're meant to do. You can walk across the bridge to ten counts.

[Counting.]

Now you can step off the rainbow bridge and look around. See what images and impressions reveal themselves before the eye of your inner vision.

Ann—I am in Egypt, in the courtyard of a temple. I am being trained as a priestess. I am seventeen years old. I have long dark hair and brown eyes. There is a necklace around my neck that looks like small pieces of burnt cork, with a green jade stone at the throat. I have on a robe and I'm barefoot. I'm in a courtyard of palm trees. My teacher is there.

Marcia—Who is your teacher?

Ann—He is a man, young, about thirty-five. He seems to be a favored one of the Pharaoh.

Marcia—He sees you now and he calls you by name. What name does he call you?

Ann—Avitar.

Marcia—Tell me more about your way of life, Avitar. Are you happy here?

Ann—I'm very eager to learn. I am also eager to be out of the boundaries of the temple. But I will be. I'll be sent to one of the outlying temples. I'm being trained to be an interpreter of the "looking girls." I will oversee them.

Marcia—So you will interpret what they see. Are the looking girls those who register psychic impressions?

Ann—I would somehow be a liaison between them and either the priest or the Pharaoh. And that's why I'm willing to do this. I guess I am not really that happy. It is a life of sacrifice. I feel very dedicated to my country.

Marcia—Does this mean you won't be able to marry?

Ann—Yes.

Marcia—What do you do during the day?

Ann—I gather flowers in the morning. That's what I like to do best. I bring them into the room. I get up early before anyone else, and bring them into the room where we all gather to meditate and chant. And I just space into the flowers. . . .

I guess one of the things I don't like about this place is that I'm always hungry. The meals are very simple; it's a discipline.

Marcia—They don't give you enough. Perhaps that helps to develop the psychic side of your nature?

Ann—I crave a big plate of food but it never comes. The mornings are filled with group lessons. There are only women teachers. And in the afternoon we have a nap and we are told to be very aware of what happens during that energy time. Then I'm with my teacher late in the afternoon and that is my favorite time. Except for the flowers. The flowers I like best.

Marcia—I'm going to ask you to go forward to your early twenties. It is five years later. New scenes come to mind. What are you doing now?

Ann—I'm with a tiger or a lion. It's in the temple where I am. I long to get out of this environment. I long to be in another place. This temple is where I went after I became initiated. It's OK but it's too confining. So this pet tiger, or lion, my special pet, is my connection to the world I don't know—that I long to be in. Sometimes I spend a lot of time astral-projecting out of this confined space of loyalty, to a life of more adventure. I long to go to Africa because it would mean living in the body and not just in the mind.

Marcia—What do you do in this temple?

Ann—I think these girls are like boundary watchers and I somehow am the connection between them and the priest in the central complex of the high city. I am not in the high city. I wonder if I want to stay in this place, but I do not have the guts to ask to be relieved because I've become a priestess. So it's like do or die. . . . I think I die.

Marcia—What came of this conflict?

Ann—I burnt my mind out.

Marcia—How did you do that? Was it from too much astral-projecting?

Ann—It was a choice and I think I did it by remembering techniques I had in Atlantis. There was some way of transferring energy into another dimension. I knew that deep inside I had the power to do that. It hadn't been taught to me in Egypt. Because I couldn't take that dull life, I chose to experiment with my past knowledge. I was twenty-six years old when I died.

Marcia—Now you're out of the body. You've found that you *could* get away from this dull life. Where are you now? What happened when you left the body?

Ann—I see myself in a pyramid, in an inner chamber. It's a resting place.

Marcia—If you can—and you have complete freedom in this—I'd like you to go back to Atlantis and see what it was you learned to do. What was the experience that tied in with your Egyptian life?

Ann—I feel like I'm home. [At this point a strong feeling of love and happiness enveloped me. It was such a different feeling from the desolation and loneliness of the Egyptian life.]

Marcia—What is home?

Ann—A lot of people who love me. These seem to be people I have touched with this energy. Somehow I was a teacher to them but I also lived with them and touched them in a certain way so that they became more lighted beings. I feel that they are welcoming me back.

Marcia—How do you appear to them?

Ann—I am a man. Wearing black trousers made like the shape of the Vietnamese outfits. They are made of a soft material, like silk and cheesecloth woven together. Belted. The top is loose with a V neck and big sleeves. There are jewels set in the V of the shirt. I am very swarthy with shoulder-length black hair, and my eyes are like deep wells. The eyes are very black; they don't have any color to them. Just black and white. I'm somewhere between thirty-five and forty years old.

Marcia—Tell me about your life.

Ann—I'm a teacher and I *know* that I have that knowledge from another planet. I'm close enough to that time so it's still in my consciousness that there isn't that conflict between knowledge and no knowledge. I know that my mission is to bring knowledge to these people.

Marcia—Why did you come to Earth? Isn't this planet rather barbaric compared to the place where you've been?

Ann—Yes, very.

Marcia—Then why did you descend into this low place?

Ann—It's a tremendous challenge. It's a growth, a privilege, first of all to teach others. And then, it's a tremendous growth experience, though I don't feel I've had much conflict compared to other lives. It was conflict compared to where I had come from. There was growth you can go through being in the flesh.

Marcia—I've often wondered why people from your planet would come and bother with the Earth.

Ann—We're all working toward a universal knowledge, and if there are those who have no knowledge, that holds back the whole universe. And it's so important that those who are on Earth be taught . . . be lighted.

Marcia—Would you say that just as we try to civilize remote barbarian lands for the sake of the Earth as a whole, the guardians of the universe try to civilize the Earth? Because it's all one Universe.

Ann—Yes, the Earth has been given the heaviest burden of any place in the universe. So it's a real privilege to work there and to try to bring knowledge to its people. It is a very heavy task and I go back every so often to be revived on my planet. Because it's very heavy.

Marcia—Do you go back between lives?

Ann—No, I have the feeling I go back within the life. I probably go back between lives too. I feel that this life I'm talking about is very close, one of my first lives, so I have to be revived. And that is who J. was [a man in my group meditation class whom I've had the feeling I was with in Atlantis]. He was my conveyor, my contact to bring me back and forth.

Marcia—He was a kind of midway person?

Ann—Well, he was a very high person on the planet but I could contact him and he would come and get me in a spaceship or something. And then I would be there for a certain time period and just by being there I'd be revived. Then I'd come back and be a much better teacher for a time.

Marcia—Did you go back through astral projection?

Ann—No, I seemed to go back through some physical spaceship-type thing.

Marcia—There were spaceships in Atlantis?

Ann—Oh sure. That was the main mode of transportation. In fact, when Atlantis fell, that's how most people got out, of those who did get out.

Marcia—Now you're at one of these stages of being revived by going back to your own planet. Can you tell me more about this planet?

Ann—I see it [with difficulty] as just light, and of course I have no body. There is red, a glow of red.

Marcia—Is it associated with one of the planets we know in the solar system?

Ann—No, it is different. The red is like the source of light, a source of energy. I feel myself—you know how you see dust in the sunlight—that's how I feel myself. Always, always moving. There is no confinement. One is always moving, swirling.

Marcia—Is that why you found it so hard to be confined on Earth—because there is no confinement on your planet?

Ann—That must be.

Marcia—Tell me more about this place. Are there others there?

Ann—Oh yes, many, many, many. We're all like flecks of light, swirling, interacting. You communicate with those who are on your light wave and those who are not you don't communicate with. There's no conflict. That's the difference. When you take a flesh vehicle you're forced to deal with bodies, whereas in this state it's just light to light. The light beams touch each other when you're in the same wavelength and those that aren't on the same wavelength just go swirling past with no conflict at all. Everything is just swirling, meeting. And that's why I chose to come back.

Marcia—Is it because you can learn through conflict? In other words, on Earth you have to confront the people who are not like yourself.

Ann—Right. There's first that physical dimension that you confront, and then there's the inner dimension. Because the physical dimension houses the inner dimension, you have to get through all that shit before you find out whether you're really in tune with this person. And somehow the flesh vehicle makes it so much harder. It's like the box around each person. That's why people choose to come back.

Marcia—Is there anything else you'd like to look into before we finish this session?

Ann—There is. Let me think.

[I knew there was something important and I scanned my thoughts—scanning, scanning, and feeling something important but not knowing quite what it was. Marcia suggested that there might be a karmic tie with a special individual.]

Donald! [Intense emotion. Crying.] His eyes, his eyes. I've been in his eyes before. His eyes seem to be like my eyes when I was in Atlantis. Perhaps that is where we were? Somehow his eyes take me into the core of who I am. *I-un-ca-ta* [a name]. Maybe he was my teacher in Egypt? He was someone I knew who taught my spirit but who I couldn't touch as a person. That's what it was. That's why I died. Because I couldn't relate to him. It's good, it's good.

After Marcia brought me back, we had tea and talked of what I experienced and of the thoughts that came with that experience.

My guess is that I spent four or five lifetimes on Atlantis. During the first three or so I had to go back to my planet and after that I had assumed enough physical substance so that I couldn't go back. I had taken on that task. I probably went back between lives for the first couple of incarnations. I had the feeling while I was doing this that it was like death—like I now imagine death to be. I got that direct correlation of movement, of only meeting those whose light beams yours run into, while all others pass by. But after death now we go to schools of learning. Somehow our earthly existence has conditioned us to go right on learning.

Although we didn't get into it this session, I felt that in one life I took those people that I loved and taught in a spaceship to Peru when Atlantis was falling. Peru and Egypt were special places where highly evolved souls went.

When it comes to descriptions of post-Atlantean cultures one can almost pick and choose at random—to me they are all fascinating. The following are examples of the kind of material that comes to light.

HYPERSENSING SESSION WITH WARD BUELL AUGUST 8, 1974

Marcia—See if you can go back to a time that sheds some light on the interests that you have today.

Ward—I'm back in ancient China at the time of the beginning of the martial arts. I see a huge courtyard. It's large enough to hold two hundred people. There is a group of men here and they are all concentrating on the same thing. They perform a kind of dance where they spar with imaginary opponents. They can continue for hours. All the dancers are students who wish to become monks in this order. It's a matter of life and death.

I'm coming near the time of my testing. . . . All right, I'll go forward to the time itself. The test lasts all day long. I get up before four o'clock and dress all in white. From four to six I sit in deep meditation. My mind and body are one.

I am being ushered into a large building with stone walls. It has a huge square door eight feet high. The door closes behind me. As I step forward it is dark with faint shafts of light. I see what appears to be a path and follow it.

There are traps set up which test one's ability to reason and think. Spears and arrows come at you. Knives fall from the ceiling. And there are pitfalls. I see the skeletons of students who have failed the test. I manage to make my way through this room and come to another door.

Now I am in a brilliantly lit room. It is filled with various kinds of weapons—swords, daggers, spears, shields, and so forth, I'm supposed to choose a weapon. I have to look for the special sign that will help me to choose the right one. I pick up a shovel and pass on into the next room. Again the door closes behind me.

This place is dimly lit. Oh! It's full of scorpions. There are masses of scorpions on the floor and walls. They drop from the ceiling. The only way to get through is to beat a pathway with the shovel. I keep pushing them back and finally I work my way into the next room.

This room is a small cube about eight feet high. There are four stone walls and no way out. One wall has two little portholes just out of reach. The only thing I can think to do is to jump up and thrust my arms through the holes. I try it and there is a searing pain in both arms. But somehow my weight has activated a pivot so that the wall swings back.

When I emerge I see that both my arms have been branded with dragons. I am now an accepted member of the order.

The following account, comprising material from two sessions, comes from Akeva.

At what point does a person realize that the experiences of former incarnations have shaped the attitudes, beliefs, and goals that define his present way of life? For me, this knowledge came with my meeting with Marcia Moore when we started a series of retrocognition sessions which brought to light the outlines of eight previous existences. Of these diverse lifetimes the most deeply felt was one during which I was a priest living high in the mountains of Peru.

When I first saw myself in this setting I was one of a group of acolytes standing in a half circle about an altar. There were about twenty of us on each side. Our heads were shaven and we wore robes with leather belts. We were watching a ceremony being performed by a priest in a feathered headdress. Behind us were the people of the valley who were also watching the proceedings. The priest was going through the motions of making a sacrifice, although no human or animal was involved.

The culmination of the ritual came when an assistant raised a circular stone disk in such a way that the priest could thrust both arms through a hole in the center. After the priest reached through the disk a woman placed a dagger in his outstretched hands. He then performed a ceremony which ended with the woman returning to the altar and receiving the dagger which he allowed to drop into her hands. Having released the dagger, he was now able to free his arms from the disk which was laid aside. He then walked between the two lines of acolytes and entered a building with a solid rock ceiling held up by two enormous side walls.

The other priests followed him and they all emerged on the far side of the building into a large clearing which afforded a magnificent view of the rising sun which was just coming up over the mountains.

In answer to a question from Marcia about our living quarters I said, "We live in a long narrow house with small rooms arranged in single file, one after another. Each acolyte has a room to himself." The long house was built on stilts and one had to climb up a catwalk and walk along a narrow porch to reach his own room. At that time I was about sixteen years old.

When Marcia advanced me to the age of twenty there had been very little change. I was still in the same place and involved in the same tasks. On inclement days our lessons were taught in the temple; otherwise they took place under the sun or stars. We were expected to keep the temple and its grounds immaculately clean. When we were needed we would go down to the town to help the people. There, if a young man met a girl and decided that he wanted to return to the life of a householder, he could do so without recriminations. A big wedding was held and all enjoyed themselves. Under no circumstances, however, could a man marry and continue to live with the priests.

When Marcia advanced me to the age of twenty-seven I saw that I had moved nearer to the end of the house where the porch began. Seniority was based on how close you lived to the entrance. I had gained in knowledge and was starting to train new acolytes, but this did not mean that I worked less.

Eventually it became my task to carry on the dagger ceremony. I now realized that when you put your hands through the disk to clasp the dagger, as long as you hold on to it you cannot bring your hands back. You have to drop it before you can free the extended part of yourself. We felt that if the people learned just that much it would be enough. You can be free only if you let go. I performed this ritual for sixteen years.

At a later date in the same life I found myself with some of the monks inside the temple. We wore peaked hats that were an integral part of our simple robes and our feet were shod with sandallike shoes made from black leather. By now I was the head abbot.

In the clearing behind the temple, which was reached by going under the thick roof, there was a disk about twenty feet in diameter. It was concave with a silvery white surface which was made to reflect the sun. Instructions for building the disk came through meditation. I would go quietly into the sacred chamber and here the knowledge of what to do would enter my mind. I had been trained to receive these messages by my predecessor and I must in turn pass the technique on to someone else. It was necessary for the disk to have many years of polishing. It was then mounted on a turntable in such a way as to follow the motion of the sun. This was done so that the rays could be directed to the same point regardless of where the sun was in the sky. The heat energy thereby created could cut stones and do many useful things.

The man whom I chose as a successor was named Enjo. At the age of eighty-two, after having passed everything I knew on to Enjo, I decided to die. I died in the temple at 2:00 A.M. It became very cold as I sat there but I did not build a fire. I just let the cold come in. As my body grew numb and became like ice, I left it with a great sense of joy. I felt that it had been a good life and that Enjo would carry on.

At this time Akeva is devoting full time to spiritual healing and is conducting workshops on this subject in and around his home Ojai, California.

8

INNER-DIMENSIONALS

I am a wanderer,
I come from realms of glory,
I come to sing the name of God upon this earth . . .

First we called them extraterrestrials. Then when it became apparent that they do not inhabit our world of time and space we termed them *extra-dimensionals,* or *inter-dimensionals.* Now we have settled on the term *inner-dimensionals,* since we reach them by turning inward to, and through, the subjective spaces of the human psyche.

At this stage of evolution man can achieve a breakthrough in his investigations of the universe only by exploring the luminous spheres of his own consciousness. He can know what lies beyond only insofar as he can know himself. He may then be amazed to find that just as his physical body is a sense-encircled casing for his overreaching mind, similarly the world of solid phenomena is but the congealed crust of an inner-dimensional realm of stupendous magnitude.

I owe a debt to Carol Griffith of Thousand Oaks, California, for being the first to open my eyes to the broad spectrum of possibilities of inner-dimensional exploration by means of hypersentience. The following excerpts come from Carol's account of the experiences which began on the morning of January 21, 1974, in Ojai, California.

As Marcia went through the procedure I found myself quite relaxed. At all times I was fully conscious of who and where I was.

We went back to the age of three and I saw myself crying. Someone was holding my hand and I can still see the wooden steps, a broken playpen, and my father walking down a dirt pathway. As I saw the child who was me crying, I found myself crying also. Marcia was aware that I was upset so we decided to go farther back.

She counted one . . . two . . . three . . . on and on. Then I found myself in an unbelievable place.

I saw myself in a pointed headdress with bells hanging from it. My dress was silver with pointed shoulders. Marcia asked me who this person was and I replied that my name is Shalamard. I spelled it for her, sharply emphasizing the letter *d*.

Shalamard was angry. I could feel her eyes narrowing and the muscles in her face were drawn with fear. People were telling her that she must go, and she didn't want to leave. I, Carol, could see and sense her anger and still separate my present life from the one I was observing.

Marcia wanted to know how I looked. "I feel beautiful and arrogant," I said. "I look down on people—all kinds of people." I kept wanting to pull the skin around my eyes and to draw it tighter, not like an Oriental but as though the eyes were set beneath a thin veil of skin. "There is a tension about the eyes," I told her.

Looking around I saw tubular windows with domes outside. The floor was inlaid with long diamond shapes. What furniture there was was curving with simple lines.

Then a man entered the room. He was wearing a long brown robe with a rope tied loosely around his waist. His hair was light and long, his eyes very wise. I felt relieved to see him and hoped he would tell me I didn't have to leave this place. We greeted each other with our palms facing upward and overlapping as we bowed our heads. When he insisted that I must go, I embraced him. Three times he told me that I am strong, and I felt that I was stronger. Then I went to the dome to make my departure. The mode of travel was by thought.

Next I found myself as a baby girl in a house made out of sticks on the Nile. I was sitting on the ground looking up at some tall reeds shooting up out of the water. Marcia proceeded to take me forward in that lifetime and I saw myself growing older. I was speaking to people in private and secret places. I felt that I was a woman who gave consolation to others, who was at peace with herself, and who wanted nothing. I died at thirty-two on a cross. At that time I felt that the cross had no religious significance. There was no pain hanging there. I felt light and unafraid because I knew I was going home. And I did, for the next thing I knew they greeted me as Shalamard. I was happy and so were they.

When Marcia suggested that we go on to another life, I saw an old man of about sixty-two with a brown shawl over his head. He was dressed in worn clothes like a beggar but seemed very calm and content. As Carol, I wanted to know more about him. So back we went. I found my name to be Simon and I could see myself as a child running and playing outside. I had no father and my mother did people's washing. We were living in Jerusalem.

At the age of twenty I (Simon) was very happy. I was working in a blacksmith shop and the children would go by smiling and saying, "Hi Simon." I liked the children and they liked me.

At the age of thirty I was walking with a limp. My leg had been crushed by a wheel. I had two boys but no wife and was feeling very weary. Marcia asked if I'd heard of Christ being crucified and I replied angrily, "Damn fool! They all tried to tell him. What made him think he would get through!" Then more softly I replied, "I guess if one person listens you have succeeded."

Simon was asked if he was a Christian. "If that's what people wish to call them, I am one. I believe what is said."

At the end of this life Marcia asked to speak to Shalamard again in order to find out why Carol was here. "Do you know?" she asked.

"Not now, but I will."

I decided to wait a week before my next visit. The thoughts going through my head were endless. This other entity . . . what is she . . . where is she from? I felt that I had come to a point of realization—but of what? I knew that I had to go back again.

Since the remainder of Carol's account is too long to reproduce here we can give only a few glimpses of her life as Shalamard.

The dwellers on the planet to which she periodically returned were obliged to live inside a network of domes and tunnels because the air had become poisonous. At one point we inspected a room full of machines, computers, and test tubes which ran from floor to ceiling. The tubes filtered the noxious gases out of the atmosphere. Since people never went outside there were no nights and days, just dark and light. People did not live in houses but in "units" which were, like most of the other places, simple and stark.

When we came to the subject of what people ate, Shalamard said, "Never thought of it." The aging process was also different from that on Earth. Asked how old she was she said she didn't know but could figure it out on a computer. She also commented, "As you grow older you become more beautiful."

Clothing did not seem important, though on one occasion Shalamard described herself as wearing green and silver. Some people wore tight clothes and tunics while others, of a higher station, wore robes.

On being asked what she did for pleasure, Shalamard spoke of riding in a car shaped like a toboggan. It was going round and round in circles in an underground recreational park. She was having a fine time and was especially appreciative of the abundance of bright colors since the rest of the planet was predominantly white. Some of the trees and grass were artificial.

Later, when we were dealing with more serious matters, she said that for the higher people recreation was found in the silence and that it was possible to regenerate oneself by going inward.

Although Shalamard liked to study, she saw no books or classrooms. There was, however, an auditorium where people spoke. While attending one of these lectures her voice took on an anxious tone as she said, "We are all worried. There seems to be some anxiety about what will happen. We are going too close to the sun or a star."

When asked, "How do you fill your days?" Shalamard replied, "Read."

"Do you read books like ours?"

"No."

"How do you educate yourselves?"

"We don't. We just know what's there."

Later Shalamard explained that when she described herself as reading she was actually looking at a screen which she called a "level bank." "You don't have to look up records," she said. "You just think about what you want to know and the information is given. You can see the past, present, and future."

With regard to the language of this place, Shalamard told us that the words were like music and would be considered foreign by us. "The high ones communicate by thought." Others used words until they too could function telepathically.

"Do people there love each other as they do here?"

"I ring void." Shalamard answered flatly.

"Isn't love important?"

"No, survival is more important, but something is missing."

When we came to the subject of the "high ones," Shalamard explained that they lived in places with peaked roofs which seemed to glow from within and which were called "sabritols." The names of these august personages ended in "su" or "u." Thus there were Jesu, Pelu, and others who formed a guiding group of superior intelligences. These "counselors" had already been through many lifetimes, some of them on Earth. Jesu, for example, had incarnated once when "we didn't know him," and then again as Jesus. "He will comfort me," she added. "He says, 'I will guide you.' "

The most accommodating of the guides was Pelu. He too had lived through many existences and did not have to incarnate again. When first seen, Pelu's eyes had a downward slant and he was wearing a monk's gown. Later, he adopted other forms in order to make the point that "the Wise Ones can think themselves to be anything they want to be."

As the conversation turned to the nature of this other planet, Shalamard said that it was called Melina and that it was a steppingstone to other spheres. It was one of three planets of learning lessons. These three included Melina, the Earth, and one other.

"Is it lawful for us to know more about this place?" I asked.

"Yes, but people won't believe."

"Would it be possible to fly there in a spaceship or must it be a journey in consciousness?"

"The latter."

"Where is your real home?"

"Wherever I wish it to be. It can be anywhere."

"Yes, but where do you wish it to be?" I persisted.

"Renena" [pronounced Ray-nay-na], she replied, spelling out the name. "A total commitment."

"Is Renena a place?"

"No, I'm not even sure of the name."

"Why do you have to come to Earth?"

"You have to come to learn. It gives a better understanding of everything."

At this point Carol was growing tired so I concluded the conversation by asking, "Who is more real to you, Shalamard or Carol?"

"That's an interesting question. I must think on that."

Later Carol answered the query by saying, "I felt that Shalamard was really me and that all those other lives were fragments of Shalamard's soul. Somehow they all blended."

As we proceeded, we could see a distinct evolution of the Shalamard personality. At the start, Shalamard had seemed cold, arrogant, and preoccupied with her own brilliant intellect. Later, after several Earth lives, she became much warmer and more cooperative. Even Carol's face grew smoother and more serene. The only real flash of resentment was aroused by her disappointment at not being able to return to her native planet between a brief existence as a Polish boy during World War II and her life as Carol.

In addition to the Shalamard material, Carol was able to make predictions concerning the future of the United States and to tune in on other people's past lives. Even so, we barely scratched the surface of what she apparently is able to accomplish. Since Carol leads an extremely busy life looking after a husband and four young children we were not able to spend much time together before I left California. Also, it seemed advisable for her to proceed slowly, since there was so much for her to absorb. At the end of her account of our four sessions together Carol wrote:

> I really don't know what all this means but I do believe that it is important. Not just to individuals but to man as a race; not just to the earth but to the solar system. It doesn't even end there. Time, space, souls, planets, dimensions—it's all infinite.
>
> Yes, it makes me very curious and concerned for mankind. I think many of the answers can be found in our own minds if we can just relax and listen to the voice of the silence. I think it must be done, for I believe that is where our salvation lies.

An intriguing feature of our sessions with Carol is the extent to which her readings corroborated information given by others. Most common are the comments that the "space brothers" can alter their appearances at will. Three other sensors mentioned scanning screens on which it is possible to look into the future. Several have also spoken of planets on which it was necessary to burrow down into underground caves because the air was becoming unfit to breathe. The impression given was that planets, like people, live and die, and that at the end souls are obliged to leave their native habitat and migrate elsewhere. One might surmise that this lethal pollution of the atmosphere is a possibility for the Earth were it not that virtually all our supersensed prognosticators agree that this planet will survive the coming destruction and that humanity will emerge into an age more glorious than any which has gone before.

The most remarkable carry-over from Carol's readings was our continuing association with the guide known as Pelu. This awesome but benevolent visitant was first contacted by Carol on February 19, 1974, during a regression session attended by Isabel Buell and myself. Two weeks later while working privately with Isabel I asked her to walk up a flight of imaginary steps to a "high and beautiful place." To her astonishment the first thing she saw was a "dirt cloud" on which Pelu was standing, along with her other, more familiar guides. At first, Isabel was so overwhelmed by Pelu's presence that she wanted to bow down to him, but he indicated that he preferred her to remain erect. Notes from this session bring out the following highlights.

> I approach him standing. He is happy to receive me this way. Now I am looking into Pelu's eyes. They are so blue they appear to be glass. His face is young for one so old and wise. He has long gray hair. His skin is incredibly beautiful—very clear with a beige tone. .
>
> Yes, he does change. Now he's transforming the figure. He is trying to tell me that he can take any form he pleases. I see him wearing a loose-fitting karate-type outfit. It has no significance other than comfort. Now his hair has become short and light. This is to symbolize power and vitality.
>
> He's showing me the inside of him, his inner health and emotions. He chose to come to us first in the outer garments of the aged one simply because that is what we expect.

In subsequent sessions Pelu continued to demonstrate his proficiency as a master of metamorphoses. Despite his changeable appearance, however, he was always on hand to open our readings. Isabel would stretch out on her shaggy gold living-room rug with a light coverlet for warmth and in a few seconds her eyelids would flutter. We would know then that she was back on her "dirt cloud" and that the guides would soon appear.

One of Pelu's many agreeable qualities was a rarefied sense of humor. On August 20, for example, he came in as a modishly dressed young man or, as Isabel put it, "a swinger." This was partly in deference to the younger members of the group and partly to inform Isabel that increasingly her work would be with young people. The following week Isabel informed me that during my forthcoming drive across the country Pelu would come and sit beside me and that he would be wearing a T-shirt and levis. As Isabel correctly predicted, the four thousand-mile journey went without a hitch.

Even though Pelu soon became quite real to those of us in the group he seemed to have a wish to prove that Isabel's clairvoyance and our own glimmering awareness of his presence were more than wish-fulfilling fantasies. This was accomplished largely through a series of predictions, some of which have since come to pass.

For example, early in the spring of 1974, Isabel announced that it would not be long before I left my beautiful hilltop home overlooking the Ojai Valley. At that time we were planting a garden, had started raising chickens, and were about to acquire some beehives. As far as I was concerned this was an ideal nesting spot, and I had invested much time and money in the house with the expectation of eventually purchasing it. Because of my faith in Isabel, however, I ceased channeling funds into the place. Subsequently, when it did became necessary to move, I was grateful not to have expended any more of my limited resources on a garden I would never harvest.

To date, Pelu's most remarkable forecast is one given early in June 1974. On this occasion he announced that he would be sending us a friend of his. This would be a girl with long dark hair, a full but trim figure, and small hands. She would be naturally intuitive, even though not formally trained along these lines. She would come to Akeva's house and I would know her by her hands which would be more delicate than the rest of her body. On the sixteenth of July, Pelu again mentioned that this young woman would soon arrive.

By the latter part of August I had virtually given up hope that Pelu's protégé would appear on the scene since, in order to prepare for my forthcoming trip, I was accepting no more applicants for hypersensing sessions. On August twenty-ninth three people were due to come to Akeva's house in Ojai to be regressed and that would be the end of it.

When Kathleen Jenks arrived for her ten o'clock appointment, I had a strong feeling that she might be the person for whom we were waiting. Our session together seemed fruitful, and I was delighted when she agreed to delay her return to New York in order to attend our meeting at Isabel's home in Thousand Oaks the following day.

Isabel had not been informed that we were bringing a guest, yet she recognized Kathleen while we were still standing on her doorstep and quickly confirmed that this was the young woman Pelu had promised to send. As I introduced Kathleen to the rest of the group, I mentioned that she had recently completed the first of a trilogy of books on the life of Moses and spoke of our confirmation that Moses had blue eyes. However, I deliberately refrained from saying anything about Kathleen's feeling that in a former lifetime she might have been Moses' wife.

Later in the morning Isabel offered to contact Pelu and the guides and see what they had to tell us. The following excerpts are taken from Kathleen's account of what happened:

"Had I known him in the Exodus-time?" I asked. "Or am I a channel for all this?"

"Yes," she responded immediately, "you had been with him. You were one of his wives that loved him very, very much."

"We had discussed that before," Marcia explained. "That's why we were asking."

"Yes, yes, you were one of his wives. And you loved him in total. You understood love. You loved him physically, but it was far superior—it was into the spiritual. You really comprehended love completely."

I was shaken and tried very hard not to show it. If her words were true, it was the most beautiful tribute I had ever been given.

"Well, that's a great confirmation," Marcia was saying in a vigorous tone of voice.

Then Isabel spoke softly again. "You gladly washed his feet."

Of all the extraordinary things she had said, that went straight through to my core. Silent tears began to flow out of my eyes. In the New Testament, one of the most profound and loving scenes for me is of the woman washing the feet of Christ and drying them with her long hair. I had often imagined myself doing that. . . . Had I washed Moses' feet? Is that why the later story about Jesus had always moved me so deeply? Did I know at first hand what it was like to love and wash the feet of a man who spoke and walked with Yahweh?

I cannot give any answer to that. I only know what I felt in my heart when Isabel spoke those five simple words. I only know that love came welling up out of me and that I felt a deep, deep loss because such a man is on earth with me no longer.

What lies in my heart as I am writing all this tonight? I keep my own counsel. Perhaps I was Moses' wife. Or perhaps I am a novelist whose emotions sometimes run away with her. I cannot say.

After a brief pause, Isabel continued. "You lived a very long life—110, I'm getting. You were with him for the better part of all that in every way, shape, and form. Yes, a beautiful relationship."

There was a question I had to ask, and I put it to her then. "Had I been the old woman who took care of him when he was a child—and then died, and then became his wife?"

"They are saying yes," Isabel replied after a few seconds. "And I know nothing about Moses as I know nothing about the Bible, so whatever comes through here is not preconceived. But they say yes. And now I see you all stooped over—you're very arthritic, as a matter of fact, and in very bad, bad condition. And, feeling strongly about this child, loving him so strongly then—you dropped your body, and you returned immediately. . . . You were not his first wife. It seems as though, oh, you were down the scale. But he prized you. He recognized you. He knew that you had been the old woman."

Isabel's voice changed entirely and then she returned to the present. "Now Marcia, does that answer you about Pelu? Anything about Pelu now?"

Marcia replied that it answered a tremendous lot and added that it certainly explained why the spirit guide had wished to get through to me with such important material.

Later, as we talked over the events of the day we were astonished to hear of the extraordinary series of coincidences which had brought Kathleen from New York City to Ojai, California, but this is a long story which has been told by Kathleen in a book she has written about her own adventures of the mind. Suffice it to say that we have had ample confirmation that it was important for Kathleen, Isabel, and me to get together and that, as Pelu said, Kathleen herself was being guided from within.

Kathleen's own feelings about the nature of this guidance are shown by the following excerpt from our first hypersensing session which took place on August 29, 1974, before our meeting with Isabel.

Then Marcia asked me to "conjure up" a spiritual guide, someone wise and kind. The guide could be imaginary or historical or anything I wished. At this point I did not wish to conjure up anything. I was more interested in seeing what would happen of its own accord. I turned back toward the temple and waited. Everything was very vague and misty. I went on waiting.

Then I saw a figure appear in front of the temple on the left. The Guide was made up of golden, peacefully swirling circles of light-energies. I was deeply touched and pleased. I felt my Guide was paying me a gentle compliment to appear in such a way. After all, light-energies are a "core" mystical image for me. . . .

So, for that first meeting I was glad not to have to bother with a properly costumed Guide. Had there been other people around up there, it would have been different. But we were totally alone. My guide's choice of manifestation moved me deeply.

Marcia asked me to concentrate on the light to see if it would begin to take some shape. I did as she asked, but I felt strongly that further "shape" would be irrelevant. The presence of the light was enough. The Being manifesting that light was one of great wisdom and compassion.

I walked nearer. I was hoping there might be some form of telepathic communication between us. Then a strange thing happened. The light simply flowed around me like balm. Not a word was spoken but I "knew" with perfect clarity what was going on. It was not the time for messages or further training; that would come later. For the time being I was to stay quiet and accept that light as balm. I was to remember that my nerves had nearly given way during the summer. I had survived an intense cleansing. I had driven myself without mercy and it was time simply to be quiet for a while. The battle was won. Now it was time for healing. I was so surprised by that compassion that I wanted to weep. . . .

When I encountered that silent compassion in my guide, a concern even I had denied myself in my "business as usual" approach to life, I began to weep. So much to heal right now. That is something I must learn to take seriously.

"Keep on," my little mundane self had said. But it is abundantly clear that knowing when to rest is also part of "keeping on."

During the year following these experiences, I remained in close touch with Kathleen. Her sensitively written book, *Journey of a Dream Animal,* published in the summer of 1975 provides a revealing description of the course of inner development which led up to the events herein recorded. At this time she is working on her Moses books and is keeping an account of her own highly successful work in hypersensory regression therapy.

One of the first groups to grow out of our workshops was an informal monthly assemblage at the home of Ray and Neva Robinson in Cerritos, California. In the reports they sent us, some of the most interesting material was that relating to Neva's experiences on Venus.

HYPERSENSING SESSION WITH NEVA ROBINSON, CONDUCTED BY RAY ROBINSON—JUNE 8, 1974

Neva was gliding through the air over a vast land of sand and jagged rocks. There were round houses that gave an impression of having glass domes, but you could not see inside. Then, when she was ready, Neva went into a round domelike house. It was her father's place.

The room was decorated in rich tapestry even to the chairs which were ranged about a long table that would seat twelve people. Neva was sixteen years of age. She had shining black hair, yellowish brown skin, and was dressed in a long robe. The house was used as a council chamber for a large city of people who were ruled by her father and another man. She was on the planet Venus and her father was called Belkar. His coruler was a man named Votar.

I asked if her life was good and she said that they had no worries because her father provided for them very well. I asked how they traveled and was told that they moved on rays of light. She did not know how this happened. We then journeyed forward to the age of twenty-four or twenty-five and discovered that she was called Tosha and was dedicated to the temple as a priestess. Her entire life was to be given over to this work. She guarded the secret temple room where the sacred tablets containing all wisdom were stored but was not allowed to enter that room herself. All her time was spent in meditation and prayer.

I asked her again about the era but she could not relate to a time period. Again she described the manner in which people were enabled to fly. They had rays emanating from their bodies and they glided about from place to place. She could not describe how the rays were activated or controlled, but she mentioned that Belkar and Votar made many journeys to Earth and other planets by this means of transport.

I then inquired about scientific matters but she could not help as she was entirely dedicated to the temple and isolated from the life of the people. Next I took her to the age of forty. At this point she was crying and stated that she was in a sleep. Her work, she was told, had been completed and the time had come for her to incarnate on Earth in order to learn more lessons.

She was breathing hard and kept saying that she was in a sleep. I asked her if all the others had to reincarnate. She said yes, except for Belkar and Votar, who had completed that phase of their evolution. Since she was feeling the strain I took her into the light where it was so bright and peaceful that she calmed down. When asked what she had gained from this experience on Venus she said, "Dedication and devotion."

On being questioned about her incarnations on Earth she stated that we all had to come back over and over until we became part of that Light. In order to pinpoint a place in time I asked her to go with me to her next incarnation. When she responded she was ten years old and in great distress and fear, so I regressed her to eight years of age. She was in a village somewhere in France with cobblestone streets and pretty little houses. She had a happy home but all were fearful because the Huns were coming closer.

Next we moved to the age of nineteen and found that she was married, had two boys, and was very happy. Then, in my next question, I discovered that I had failed to ascertain her sex. When asked what her husband did for a living I was told, "My wife stays home and takes care of the children. I gather wood and sell it to the villagers."

At this point Neva was tired so we brought her out.

It is interesting to compare Ray's account with Neva's own description of her life on Venus. She writes:

I entered my life on Venus by gliding three feet above the ground. I was propelled by rays emanating from my body and could soar higher or lower at will.

In this sphere I lived in the Temple of the Wisdom, a circular structure with a domed top made out of a shiny material that seemed to glow. There were no visible doors or windows and it was not possible to see inside. The entrance was a panel of an iron wall which slid back automatically. Inside was a long table with twelve seats around it. At one end was my father Belkar's seat, at the opposite end was Votar's seat.

The furnishings of this room appeared to be made of the same shiny material as the outside of the building. Curving divans followed the curves of the walls and, like the seats, had silken tapestrylike coverings. The walls, too, were hung with silken tapestries woven with symbols. My symbol was among them; an inverted triangle with a wedge slanting through it.

I was tall, black-haired, and robed in a long white silken garment with a red sash that went over one shoulder and tied on the opposite hip. Although it was not possible to see my own face I knew I had a chain with a symbol at my throat.

Later, I went through a period of solitude, spending my days in meditation and study. My small isolation room was furnished only with a table, bed, and meditation stool. These furnishings were of the same material as those in the council room. I now knew that I was a priestess with the right of entry to all but one of the rooms. This forbidden chamber was the Room of the Wisdom where the records of thought were kept. Only Belkar and Votar were allowed there.

We all traveled by what appeared to be rays from our body. The process seemed to be a kind of levitation which we could speed up or slow down.

My hours in this place were never lonely, even in isolation. There was a sense of complete peace, harmony, and love. I knew I was loved by all and returned these feelings.

The next scene came when I was in the sleep room waiting to be reincarnated. Despite the great drowsiness that was overcoming me I was very sad at having to leave. I had learned as much as I could at this stage and must now broaden my experience. This meant being born on Earth.

The odd thing about this hypersensing session was that while I saw all the pictures and knew mentally what was happening I do not remember anyone asking me questions or my own answers. In fact, I cannot even remember talking during this experience. Whether I was in a deeper state I do not know, but this was the most vividly real of all my experiments in retrocognition.

By mid-1975 Ray and Neva were conducting a highly successful psychic development group in Oxnard, California. Neva, who has learned to put herself into a trance at will, contacts Votar psychically and brings through messages from his dimension. There appears to be much vitality in this group and we look forward to future developments with intense interest.

What and where is Kumerae?

Judy Olsen, a lithe and attractive yoga teacher from Laguna, California, cannot give the precise location of this place but nevertheless she has been there. During our first retrotrip on May 19, 1974, Judy made a connection with a spiritual guide named Darius. We reviewed some scenes of her past experiences including an incarnation on Atlantis during which she sowed the seeds of certain relationships which she is continuing to work out in the present lifetime. While in Atlantis we also encountered a benevolent mentor known as "the white priest."

The second session, conducted the following day, commenced by invoking the same guide and asking his blessing on our venture. The following transcript is a complete recording of our conversation.

Marcia—We are going up the mountain path to that high and beautiful valley, the place where you can find your spiritual teacher. When you've taken your fifteen steps find your resting place and look around for Darius. Let's see if you can find Darius, and then when you have found him you can tell me. There is no rush about this. I want you to do it for yourself this time.

Judy—He's here.

Marcia—Good. I'm so glad he's here. He must have been waiting for you all the time. How does he look? The same as yesterday?

Judy—Yes, the same. White, white. Robe is white. There's purple on the stitching.

Marcia—You should take time to have a little visit with him. And without being presumptuous, I'd be interested to know more about him. That is, is he someone you've known in a past life?

Judy—He's nodding.

Marcia—He's nodding. You've known him before?

Judy—He says we're old friends. It's funny, he's not speaking, but he's saying it anyway.

Marcia—I imagine he can speak to you without words.

Judy—Yes. It's with his eyes. Seems to be with his eyes.

Marcia—Has he a message for you? Anything about your personal life, or future, or that he feels you should do?

Judy—He says I'm moving faster now. Coming along.

Marcia—Good.

Judy—I was a laggard last time. I've been lagging behind.

Marcia—You don't seem like a laggard.

Judy—Some other life I was a laggard.

Marcia—Is there anything you should do? A thought for meditation? Or any kind of information or advice?

Judy—Well, there's two things he's saying. With the right eye he's telling me that if I think on him it will help my meditation. Then with the left eye he's saying that in meditations we'll go beyond the causal.

Marcia—You were afraid that if you had an inner guide of this sort you might yearn for him too much, but that doesn't seem to be a danger, does it?

Judy—No, he doesn't think so.

Marcia—Perhaps it will be a way of focusing?

Judy—It's all right. It's all right to think of him the way I see him now.

Marcia—Why don't you have a brief meditation right now with him. I'll turn off the tape and you can just sit in his presence. Then after you've had some time to meditate with him we'll go back and look into the past again. . . . Just let yourself go as though you had no body. You don't need the body now.

Judy—I'm here. He's here. He's just a point of light now, and I'm just a little tiny, tiny dot. But it's OK. I don't have any body to feel in, but I feel all right. It's like I'm all compressed into a little nugget. But it's all there. I'm still feeling separate because I'm not aware enough yet that I'm part of the whole thing, but we'll learn how . . . to get me to feel less individual . . . and more . . . part of the whole. But not the individual consciousness. It's a beautiful feeling I'm beginning to have. A great warm bath [chuckle]. Everyone else is in the bath.

Marcia—Wonderful. You should just enjoy this for a while.

Judy—Oh, we're moving.

Marcia—Where are you moving to?

Judy—Space. Like there were galaxies going by. . . .

Marcia—Let yourself go on this journey and see where he takes you.

Judy—It's all just dancing around, like the whole universe is dancing around, but in just one little speck of my . . . what I can see. It's over in one corner, the dancing around universe. He's telling me that that isn't even all. That's only in one corner, but there's more. . . .

Marcia—Yes, even that isn't all.

Judy—Now I'm big.

Marcia—First you're little and now you're big.

Judy—Now I'm spreading out. I'm so big that you could stick a whole universe in this little portion of my consciousness. We're going to go . . . Getting heavier.

Marcia—Yes, you're getting heavier. You're coming down onto this other place.

Judy—Yes, very heavy.

Marcia—Let it happen.

Judy—Heavy, but not as heavy as really. Like a heaviness when you're in water. Lighter, there's a fluid feeling like that. Only there's an atmosphere. It isn't water, but it feels fluid.

Marcia—Yes.

Judy—Everything's translucent. You can almost see through everything.

Marcia—Yes, what sort of things are here? What does this place look like?

Judy—I can't get it yet. There's a . . . colors, and there are forms. I don't know what the forms are. They're shapes.

Marcia—It will come more clear.

Judy—It wants to come clear. There's shapes, you know. There's tall things, but they're not trees. And pastels, almost see-through, pearllike.

Marcia—Yes. Opalescent.

Judy—Oh yes, there are other people . . . and those have got to be buildings.

Marcia—Like buildings.

Judy—OK, we're kind of flying around. Very, very, very, very pretty birds in this place. But you can see through them, too. You can't quite, but it's like you could.

Marcia—A finer kind of matter than we're used to?

Judy—Yes . . . more subtle. This is a place that is a planet.

Marcia—Another globe?

Judy—But it isn't. I guess you can't see it from earth, physically. It's not that there aren't telescopes to see it; it's just that it can't be seen.

Marcia—Yes, it's in another kind of matter. Another realm. Does this place have a name?

Judy—Well, he's telling me . . . something like Kumerai.

Marcia—Kumerai is a beautiful name.

Judy—Nobody talks, though.

Marcia—Oh, they communicate in some other way?

Judy—Yes, but I feel that's what they call it . . . Kumerai.

Marcia—You can continue now to explore. See what comes to the eye of your inner vision and then report back.

Judy—The people seem to be engaged in different kinds of activities.

Marcia—Are they humanoid-type people?

Judy—Yes, but I don't see any children. No children. I'm looking for some. But I don't see any schools.

Marcia—Yes.

Judy—And I don't see any trains, no cars, no vehicles. They just get places. They . . . we're just kind of flying.

Marcia—On wings of thought?

Judy—Yes, that's it. I was looking over there . . . and then I was there.

Marcia—What do the people do? Is there any kind of music on this place?

Judy—It's a sound.

Marcia—Sound. I was wondering what you hear.

Judy—It isn't like any instrument I ever heard, but it's like eighty orchestras. It doesn't seem to have any musical form like one, two, three, four.

Marcia—Yes, A different kind of sound.

Judy—A flowing sound . . . and nothing's repeated. Very, very beautiful. The closest instrument is like strings, but it isn't violins. Doesn't seem to repeat. [Chuckle.] It's like you could climb aboard one of those sound waves and go away with it. That's what it is . . . it's sound waves. You could get on a beam.

Marcia—Do you have Darius here to guide you? I should think you would need him.

Judy—Yes, he's telling me that you could get on one of these sounds and go to its source. You would find the source . . . the source of all. . . . This seems to be a natural home between homes.

Marcia—What does that mean, "a natural home between homes?" Do people come here from the Earth?

Judy—Yes. I don't think it's just the Earth. Everybody's very nice, but they're not paying much attention to me, but it's all right because . . . I'm kind of thinking . . . that great group thought. All these people over here . . . they all have one big thought at one time.

Marcia—How is that? You mean they all think together?

Judy—Well, it seems like it. I'm in this group now, and I'm thinking and it's like they're all thinking it, so we all are. One is the same as all.

Marcia—Yes. There is a communion there.

Judy—Yes. So that you can't have . . . you can't really own a thought at all. As soon as one has it, it becomes the property of everybody in that group.

Marcia—That's something that earth people should learn. You can't own a thought.

Judy—And then there's others having their thoughts. . . . Nobody seems to eat anything. There doesn't seem to be any need for anything. There's nothing to do but think. That's what this place is. That's why there aren't any trains or cars.

Marcia—It's a place made out of thought?

Judy—Yes, that's all you need to do.

Marcia—You're not burdened down with mundane work?

Judy—Nope. There's nothing to do.

Marcia—What about making garments? What do they wear?

Judy—Everybody's kind of translucent. And I can't tell men from women. In fact right now I look like all the rest of them.

Marcia—What are you wearing?

Judy—I'm not wearing anything.

Marcia—Are you also translucent like these people?

Judy—Yes. I've still got arms and legs though, and I don't have any female organs that are noticeable.

Marcia—So this is a place for people to go and think and hear. Are there colors too?

Judy—They're magnificent. Very vibrant. . . . Ah, they're not heavy but very, very strong colors. But not of the heavier shades. They're all like pastels, but extremely vivid. Rose is almost unbearable. It's because I'm not tuned up for it.

Marcia—Yes.

Judy—It's time to go.

Marcia—All right. Can you return here again sometime? Ask him if he'll take you back sometime when you need to go.

Judy—I can go in a dream . . . and I'll go again between this life and the next.

Marcia—Oh, you can go there between lives?

Judy—Yes. Oh, now we're getting into . . . It's like an ocean.

Marcia—Yes.

Judy—It's not wet, but . . .

Marcia—Yes, it's like an ocean.

Judy—Oozing all over me, but it's not wet. . . . OK, we're coming out.

Marcia—Coming out?

Judy—Oh, we're back in the meadow.

Marcia—Back in the meadow. Good. I'd like to ask Darius if this is the sort of thing you learned to do when you were in Atlantis working with out-of-the-body experiences?

Judy—He's the priest.

Marcia—Oh, Darius was the priest then?

Judy—He's the white priest.

Marcia—And so you knew him then, is that it?

Judy—I didn't know that.

Marcia—You knew him as the white priest. He must be a very high being then.

Judy—I didn't know that!

Marcia—Who was the man you loved . . . Gregor? Is he anybody you've known in this life?

Judy—My husband.

Marcia—He was your husband in this lifetime. First you wanted him and couldn't have him, and then you had him and didn't want him. Is that how it worked out?

Judy—That's right.

Marcia—Was there something to be learned from that . . . any lesson in it?

Judy—I broke a law by loving him. This time he broke a law by loving me.

Marcia—Well, the really important thing was the priest, Darius.

Judy—He's so wonderful!

Marcia—Yes, he's the one who will sustain you. . . .

One point on which our sensors have been unanimous is that the higher-dimensional beings function in group formation. The following readings deal with the nature and activities of these telepathic communicators.

EXCERPTS FROM TWO HYPERSENSING SESSIONS WITH MICHAEL
MATTHEWS–JULY 29, 1974

Michael—I worship the sun which sets over the water. This place is very high, so high that I can't find the path that leads to it. I am alone and have always been alone. Yet there are many people who come and visit me here.

I am standing on a cliff looking out over the ocean. There is a small temple behind me. I am wearing a robe like they did at the time of Christ. It has long sleeves and falls to the ground. I am the priest-healer of the temple. I have a long beard and hair.

The sky is full of shades of pink, but the setting sun is my God, full of healing and compassion. My heart is filled to overflowing; my cup runneth over. Creation is good and just. It is concerned about each of us. I act as the human side of its concern. The impersonal becomes personal through me. I act as the personalizing agent.

This is the place of the funnel. Energy is taken from the cosmos and funneled through me. Compassion is the tool I wield. What I treat are not so much the physical ailments as the deep problems of the mind. Compassion and healing are renewed with the setting sun.

I have come to succor the sick, to heal, to comfort, for it is a long path we must march, a long distance we must travel. Let us soothe the travel weary, that they may find peace along the trail.

I am him and he is me. I am his projection onto the physical plane. There may be others. This is where my consciousness stems from. I have always been here. I am always ready to receive and comfort my parts which are incarnate, as well as many others who have made associations with me over the centuries.

I can't leave here. I am of the temple. Mostly I stand upon the balcony and watch. Occasionally, part of me incarnates in the world. I have tremendous compassion and love for all my people. Yes, I care for them in every way. My heart bleeds for them. My eyes are full of tears. For each of them must suffer for himself, but I must suffer for all of them.

Marcia—Were you ever one of the people?

Michael—No, I have always been old and set apart. As the cliffs are ancient and far from the sea, so I am old and far from my people. My people are not in this place; they are on Earth. I feel their presence as if they are very near. I talk with them and soothe and comfort them.

JULY 31, 1974

Marcia—. . . Can you see yourself in a more congenial sphere?

Michael—A large hall. Many of us are there—all men. A Jewish patriarch sort of trip. Old men. Someone is talking but not using words. Speaking in waves of emotion. A different language, based on empathy. I can't quite follow it. I can't begin my work until I can understand that language. It's like reading a book in a dream without understanding the words. I'm not hooked up yet. There is a whole group of telepathic communicators sending support and training. Some are incarnate.

Marcia—Are you one?

Michael—I'm at the end of the stick. I am like their puppet. There's still a block of ignorance I have to remove. They are a network with each joint representing a telepath. Arranged in triangles and pentagrams—like a geodesic dome of the third magnitude. There is such a close relationship between each member, yet each one is different.

Marcia—Is this your group?

Michael—Yes. The question is, why have they kept me isolated so long? I have to build up my own strength. If I am going to receive, I must have the strength for the dry periods between receptions. They are brothers—an order of men. That seems chauvinistic. "Metaphysical midwives." They deal with the whole range of evolution. The network is only part of them. I have to incarnate to focus and direct the energy, like playing music. There is a whole symphony going on. I'm the horn at the end with the musician behind me. In other words, I'm a transformer. Those missing aspects of my personality which other people have were left out for a reason. The companionship which I cannot get in the world is there completely on another level.

Marcia—If you were complete on this level, you might not have to look to the other.

Michael—Yes. . . . Now I'm going to see if I can get into the group mind of the members of the order. [Pause.] It seems to be a network of tremendous compassion. They are like parents who see the follies of their children, and yet must let them screech and yell. The rules are that they must be asked for help before they can do anything for us. They are very gentle. One must ask with the whole of his being. It has to be an earnest request. They are searching for a few people who can understand.

I don't think these people are like us. They have this tremendous reservoir of spiritual knowledge that they want to drop into humanity. Answering prayers is a minor kind of thing. They are looking for receivers and find very few who are capable of taking what they have to give. We don't dare all incarnate at the same time; the world could not stand our vibration. There were many of us in Egypt.

Marcia—What about other civilizations?

Michael—There have been many civilizations between the Ice Ages. They take those who are ready. The rest have to start all over again, like wiping the slate clean. There were some people in China, like the Taoists. Tibet— very good receivers there. Their arrogance caught them. Their connection wasn't pure enough. Tibet's problem was mainly indiscriminate teaching— black magic resulted.

Marcia—What about America?

Michael—We brought in too many from Tibet. The black magicians along with the white. There seem to be a lot of people from Tibet in America. That is why the psychic movement is so popular now. They had the physical grounding of power. Looking out over the United States I see pillars of white and pillars of black. Whole areas like advertising are predominantly black. Why isn't the white doing something about it? The cycle's coming to an end. They prefer those people who can pick them up telepathically.

This decision again. Atlantis, Roman times, French Revolution, and now.... Last time for a mature choice. It seems so unfair. I see what the blacks are doing, but what are the whites doing?

They are giving a barrage of telepathic messages—symbolized by radio and TV. Quiet listening is needed. People are not listening to the right things. They should turn off all those dials and really listen.

Marcia—How can one become more receptive and telepathic?

Michael—The use of tobacco and alcohol make reception difficult. Meditation on the seven colors of the rainbow is extremely helpful in developing telepathic ability. Start with red and go to the other colors through orange, yellow, green, blue, indigo, and violet. Each time you meditate on a given color you should try to feel and visualize that color.

It is also very useful to sound the chakras. Start with the lowest chakra, the muladhara, and sound the AUM, holding the note as long as you can. It will take some experimentation to find out which notes correspond to which chakras. Seven chakras, seven notes.

The first and easiest exercise for a telepath is for one person to send another the thought of one of the colors of the rainbow. This practice is extremely useful because it develops clairvoyance and telepathic ability at the same time. Gradually shift to guessing what is contained in sealed envelops or desk drawers. Use the color gold to wipe out anxiety and confusion. In the first stages one tends to feel quite anxious and to have a lot of fear that the answers may be incorrect. All answers are correct, each in their own way.

Shift gradually to whole sentences, whole concepts. The secret is in the verb ... let it be action oriented. The emotional content is extremely important.

Concentrate on breathing beforehand. Make it slow and steady. You will receive best with your breath out. Gradually you will notice a buzzing in your ear when you are receiving.

In a group it will be very useful to start with an opening prayer and then sound the chakras. Have one of the members lead you in a color meditation and proceed with practicing your telepathic exercises. Allow no one to criticize another in the group. Accentuate the group's willingness to serve all humanity and not just the personal development of its members. Ground your work by saying the Great Invocation [from the Alice Bailey books] at the beginning and end of your meetings.

The following reading with Lourie Dildine shows what can happen when we veer away from our preoccupation with past lives and encourage the sensor to register whatever spontaneously comes to mind.

HYPERSENSING SESSION WITH LOURIE DILDINE, CONDUCTED BY AKEVA—JULY 8, 1974

Akeva said to speak of anything that came into my mind.... Then the images began to form in geometric shapes. The clearest picture was of two triangles set point to point, the one on top of the other. When Akeva asked what they meant I related it to an hourglass and felt that it symbolized "ancient time."

Then Akeva said to imagine that the lower triangle was large enough to pass through. I followed his instructions to go through the opening and found myself in a space not of this Earth. I felt as though it were pre-Earth. Soon a sphere which might have been the Earth began to form, but it was very far away. I was looking "down" at it from space with a feeling of being part of a great body of spirits. We were all one, yet there was a sense of being an individual as well. I then began moving away from the sphere until it disappeared from sight.

Akeva asked what I saw. It seemed as though blue and red strips of light were going by. He said to move in the direction from which they came. Then I saw a large shape like a cone. I went into the cone which was like a tunnel growing smaller as I proceeded. Through the opening in the small end of the cone was a bright light. Passing through this opening I came out into a desert area. I was standing on a hillside looking out over a scene similar to this. [Here Lourie made a sketch of a desert with stones, cacti, and a rocklike natural bridge.]

While observing this desert terrain I became conscious that a spaceship was hovering behind my left shoulder. In the same position on my right were two identical ships. Akeva said to go to the one on my left. I said "No, I am supposed to go to the first one on the right."

As I went over to the ship it lowered to about six feet above the ground. A sliding door opened and I floated up into the opening. As I went into the ship the feeling of having a body was not so great. It was like having an energy body rather than a physical one. The other people were also vague with regard to their material bodies. The inside of the ship was large and had a lot of open space with panels of light around the edge. There were large windows around the outside of the ship. I felt that there was much more than this room, which was located at the top of the craft. [Here Lourie drew another illustration showing the spaceship to be shaped like a disk with a horizontal row of windows around its equatorial band.]

Akeva asked what we were doing. I said we were looking for a place to settle. He asked if we would blend in with the other people. I said, "There are no other people."

We came from a large city where everyone else lived. Other search parties were also looking for a place to go to live away from this city. My impression of this city was that it was extremely "modern" in the sense of being technologically advanced.

When Akeva asked where and when this took place I said, "Earth—in ancient times." At that point he brought me out.

Thus far about a dozen sensors have independently reported seeing an image shaped like an hourglass, infinity symbol, or mobius strip. In every case this form was associated not just with time travel but with the process of passing through the dimensions from one state of being to another. The following quotation from Kathleen Jenks is typical of these experiences.

This time Marcia suggested that I deliberately try to tune into an Atlantean life. She counted me back into it. When she had finished, I found myself engaged in a perfectly natural activity—one which spontaneously springs to mind whenever I wonder if I have ever lived in Atlantis.

I was flying in a small crystal sphere about six feet in diameter. It flew through thought control. I was standing up inside it. Had I wishèd to sit down, I would simply have leaned against a curving wall and it would have given way to make a comfortable form-fitting seat. . . .

Then Marcia asked me to land. I saw a vivid image of an hourglass in front of my eyes. It seemed as if the flying sphere had to fall down through the glass, pass through the narrow neck, and continue on into the lower half. It was a clear symbol for passing through a time-warp—but that makes no sense to me. . . .

This next account, written by Jack Kerollis, summarizes the information gathered in four hypersensing sessions conducted in March and April of 1974 in Ojai, California.

Yes, I have remembered myself in many past times. I have seen dreams of many lands, images, reflections of ageless beings traveling the path of Earth. A glimpse here, a flash there, and the knowledge that "I was here before."

My path has been one of ever-growing conscious activity, experimentation, and trial. Upon contact with hypersensing I became concerned with the many layers of illusion in this new technique. Diving into the experience of my locked subconscious I have gained tremendous insight into the creative play of my infinite self. My first experiences were concerned with the unfoldment of the knowledge of other times.

How beauteous the images and how clear! There I was working diligently in a hidden monastery located near the Gobi Desert, the highlands of the Uighur civilization. I became a scientist, working with the tremendous columns of light which generated energy for our lost cities. A man of devotion and dedication to a civilization long since forgotten.

Ah, I see myself as a small child being trained with others in the art of levitation, three children alone in the Black Forest playing with the energy of gods and men. We flew throughout the trees, lifted heavy objects by the power of thought, and participated in the design of the universe. But the forces with which we tampered were beyond our capacity to control and we were crushed in a rock slide that we had inadvertently launched.

Atlantis. I see in the distance a great city, a crystalline image, yet surrounded by a haze of transgression. I signal my fellow airmen. We travel in threes, our ships almost invisible to those below. "Beam into manifestation," I say, as we descend upon the distraught residents of the fallen continent. We are a fleet designed to transport those who have the message of light and love to spread throughout the Earth. I see them as we approach; what bewilderment and fear they exude! "Life is only a play of energy," I telepath. "Do not fear, young Earth peoples. We go out to cover the planet, to distribute the children of Atlantis to all corners of the globe. Our translucent silver ships are mere extensions of our will to render service."

What of my immediate past? I see myself as a Jamaican dancer destroyed by the power of alchemical experimentation. There are so many of these lives. I could search myself and see thousands. There is no limit to the power inherent in the unconscious mind. Yet I become dissatisfied with the glorified images of days unknown.

While in this state of disenchantment, I arrived on a plateau in Peru. This was the home of my teacher and divine father-being. Our first meeting was merely an introduction. I visited his house in the Andes, communed with him and his fellows, and established my archetype for future development. I sought no more past images. It was enough to be present, to live in the here and now in communion with my higher self.

Since that session I have visited this plateau many times. Often I have experienced this presence while in the midst of my friends and associates, many of whom have also sensed the overshadowing influence of the great ones. Many have even traveled to this spot and seen the same vision. My Peruvian master has taken me into his temple and given me experiences of light as yet unknown. . . .

Often I have wandered through the heights and depths of consciousness, experiencing, activating, and being engulfed. Hypersensing has been a step in piercing that veil.

Finally, I would like to relay in detail the last session with Marcia. We began by walking up twenty-five steps to the valley in the Andes. On the way to the stone house I noticed that the valley was planted with fruit trees. The gardens leading to the house were awe-inspiring. Strange varieties of plants kept changing, glowing translucently with the fruitful magic of life. In the far distance I saw a town and realized that this hidden plateau could not be seen from below. It just looked like part of a mountain northeast of Lake Titicaca.

The house is very large, like a castle cut out of rock and surrounded by walls. It seems like a huge commune of beings. I know them as "The Keepers of the Gate." There are forty-nine of them altogether—forty-two in bodies and seven great beings who remain formless. Each one is engaged in an activity, organizing, meditating, communicating. I am with a high-frequency teacher who is raising my vibrations. There seems to be an open hole in the top of my head and I breathe in and out from this center of consciousness.

To the right of the house there are three indentations in the mountains like landing strips. There is a craft above the house, a flying vehicle, spherical in shape. As I go in deeper, I realize that the airships are connected with the people in the house and that they exist together in the higher dimensions of consciousness. I try to dive deeper into a blue hole, and everything turns violet. I feel myself tapping into the consciousness of the Great One, the mastermind of the ship. . . .

There are vehicles everywhere, all around now, all the time. You can see them if that is what you're looking at.

Images of spaceships have so often appeared during our hypersensing sessions that it has become evident that we shall have to devote several chapters to this subject in our next volume of research findings. This work, which is already underway, will deal primarily with the nature and activities of our "space brothers."

According to our sensors the most impressive feature of so-called unidentified flying objects (UFOs) is their number. Apparently the universe swarms with them. They are not strictly physical but come *through* the dimensions so that they may appear at one moment and be gone the next. This transdimensionality means that they are not bound by the speed of light; hence they may even come from other galaxies.

Most UFOs function in the etheric realm of super-rarefied matter. Objects created out of this subtle substance can sometimes be discerned by sensitives but are not visible to the average person. Like colors at the edges of a spectrum, they may lie just beyond the border of visibility.

The range of sizes of these spacecraft is astonishing. Some may not even be measurable in terms of our customary ways of thinking. In general, the larger ones originate outside the galaxy while the smaller ones are intragalactic. The diversity of their forms is also beyond our power to comprehend since they come from so many spheres.

Spaceships have always been with us, and may even antedate the formation of the Earth. In Atlantean times they were generally recognized, but for reasons inherent in the working out of planetary karma the knowledge of their presence has been withheld from the human race for millennia.

Now, once again, humanity is being permitted to recognize the existence of the space brothers. The science fiction movement in literature and drama has been one way of preparing men's minds for their advent. Unfortunately, this stream of revelation has become polluted, so that the missionary spirits from more civilized regions of the universe are too often portrayed as super-mechanical monsters who magnify men's materialistic traits. Hopefully the future will bring more emphasis on their superior capacity for compassionate understanding.

At this time increasing numbers of people, including a handful of prominent scientists, claim to be in conscious touch with the space brothers. According to our communicators many more respected people will admit to having established contact with them over the next few years and the general public will, almost without realizing it, come to accept the probability of their existence. Ultimately, this widespread recognition will force the authorities in churches, laboratories, and government offices to take heed. This will be a grass-roots movement which in the 1980s may culminate in the visible appearance of some of these emissaries of goodwill from the living heart of the cosmos.

While a few individuals can even now establish a telepathic rapport with the occupants of various kinds of spacecraft, this is not necessarily advisable. In exceptional cases, where there is some valid reason for wishing to tap the minds of higher beings, it is better for people to work in group formation. Even then, caution should be exercised. While most of the space brothers seem to be morally as well as technologically far ahead of us, there may also be some who are neither friendly nor considerate.

Perhaps the greatest danger is that of low-grade astral entities masquerading as extraterrestrials. Already many weak-minded people have had their mental underpinnings knocked out from under them by real or fancied contacts with alien intelligences. Undoubtedly there will be many more casualties of this sort, but that is part of the calculated risk that must be taken to rescue humanity from its present impasse. "By their fruits shall ye know them." Communicators who are genuinely in touch with higher beings will be recognized by their ability to function as wholesome, level-headed, productive members of society.

The only safe way to contact the space brothers is through the elevation of consciousness to a point where it is possible to gain an intuitive grasp of the wisdom they wish to impart. No amount of curiosity or personal ambition can accomplish this task. Closer rapport can be achieved by dedicated servers of humanity who are sufficiently altruistic to use the energies released for the good of all.

In the nineteenth century most people saw the world in terms of static structures and sharply defined boundaries. Now, thinkers are becoming increasingly preoccupied with dynamic force fields and interpenetrating spheres of influence. Only in death do forms remain rigid and inert. Everything that lives must vibrate, circulate, and flow through space. Similarly, worlds may not be as isolated as we have supposed. If there is life on other planets and in other dimensions, then there must also be much movement of individual particles of sentient substance back and forth and round about the energized field of consciousness that encompasses the many realms of creation.

As materials become radioactive they send off showers of atomic particles. If, therefore, the Earth is becoming spiritually radioactive, then it may be that now, as never before, the opportunity is being offered for human souls to transcend the psychic gravitational field of the planet altogether. Hence, we can prepare to reach out to our friends from space and to heed their message that, far from being dark and deadly, the skies are beckoning us on to new and more enlightening voyages of exploration.

Although we have collected many stories about the "inner-dimensionals," it is too much to expect that this accumulation of data will be called scientific in the currently accepted meaning of the term. Nor is there any real need, at this stage, to argue the pros and cons of their objective reality. For a while it should be enough for us simply to act as a clearinghouse, processing information from independent sources and giving it out in periodic reports.

It is possible that the endeavor to learn more about the brothers from space will stimulate various lines of research which will be carried out in the coming Aquarian Age—the age of true democracy. At present, the people deemed worthy of conducting scientific investigations are usually highly trained specialists with advanced degrees, expensive laboratories, and extensive funding. But what if for some reason the space brothers did not choose to reveal their presence via the academic establishment? What if they would rather make themselves known in quiet ways to those who are willing and able to tune in on their frequencies? Then, regardless of money, status, formal education or worldly sophistication, even the humblest cooperator could share the glories of laying the foundation for the most sublime of all New Age sciences.

Despite the scoffing of skeptics, those who believe that they have made a link with the inner-dimensionals seldom worry about what the world thinks of them. They are all too poignantly aware that in terms of the cosmic scheme this is still a backward little planet whose inhabitants can hardly be expected to grasp more than a few elementary rules of the road as they journey through the sunlit immensity of metagalactic space.

It is important to remember, however, that if there are superior forms of life elsewhere in the universe, then the task of contacting these intelligences is not entirely in our hands. With each new recognition, the brothers of the stars draw closer. As we accept their help, their ability to communicate is correspondingly enhanced.

In some respects this growing cognizance resembles the building of a bridge. When we put forth a span from our side, we glimpse a similar span arching out from the other shore. Thus, we meet at the center. We have not yet laid the final connecting span, but the time may be coming when this last extension will be made and we will see them face to face. As one spiritual guide put it: "There will be a place where we can meet, and you and I will walk together. I wait for you now—at the threshold of our reunion."

9

THE OTHER SIDE
OF DEATH

The experiences which await the soul after death vary as greatly from one person to another as those which occur while in the body. As always, education makes an enormous difference. In addition to leading a good life, the best preparation for the great transition appears to be knowledge (or remembrance) of what to do and where to go after quitting the body.

For a while there may be some awareness of what is happening to the abandoned shell that has been left behind. Our colleague Akeva, after having passed through a life as a Chinese scholar named Kwang, died peacefully in bed. Prior to his passing he had given strict orders that his relatives were not to grieve. However, as he looked down upon the death scene, he could see his devoted wife weeping by his bedside while servants scuttled about preparing for the funeral rites. As he surveyed the scene, his consciousness slowly seemed to withdraw into his eyes. Finally he felt as though he were just one big eye. Then that too blinked and went out.

In a subsequent incarnation Akeva was a Persian administrator named Armin. In his late forties Armin was riding in the desert with his wife when his horse stepped into a hole causing him to pitch forward and hit his head on a rock. Although his death was instantaneous, Armin could see that his wife lay on the body a long time and cried. Then she went back to the town for help. A group of men came, put the body in a bag, slung it over a horse, and carried it home.

On the whole, the departing soul seems remarkably unconcerned about the disposal of the corpse it has left behind. Only once did we encounter a sensor who was depressed by the thought of his own decaying body, wishing it had been disposed of more cleanly. More typical is the attitude of a man, now an airplane pilot, who had the unusual experience of being beheaded atop the Great Wall of China. "The blade is falling," he said. "It falls forever—but it can't hurt me. Because I don't care. It never fell; I never saw it stop." Afterward he described his indifference to the callous manner in which the executioners tossed his severed head over the parapet, allowing the body to remain unburied where it lay.

Only in the rarest instances does a cast-off body exert an earthward pull upon the soul for more than a brief period after death. Maria Comfort has reported one such case in which a girl she was regressing went back to a life in the mid-eighteen hundreds where she was a young man who went to Colorado to work in the mines. When Maria counted the subject forward to the age of twenty he said, "I see only dirt." At twenty-one the reaction was still, "I am in the dirt." At twenty-two he said, "I am nowhere." Going backward it turned out that this young man had died at the age of eighteen when the mine in which he was digging collapsed. Unable to grasp what had happened, his spirit hovered around the body for four more years.

"Why are you staying with your body?" Maria asked.

"There is nowhere else to go." Nevertheless, this soul did shortly thereafter ascend into the light.

People occasionally attend their own funerals, but it can be an ironic experience. "How can they think that thing in the coffin is me?" the liberated one will exclaim. "If only they knew where I really am! I want to tell them how much better it is over here."

One who had been a successful businessman chuckled heartily to see his remains laid away in fitting style. A plainsman killed by Indians was touched when his buddy fashioned two sticks into a wooden cross and laid it over his grave. In another instance a woman saw herself as a spirit, perched cheerfully atop her own tombstone, watching her sister plant flowers by her grave. "Why are you hanging around that cemetery?" I asked. "Well, she never paid me much attention while I was alive," she replied, "so I figure I ought to get what's coming to me now."

Only if there is some unfinished business such as leaving a family in need does the entity feel a sense of distress which may pull him back to earth. A man who had been a farmer grieved because he had died prematurely, leaving a wife and small children with no means of support. A bandit, unrepentant when he was hanged for his crimes, felt sorry afterward about the people he had slain. However, the instances in which there are regrets constitute a small minority. Undoubtedly there have been, and are, earthbound souls, but the people who come to us seem not to be of the type to encounter this difficulty.

A poignant instance of a deliberate effort to maintain contact with the earth plane is that of a happily married woman who was wed to the same man in an East Indian incarnation. In that embodiment she had been the pampered daughter of a wealthy household. At an early age she married a kindly merchant many years her senior. Immediately after the birth of her first baby, she died. For the next twenty years her spirit lingered lovingly about the house where she had gone as a bride as she watched her son grow to manhood and her husband decline into old age. Then, when he finally passed on, she was there to greet him. Her description of his astonishment and delight to find her waiting when he "woke up on the other side" made a touching epilog to her story.

When departing souls are met by their loved ones, they seldom tarry around their mortal remains. Even though members of the welcoming party may have died years before they evidently have the capacity to return in a familiar guise to greet the new arrival.

Robert Thomas of Mill Valley, California, recollected a particularly depressing life in which his wife and two small sons were beheaded in front of his eyes. He, the bereaved husband, lived on for years after but never recovered from the shock of the experience. Finally, when his turn came to pass over, the first thing he saw on the other side was his beautiful young wife leading the boys by the hands. They had come to welcome him and guide him on his way.

A case like this provides a good argument for taking the regressed subject through the death experience. Had we left Robert with nothing more than the horrible memories of watching the execution of his family, the whole retrotrip could have been unendurably depressing. But thanks to the catharsis at the end when his wife and children came to greet him the situation was redeemed.

The following letter, reprinted in its entirety, describes the case of a soul who chose to remain close to the physical plane until he was sure his beloved dogs would be in good hands. Yet he too found a helping hand to ease the great transition.

Dear Marcia,

This is a regression done February 6, 1974, by Isabel Buell. Subject: Eileen Hyatt.

It was suggested that my most recent life be explored. I had been regressed before but this experience came through so colorfully that I felt it for days. Notes were made at the time and from these notes I read:

So much light, color vibrating, rainbows, electric, Aurora Borealis—I must be looking at the northern lights. The feeling was of strong, pulsating, and rhythmic vibrations of light which became so brilliant that it was blinding. All colors and bright snow. I became aware of an Eskimo man standing in awe. This is his religion. He is worshipping and ecstatic. God is light and color.

I am an Eskimo man with dogs. Six dogs. I am thirty years old—very happy. Asked if I knew white men I said, "Down at store; they drink whiskey."

"Do you drink?"

"No, I have everything I need. I have furs, dogs, the lights. I carve my animals—seal, walrus, beautiful animals. I learn to speak English from white man. White man smell dirty. They stay inside too much. Air here is fresh. So good to smell. It helps me to carve and to see the lights."

Asked about a wife, I said her name is Namea. Was she beautiful? I laughed and said, "For an Eskimo. White man think wife should be beautiful—not important."

There were lots of children, fat happy babies. Did I love them? "Sure, why not. Simple."

My name was Jomo, which meant "hunter." The lights were my god. My wife's god was the moon. I came out to be alone. I see my hands, very brown and very strong. I have much power in my hands. "I use for good. I am a strong man. I make beautiful animals out of stone, walrus tusk, or whatever I find. I eat fish, walrus blubber—white man think we smell. White man go ugh! I don't see them much. They don't matter. They teach me about cross. I see cross in sky. I see everything in sky. Sun is setting now. Clouds deep yellow. I feel the sky coming down close on me like a cover."

Asked what year it was, I read 1902 on the calendar at the store. I could count to ten and got rather arrogant about it. Brought to my death scene everything changed from brightness to a gray color. "Lots of water— summer logs jammed in river—too deep, too deep. I fight hard but too much water. Stupid white man always cutting trees. Jomo's furs weigh too much. I can see them sinking down through the water—good furs."

"Too young to die. Stupid white man make mistake in river. Year? 1912. I miss my dogs. Dogs are best friends. I can't leave my dogs. They don't know where I am. White man don't know how to take care of dogs."

There was much anguish over this until I see Namea coming and she sees the dogs. "She's pretty fat." [Is she pregnant?] "No, just fat old lady—forty. She just woman—not like me but she try. She get another man, he take them. My dogs were me! Same, same! They are me and I am them. Same— we think alike. I watch over them. I watch for a while."

Something seems to open up in the sky—a door but it opens from the center out like an accordion. [Voice changes here.]

"Poor Jomo." [Who is talking?] "Jomo went into the little door. The lights shine brightly. He was a good man. You come into the world with light. He felt it but didn't understand. None of us likes to go really. It's so difficult to be here and watch suffering. Beauty bores you so you go to help people."

[What is your name?] "I have no name. I don't really know what I am. Whoever I am I came to help Jomo to the light. I help souls to come through. That is hard work."

After death and the release into the other world Jomo moves among colors and shapes that are geometric and shifting like a kaleidoscope. Triangles change to diamonds and then to rectangles. All movement is effortless and gliding. Tubes of light, prisms of light and color. Transparent clouds. Everything moving and shifting and somehow scientific and exact. Jomo didn't like to leave the earth.

I hope you enjoyed reading this, Marcia. I hope to pursue this further as it is a fascinating world I glimpsed. I felt like Alice going through the looking-glass. I know little about the Eskimos but have researched it some since and find that they did make carvings of stone and ivory. Also they believed that animals had souls like theirs.

Sincerely,
Eileen

In a follow-up letter dated May 27, 1975, Eileen wrote:

On May 5, Isabel regressed me back to the Eskimo life because I wanted to know the exact location, which turned out to be Fairbanks, Alaska. Then she asked that we contact whoever or whatever came through to help Jomo to the other side. My voice changed and became masculine and deep. The words came pouring through.

When asked who he was, the being who spoke through me said that his vibration was "E." He was the "E" note on the musical scale, and could best be understood by plucking the "E" string on the harp. A guitar or piano came close, but the harp was the truest. He said he had twenty-four people under his protection at the time. These people were like the facets of a diamond; each representing an aspect of the whole. He named several. He gave Isabel a reading and said other things of interest.

On the 22nd I decided to try to reach him on my own. I lay down and used a pyramid that Ward made. The entire plan for a book was revealed to me. Ideas and words poured forth and I sat up and wrote my first chapter. I am now on chapter seven. It is a children's book and in a subtle way will explore ESP and various other aspects of the psychic world. I see not one book but many. Each time before I write, I go into a meditative state, and the ideas come. I never plan what I will write; I take what is given me.

One of the rare psychics who can function with as much facility on the astral plane as on the physical is the writer Joan Grant. In her book *Many Lifetimes* she relates the story of the gardener "Old Morgan" whom she nursed during the days before his death at the age of ninety-three. The night after his passing she had a clairvoyant vision of him lying in his open grave. When she told him to get up he replied emphatically, "This is my grave and in it I shall lie until the Last Trump."

Later when she found that he insisted upon remaining in his grave she says, "So on the following night when, in spite of my best persuasions he remained obdurate, I left him while I achieved a convincing semblance of the conventional angel, complete with wings, white draperies, and a madonna lily. This apparition caused him to peer over the side of the grassy trough, but seeing that none of the other graves showed any signs of disturbance he declared, 'I'm not going to cheat my friends by going to heaven before it is officially declared open.' "

Suddenly, Joan Grant found herself in the guise of a young woman in an Edwardian dress. Carrying a parasol and a basket of roses she said in a kindly but peremptory tone, "Morgan, get out of that grave immediately! It is quite ridiculous to stay there another instant, for I require you to help me with my gardens."

With a smile of ineffable joy he exclaimed, "Very good, Your Grace," and sprang lithely to his feet. Joan then goes on to recount:

> I found myself, still the Edwardian lady, standing with him on a rustic bridge which spanned a stream alight with water-lilies. His delight at the height of the rhododendrons and azaleas, the profluence of primulas, the profusion of water-loving plants beside the lake, showed me that he had known them when they were planted to translate a dream into reality. I remember seeing the great yews clipped into masterpieces of topiary, roses

and yet more roses, swathes of lawn and leaping fountains. Suddenly he noticed that each flower, each leaf, even each blade of grass, was in its perfection. It was then that he exclaimed, "I am in heaven!"

Through discreet questioning of Morgan's sister Jemima, I learned that his ideal of womanhood had been the Duchess of N, for whom he had worked as a very junior member of a team of thirty gardeners during his early twenties. Jemima looked at me very straightly with her penetrating gray eyes and said, "Morgan made a vow when he was only a boy that he would not enter heaven, even if St. Peter himself opened the Gates, until the Duchess told him to come in!"

While the souls of the departed may be hastened on their way by the prayers and good wishes of their loved ones, their progress may also be impeded by the wrong kind of thoughts. Perhaps they may even be called back to the world of the living? In view of the current resurgence of interest in medieval magic, it seems worthwhile to pass on the following dialog, received in a report from Juanita Steele of Austin, Texas.

> *Nita*—We're going back to a time when you were involved in the handling of magical energy. . . . Where are you now?
>
> *Sensor*—It's all dark . . . walls . . . a castle . . . looking into a room.
>
> *Nita*—What are you doing?
>
> *Sensor*—I'm watching a magician. . . . He's reading from a book, mumbling words. His back is turned to me. He has a pointed hat, robes, predominantly blue.
>
> *Nita*—How are you dressed?
>
> *Sensor*—I'm not.
>
> *Nita*—Well, what do you look like?
>
> *Sensor*—I'm . . . I don't think I'm here.
>
> *Nita*—Where are you?
>
> *Sensor*—[A long pause.] I'm in a space outside the magician's sphere. I don't have a body. . . . [Long pause.] I have a head, and part of a chest. . . . I think I'm dead.
>
> *Nita*—But why are you here? What are you doing in this castle?
>
> *Sensor*—He conjured me here.
>
> *Nita*—Whatever for?
>
> *Sensor*—I think he wants to know something about the town. . . . I think he wants to know something about business deals.
>
> *Nita*—But why you?
>
> *Sensor*—I was a businessman.
>
> *Nita*—Well, let's leave the magician to his meddling and go back to the time when you were a businessman.

Another example of the kind of unexpected development which can occur during a hypersensing session is the case of twelve-year-old Betty. The girl's recently divorced mother had just moved into a spacious new home, and Betty was delighted with her sunny room and new friends. Nevertheless, she appeared pale and languid—in contrast to her usual ebullient disposition—and spent an inordinate amount of time in bed. Since Betty had been regressed several times by her mother, she was familiar with the technique and knew it had helped her in the past. Therefore, she asked her mother to work with her in order to ascertain the cause of her malaise.

As Betty sank into a trancelike state she reported that a bushy-haired young man was bothering her. "He keeps pushing and pushing at me," she complained.

"Does he have a body or is he in the spirit world?" her mother asked.

"He is in spirit. But he is in the dark. He seems to be afraid."

Gradually it appeared that Betty had contacted the spirit of a young man who had died so suddenly that he still didn't realize what had happened or where he was.

"Can you find someone to help him?" she was asked.

"I'll try. Yes, there is someone here who can help."

"That's good. Now, see if you can take him into the light and entrust him to his spiritual guide."

After a pause Betty announced that she had followed these instructions and the young man was now in the light. Thereupon she woke up and went placidly to bed. From then on she was her normal cheerful self and there was no further harassment from the fretful phantom.

What Betty did not know at the time was that the year before a young man had been murdered on the back doorstep of the house in which she was now living. He and some friends were giving a party when a band of motorcycle riders appeared in the driveway. With the intent of frightening off the intruders he went into the house and returned brandishing a pistol. One of the cyclists panicked and tried to disarm him. In the ensuing tussle the gun went off shooting him through the head. Whether this was the same young man that Betty saw in her vision we never knew, but the house was thenceforth free from ghostly visitants.

It frequently happens that when a sensor is instructed to search for a spiritual guide he receives the vision of a deceased friend or relative. Even though these instances may represent little more than exercises of the imagination, a few, such as the following, give pause for consideration.

The sensor, Marie O'Neill of Carmel, California, had recently become engulfed in problems not of her making and apparently beyond her control. During her first retrotrip she encountered a spiritual guide in the form of a wise American Indian. The Indian guide advised her on a number of matters, including the measures which she should take to overcome her painful arthritis. With the guide's permission, we also went back to a life in Scotland during which she had enjoyed a happy relationship with a young man who is now one of her children.

During a subsequent session I asked her to imagine herself ascending a flight of thirty wide, shining white steps. On arriving at the top of the stairs she found herself standing on a marble balcony. The view was breathtakingly beautiful with mountains all around and a lake glinting below. A yellow butterfly fluttered by. Her hair was blonde, she was wearing a blue gown, and she felt young and beautiful.

Turning around, Marie saw that the balcony led to a spacious white mansion with heavy carved doors and many windows. As she walked into a room with tiled floors and an arched colonnade I said, "See if there is someone who will meet you here."

"Yes," Marie replied. "There is an elderly man who comes to greet me. He seems very old and loving."

"What does he look like?"

"He has blue eyes, hardly any hair, a bit of a beard, not very tall."

"Does he see you?"

"He holds both hands out to me. He seems glad to see me. But I don't know who he is. [Addressing the old man.] I don't remember seeing you before. Who might you be? [Pause.] He smiles. 'Don't you remember?' No, I don't remember. Oh, now it comes to me. He was my mother's friend when I was a little girl. He was very old then. *He* remembers."

"Who was he?"

"He reminds me of how he used to visit us and take care of us when my mother was in the hospital. We called him Uncle—Uncle Jack."

"Please tell Uncle Jack that we are grateful for his presence and will appreciate any help he can give. Has he a message for you?"

"Uncle Jack, right now I need a golden ray of light. [Pause.] He tells me there will be some money shortly. We will find a place to move. It will be a happier house. I know it isn't going to be easy but I can do it."

"What is he doing now?"

"He holds my hand and we turn and go through the door into a courtyard with a fountain. There are birds singing ... music. He still holds my hand. He's assuring me everything's going to be all right. The flowers here are very pretty."

"Ask him if it will be possible for you to return."

"Uncle Jack, may I return? [Pause.] Oh yes, just climb the stairs."

"Ask Uncle Jack, 'Where is my true home?' "

"He shakes his head. Not at this time. He's going to find out for me. He promises he will.... There's someone else here. A very large man, bare chested. He has a turban on his head. He walks to the edge of the room by the arches and tells Uncle Jack that it is time to go. But he will return and meet me here. I just have to come back to this place. There are many rooms off the courtyard with big doors to each one. Not closed. I'm welcome here. I can hear the bells in back, like music. I feel so good when I'm here."

Afterward Marie told me the story of Uncle Jack. In the 1930s during the depths of the depression she had, at the age of twelve, been the eldest of six children in an impoverished, fatherless family. They did, however, have a cow. In order to ensure a supply of milk for the children the government would occasionally give them fodder for the cow. One day, in desperation, the mother tried to cook the cow's food for the children, but it was too rough and they all became ill. At this juncture, the mother had to go to the hospital to have a baby.

At the height of this crisis an elderly man known only as Uncle Jack would walk every day to the house to help Marie take care of the brood of sick children. Through the intervening years the memory of his kindness had faded, yet here in the year 1975 was Uncle Jack, happy and well at the top of the stairs and still extending a helping hand.

THE TIME BETWEEN

No set formula determines how long the soul remains out of incarnation. Apparently there is about as much free will on the "other side" as there is in this terrestrial sphere. That is, some individuals have far more personal choice than others with regard to how, where, and when they will return.

Occasionally the in-between state allows considerable leeway for weighing the pros and cons of entering a new body. Arlene Robertson of San Diego, California, has touched on this in the following transcript taken from a hypersensing session conducted on August 29, 1974.

Marcia—You're out of the body, in the light, and you realize that you're free again. Where do you go from here? When you're not in the body where are you?

Arlene—I'm under a tree with some other friends and we're just sitting there talking. It's lovely. It's sunny and clear. It's sort of like a university and we're all gathered outside. We're talking over our ideas and thoughts.

Marcia—This is not a place on earth, is it?

Arlene—No.

Marcia—Let's dwell on this. Tell me about it.

Arlene—It's very clear and beautiful. The sky is blue. It has a clean feeling about it.

Marcia—What sort of people are with you?

Arlene—They are very learned people—scholars.

Marcia—Is there a teacher there? Who teaches these people?

Arlene—It looks like Jesus.

Marcia—How does he look?

Arlene—He looks like the light shines out from him.

Marcia—What else do you see in this place? Are there any kinds of buildings? Is it all outdoors?

Arlene—It's all outdoors. Beautiful flowers. The word *wisdom* comes to me.

Marcia—Is this where you learn wisdom?

Arlene—Yes.

Marcia—Will you ask one of these people where is this place?

Arlene—They say this is the life between lives.

Marcia—Where does it take place?

Arlene—It's another dimension that we can't understand here.

Marcia—If this place is so beautiful why do you come back to earth again?

Arlene—To learn more wisdom on the Earth level.

Marcia—Why can't you learn the wisdom in between?

Arlene—You can learn it but then you have to go back to Earth and apply it. They all sit around and decide when you're going to go back. They suggest when you should go back and use the wisdom that you've learned here—use it on the Earth level—and you can go back when you choose. There's a lot of kidding about it—they're joking. Like—you've been rather lazy; don't you think you should go back again, Joe? Like that. One of them said, Well, I haven't been here long enough. I want to stay a little while longer before I go back. And another one says, Oh, come on, you're getting lazy. And they all laugh.

Marcia—Now you're coming back to earth. What special lesson do you have to learn this time around?

Arlene—I feel that I have to give love.

It should be mentioned that Arlene is a remarkably lovely, multitalented lady who could certainly be expected to find an agreeable niche in the "summerland" of postmortem experience. We have also encountered subjects who face the prospect of their return with all the trepidations of a reluctant exile.

The following account by Valerie Brock of London, Ontario, describes an interlude which occurred at the end of a hardworking lifetime in early New England. Our conversation ran as follows:

Marcia—Where are you going from here?

Valerie—I think a little way by myself.

Marcia—Where are you going?

Valerie—Erica.

Marcia—Tell me about this place?

Valerie—Full of light, and it's lovely.

Marcia—How do you look?

Valerie—I don't think I look.

Marcia—You're one with the light?

Valerie—Yes, I think so.

Marcia—Is this the place you go between lives?

Valerie—Yes.

Marcia—What do you do here?

Valerie—There are people you talk to and they talk back and explain to you their understanding. They have a lot more information now; they have been doing lots of studying. They don't expect too much of me as we're not very highly evolved.

Marcia—Where is your true home? Do you live on Earth?

Valerie—Earth and here. I have to keep going to Earth; that's my lot.

Marcia—Have you had many Earth lives?

Valerie—Yes, oh, yes, many.

Marcia—Tell me, have you a teacher?

Valerie—Yes, he is all light, very bright.

Marcia—Does he have a form?

Valerie—Yes, it is long and thin with a big sun around his head. I don't look too much as he is so bright. He will speak to me though.

Marcia—Could you speak with him now?

Valerie—He says we're too busy. I have to learn more. I'm supposed to learn all the time here.

Marcia—Tell me about this light land.

Valerie—Well, you don't walk, you spring along.

Marcia—Do other people come here between lives?

Valerie—No, not always. Sometimes they just keep going back. People who have done a good job come here. Some people don't do anything and they have to keep going back and go through it all again and again.

Marcia—Why did you come back as Valerie?

Valerie—I'm supposed to help. I have to be there to help. To help quietly and don't let them know.

In a subsequent letter Valerie went on to say:

The whole feeling was one of being joyously happy. I wanted to laugh and laugh. I felt that the great being there just radiated light and smiled benevolently at me most of the time as though amused at my efforts but understanding my potential. It was as though he were patiently waiting for time to take care of all things.

I saw that there were other beings around but I was drawn to the main one who directed me. The others seemed to think me slightly dumb but the Sun one seemed to think there was hope. I had the feeling that everyone was exceptionally intelligent and understanding of the higher laws.

I did not regret leaving my Earth life or the people in it. I accepted the idea that I would again return to the Earth planet and to the people who meant so much to me. Then when it was time for me to leave Erica again I felt no sorrow—just that a job had to be done in the best way possible. I wonder if the spaces where we go between lives are all the same place and we each give it a different name. Whatever it is, whatever it was, it was beautiful.

HOW MANY LIFETIMES?

A question often asked is "How many times must a soul incarnate on earth?" Its corollary is, "What is the duration of the periods between lifetimes?"

The answer I always give is that there is no set rule about this. People have about as much free will on the "other side" as on earth. This means that some have quite a lot of latitude for personal choice and others hardly any at all. In general, the so-called younger souls seem to wheel rapidly in and out of incarnation, while the older souls require more time to digest their experiences and may not even come back at all. Occasionally, a highly evolved entity will undergo a series of closely spaced lives in order to accomplish a particular task.

Thus far we have not been able to draw any cut-and-dried correlation between the age of the soul and the length of the interludes between lives on Earth. One well-known scientist who possessed manifestly superior qualities of intellect remarked that he had been born only about three times since Atlantis. Most people can recollect numerous lifetimes but a few seem to have undergone most of their development on other spheres.

All the available evidence shows that people who die prematurely are apt to return quickly in order to complete the lessons they were in process of learning. Many who were cut down during World War II came back within a few years, often retaining antiwar sentiments. One can, therefore, speculate that numerous young people who were actively engaged in protesting the Vietnam War had reason to feel that they had already seen their share of senseless slaughter.

Carol Griffith (Shalamard) reported that in her previous incarnation she had been a Polish boy whose father, mother, and sister were killed by the Germans when he was eight years old. After two years in hiding, the child was shot by the Nazis. The death date of this former personality was three years later than Carol's present birthdate. Evidently this soul moved into a body that was already sufficiently mature to allow her to avoid repeating the trials of birth and infancy.

When asked about the displaced owner of the body Carol replied, "She was just a dumb kid." At this point Shalamard became upset because she had missed the chance to go back to her own planet. Later, describing this incident, Carol wrote:

A couple of days later I really put my head into Shalamard. I questioned the idea that I had entered Carol's body at the age of three. So I proceeded to regress myself back to that time. I saw myself walking through a tunnel asking for Pelu. Pelu appeared and I asked him why I chose Carol.

As Shalamard, I saw Carol and her two brothers out in the back yard. There was a broken playpen with no one in it. The house was wooden with four or five steps and a rail missing from one side. A dirt path led to the road. There were trees all around. The mother, in a printed dress, was holding Carol's hand, and the father was walking away. The child was crying very hard. I, Shalamard, observing all of this, try to figure out—Why the choice?

The first time we regressed Carol this was her earliest childhood memory. Could it have been that the distressed child no longer wished to remain in that body and was, therefore, ready to relinquish it to someone else?

Dr. Ian Stevenson and other investigators of spontaneous recollections of former incarnations have described similar cases in which the soul of a person whose life was snuffed out by an accident immediately appropriated the body of a baby or young child. (Note the case of "Jasbir" reported in our book *Reincarnation, Key to Immortality.*) [1] Instances also appear in psychiatric literature of children who, having been retrieved from the brink of death, undergo drastic personality changes.

Owing to the accelerating pace of life in the twentieth century, souls now seem to be wheeling in and out of incarnation with unprecedented rapidity. There is so much to feel, sense, and experience; multitudes are flocking in for the show. Their eagerness to grasp this opportunity to undergo crucial tests may partially account for the present problem of overpopulation.

Should it be true, as we have surmised, that Earth has supported many teeming civilizations of which no records remain, then a far larger "pool" of souls may be feeding the mainstream of human evolution than one might suppose from a study of known history. In addition, entities coming in from other dimensions as visitors may be compounding the current crowded situation. This era offers extraordinary opportunities for growth, but it may also be setting the stage for a karmic purgation comparable to that of Atlantis. Perhaps some of these venturesome ones want to be able to boast in regression sessions of the future, "Oh yes, I was there—right in the midst of Armageddon. I remember it well."

COMING TO BIRTH

The innocence of children is our eternal reminder of the purity of spirit from where we all originally come. Every personality is the expression of a power that strives continually to renew itself, a power as incorruptible as a flame cast forth from the incandescent core of creation.

---

[1] Marcia Moore and Mark Douglas, *Reincarnation, Key to Immortality* (York Harbor, Maine: Arcane Publications, 1969).

In the realm of procreation, however, the newborn infant with his preprogrammed genetic code and phylogenetic conditioning is as old as the earth. Already he is stamped by that which has gone before. In his spirit he is free, but in his body he is bound to abide by the consequences of choices made before he entered his fleshly abode.

Sometimes the memories linking one life to another are as tightly woven as those reported by Joyce Ween:

> My death at a fairly advanced age was at the hands of a soldier. I was stabbed, saw and felt the wound vividly, and felt reconciled to dying.
>
> After death my consciousness became a point in space that was in a dimension other than that of the Earth and its environs. The point became a pivot of an axis whose turning generated hemispheres of light in complementary color pairs—red-green, yellow-purple, and so forth.
>
> Then my awareness became that of a tiny, bluish gray sluglike creature. I saw a water-filled channel, wide at the top and tapering to a narrow opening; then my this-life mother looking young and serene. Finally, I felt a sensation of warmth and of being held, first to a soft chest and then to a fuzzy one.

Usually there is an interlude prior to birth when we can say to the sensor, "You are looking down at the earth, knowing that you are due to return. You are coming back to new parents, to another home, a different set of circumstances. Why are you doing this all over again? Is there a particular lesson you must learn this time around?"

Answers to this question are remarkably diverse. Some subjects speak of the spiritual qualities they wish to cultivate. "I have so much to learn—kindness, patience, reaching out to others—a lot of helping." By contrast, the teen-aged son of wealthy parents said, "I am coming to this family because they can help me to make a lot of money."

One girl was hastening to be born because her lover has already incarnated and she was eager to meet him again. Another young lady was returning in order to help her mother with whom she had a long-standing karmic relationship. Still another was so dismayed to be burdened with a body of flesh that all she could do was weep dismally. A woman who believed that she belonged on another planet explained, "I am going to try to settle all my karmic debts so that I won't have to return to Earth anymore. It isn't going to be easy but I think I can make it. Then, I shall go home again to stay."

The common denominator seems to be that we are all here to continue our education as citizens of the universe. Souls return to be with loved ones, to deal with ancient enemies, to work at assigned tasks, and to instill qualities of character. Once anchored on terra firma they may forget their mission. It appears, however, that at the magical moment of inception they know from where they come, why they are at this stage of the journey, and where they are heading.

10

QUESTIONS

In discussion groups and private conversations on the subject of hypersentience the same questions repeatedly arise. Here are some of the answers customarily given.

To what extent can retrocognitive experiences be verified?

Thus far we have some, but not much, proof that the lives described actually occurred. Even though I have tried to make it clear that the scientific validation of the reincarnation hypothesis is not the issue with which we are concerned, it is nonetheless gratifying when a case does check out. Eventually we may have a weighty enough mass of evidence to convince the diehard skeptic—provided he is willing to look at it. In the meantime the work must proceed on the basis of enlightened conjectures concerning the whys and wherefores of man's existence on Earth.

With regard to presumed validity, our cases can be ranged from the extremely probable to the extremely fantastic. In the former category are the experiences of sensors who recall lives of recent vintage. Names and details they never could have known turn out to be exactly as described. For example, one girl refused to go to California because an enemy from a previous lifetime was still living there and she did not care to risk a confrontation.

At an early age Ward Buell remembered having been a Japanese kamikaze pilot who died in World War II. In his baby pictures he looks astonishingly Japanese while to this day his features have an Oriental cast that is not characteristic of the rest of his family. Although he has not yet been to Japan in this lifetime, he has a natural understanding of that country's ways and customs and makes his living teaching the Japanese martial arts.

My first regression sessions with Tony Joseph occurred during the summer of 1970. In one lifetime Tony took on the identity of the nineteenth-century journalist and explorer Henry Stanley. (Like Stanley, Tony is a writer and lecturer who travels extensively.) In a letter dated 1 August 1975 Tony writes:

An amazing feeling swept over me when I was deeply absorbed in listening to a group of Congolese singers and drummers. I saw myself in Africa and knew that I had experienced a lifetime there.

I am now convinced that our exploration of one of my previous incarnations is genuine. In that journey into my past I visualized myself in England at a social gathering. It appeared to be a going-away party, though for whom I was uncertain. I was wearing khakis and hurried over to see what the excitement was all about.

It was a farewell to Henry Stanley who was embarking on an expedition to the African highlands near Victoria Falls. Stanley was deeply committed to the mission of rescuing Dr. David Livingstone who, it was assumed, had been lost or captured by African natives. The crowd seemed to be speaking of the expedition as a "crusade" to save one of the great bearers of civilization who had risked his life to bring "truth" and "the knowledge of Christ" into Africa.

On being asked to go back to an earlier time in that life I was sailing for the southern part of the United States where I hoped to begin a new life. I met some extremely kind people who cared for me and considered me as their own child. In gratitude I took the family's last name—Stanley.

After gaining experience with a printing office and then with a small newspaper in New Orleans I felt an urge to return to England where I might make use of these skills. There I wandered from newspaper firms to odd jobs as a beginning reporter and was unaware of any great activity in my life.

On being asked to go forward ten years I found myself in Africa. There was a great sense of anticipation as I climbed over a ridge and set eyes on Lake Victoria. I was overwhelmed by its beauty and wanted to explore the area, but felt compelled to continue the search for Livingstone.

There was much difficulty in locating Livingstone, but I was encouraged by the legend of a "great white doctor" who lived among the natives. After an arduous trek through previously unexplored parts of Africa we arrived at the village where it had been reported that the "white doctor" could be found. We entered a clearing in front of a row of huts and were suspiciously greeted by the villagers. Next we were taken to a secluded hut where Livingstone was lying down, apparently suffering from a minor illness. He was unimpressed by our presence.

During the last part of the session I was preoccupied with vain attempts to encourage Livingstone to return with us to England. He blatantly refused and kept talking about his love for the people and the importance of his work. Our emotional reaction to this was very strong as we set back to England without him.

An interesting detail is that when asked my name I replied, "John Rowlands." Later I learned that this was the original name of Henry Stanley. In the present lifetime I also ran away from home, was adopted, and changed my name.

At the other end of the probability scale are accounts such as the following, received from Barbara Lee of Petaluma, California.

6 July 1974

Dear Marcia,

I have been hypersensing people like mad ever since I attended your workshop in Santa Rosa. . . . There was one thread of continuity throughout all the interviews. The purpose of life is to learn to love. Of course we've heard this idea since forever, but that really is what the task of the moment is—to love. To love each moment, each place we are in, and each person we encounter with our highest Godly Self.

My fourteen-year-old son had an interesting story to tell. At one point either ten million or ten billion years ago he was riding a winged white horse with a golden mane over the Earth and sprinkling something down. When I asked him what it was he said, "Love." He also said that he didn't have to come back to Earth again but that he did return to spread love and help little children.

I've sometimes been concerned because life seems so easy to him. (Some leftover Puritan ethic on my part!) I can now see that he probably won't be spoiled by that fact.

Frequently we gather corroborating evidence from several sources. Subjects commonly pick up on lives which have been described by psychic readers or vice versa. For example, a regression session with Carol Griffith at which Isabel Buell was present contained the following dialog:

Marcia—Can you see other people's past lives?

Carol—Yes.

Marcia—Can you see one of Isabel's lives?

Carol—I see a priestess in a temple, long before the Aztecs. She is buried under the Aztec ruins in Mexico.

Marcia—What kind of priestess is she?

Carol—She prepares the maidens. . . . I don't like what she is doing. I don't want to watch.

Marcia—Are you there?

Carol—No, I'm nowhere around. I'm just looking down on it.

In a later report Carol added:

I realized that Isabel was still in the room and purposely left out describing her headdress, for I was afraid she would put it in her subconscious mind.

Later Isabel went through her session with Marcia and did pick up on the life I had observed. She mentioned that the headdress seemed more significant than her own personality, and that without it she was nothing. As we were driving home I asked her to describe the headdress for me. When she did so I was amazed to find out that it was just as I had seen.

In my own case, one of the first past-life memories that came to me was an experience as a dancer in ancient Greece. Later I became one of a class of women known as hetaerae who had their own homes, relatively good educations, and many generous friends of the opposite sex. My impression was that I entertained numerous interesting and intelligent men and enjoyed life thoroughly.

Curiously, the same life was described by a clairvoyant in England who added that although I started out as a dancer—a low-class occupation at that time—there had been no necessity to have demeaned myself this way since I came from a well-to-do background.

Later a man came into my life whom I seemed to have known before. During a retrotrip he too described me as having been a dancer in classical Greece, adding, "But you didn't have to lead that sort of life because you came from a good family."

In present-day terms all this fits the fact that I have made a career teaching Hatha Yoga and that this course of action brought much criticism from those who thought that I could have used my social and educational assets to better advantage. (That was in the days before yoga was as generally accepted as it is now.) It has also been extremely important to me to have a home where friends could be graciously entertained in an intellectually stimulating atmosphere.

How can you distinguish fact from fantasy?

We have found that those who work with the technique of hypersentience learn to discriminate between experiences which seem intrinsically real and those which are symbolic or make-believe. One can usually tell from rapid eye movements, tone of voice, emotional reactions, and vividness of imagery whether or not the sensor is merely exercising his imagination. The unexpectedness of the material which comes to light and the way it ties in with the person's present situation, as well as with past epochs, gives most of our sensing sessions an ineffable ring of truth. For the most part it would seem far more remarkable that people could make up the stories they report than that they should remember them.

Occasionally one does run into cases in which a subject's fantasy life overshadows the reality of what might actually have happened. In the book *Many Lifetimes* the psychiatrist Denys Kelsey tells of hypnotizing a young man who, as he regressed to a previous lifetime, described a series of scenes in which he identified with an elegant young woman who appeared in a variety of glamorous poses. At this point Kelsey's wife, Joan Grant, who had been tuning in psychically, handed him a note saying, "This is a genuine recall. But he is not seeing the girl he really was; these are the girl's daydreams of the woman she longed to be. Tell him to see the girl herself."

It then turned out that the young woman who had been fabricating these idealized images was actually the daughter of a tradesman. She had fallen in love with an aristocratic young man who, she hoped, would make all her dreams come true. Instead, she became pregnant, was deserted by her lover, and died of a botched-up abortion. Kelsey goes on to say:

> When discussing the case with Joan I asked her how she had recognized that these fantasies, although highly relevant, were not memories of actual

events. She explained that the clue lay in the fact that they were static and contained no action. This was because the girl was able to visualize how she would appear, but not what she would do, in situations that were outside her social experience. Had she belonged to the same milieu as the man she hoped to marry, she would have seen herself playing an active part in her daydreams, in which case their true nature would have been more difficult to discern.

If the sensor is inclined to dwell upon the fantasies of another lifetime, we usually give him free rein, since they are bound to have some relevance to his thought processes. One young man went back to a dull existence in early Christian times during which nothing of interest occurred. The only real excitement he seemed to have known was in his thoughtlife. Once while on a journey this former personality fell asleep and had a series of vivid dreams. In one of these reveries he entered a cave where Satan was standing on a rock. The archfiend was described as being humanoid with pointed ears, a dark beard, mustache, close-cropped hair, and bats' wings extending from his body. A light from below cast weird flickering shadows which were supposed to be frightening but which only provoked a burst of derisive laughter followed by the comment:

> It's supposed to be terrible—like every image you've ever seen of Dante's Inferno—but really it's wonderful. Satan doing his gig, like Bela Lugosi doing his Dracula thing. All the images of Hell are there—little demons tormenting people, screams and cries, burning flesh. Lucifer is standing there at the entrance to the cave to give everyone a hell of a shock. It's just pits of shit, but the people there, they're all like windup dolls going through their motions. . . .
> Now I'm coming out of the cave and it's a beautiful day. I am standing behind my body. Now I enter it and walk on toward the village.

Possibly these fantasies were part of the religious tradition of the young man who was traveling from one town to the next a thousand years ago However, there was never any question of their being confused with the reality of his everyday experience.

Do regressed subjects often believe they were famous personalities?

It is a matter of amazement to us that uninformed critics still drag out the old cliché (which never was true) that people on a retrotrip invariably want to believe themselves to have been some well known historical personage. In actuality, most lives turn out to have been so mundane that it soon becomes boring to dwell upon them. In order to sustain interest in a series of regression sessions with one individual, we usually turn our attention to the exploration of lost civilizations, intervals between lives, and karmic patterns. Unless the subject is specifically instructed to return to a happy time we seldom find an incarnation anyone would want to repeat.

On the other hand, many well known people have lived upon this earth and it would be extraordinary if, after regressing so many talented individuals, we had not encountered some bygone celebrities. Hence, we have come across a few who could find their names in history books. In addition, a number of our sensors knew or encountered such figures as Cardinal Richelieu, Anne Boleyn, and Jesus Christ. But far from wanting to boast about it, they prefer not to be mentioned by name.

Some recollections seem extraordinarily real. Once at a workshop in Malibu, California, professional clairvoyant Gayle Eaton recapitulated an incarnation as a prophetess in the Holy Land during which she saw Jesus on several occasions. Toward the end of a detailed account during which she actually relived the incidents described, her voice rose to a piercing wail as she shrieked, "They're crucifying him!" Looking around the room I saw tears coming down the cheeks of most of the spectators. No one who was there will ever forget that afternoon. It is hard to make a scientific case for this type of recollection, but the sense of reality was such that it is easy to accept the possible historical truth of Gayle's account.

It is our impression that Jesus often used to lay his hands on people, and that, when this occurred, a link was established which would hold for all eternity. Thus, a young man recollected an incident in Palestine in which the Master touched the center of his forehead. To this day he feels that a current was set in motion which is still stimulating his spiritual growth.

Certain archetypal figures have exerted so compelling an influence upon the human imagination that they are represented by powerful thought forms. Hence, anyone who recalls having been burned at the stake may fancy she was Joan of Arc, even though thousands of hapless women were consigned to the flames. Similarly, the holy prostitute is represented by Mary Magdalen, the eternal seductress by Cleopatra (actually a succession of Egyptian queens bore that name), the good physician by Saint Luke, and the conquering monarch by Napoleon. There is obvious danger in taking too seriously anyone's allegation of having been one of these personages, since the sensor may merely be tuning in on the thought form which has been reinforced down the ages. At the same time, there is no need to be closed-minded. At this crucial juncture in human affairs it is probable that many great leaders of yore actually have returned to guide mankind through the present crisis. As popular as the hypersensing technique is becoming, it is inevitable that some of these noted people should turn up.

What determines which of many lives a person recollects?

Although we sometimes ask the sensor to explore the situations which bear on a current problem, usually we leave the decision to him. Most of the time the experiences recalled are those with which the present personality naturally resonates.

A fifteen-year-old boy whose hobby was collecting German war mementos relived an episode as a Nazi pilot who was shot down over the Dutch coast. The airman maneuvered his craft to the ground and started to walk away, but was killed when a piece of the exploding gas tank pierced his back. (As a baby this boy cried when anyone tried to burp him, and he still hates to be slapped on the back.) In addition, he recalled incidents from a life in Gaul when he was a barbarian fighting Caesar's legions, and a dreary interlude in the Middle Ages when he yearned unsuccessfully to be a knight. These militaristic memories seemed appropriate for one who in childhood had been exposed to countless hours of war films on television.

At the age of twenty he became interested in Oriental culture and traveled extensively in Nepal. This time, when regressed, he became the abbot of a small monastery in Tibet. In distinct contrast to his normally affable nature he was now a veritable personification of the inscrutable East. When asked what he was wearing he replied ponderously, "I am wearing Life." Further efforts to elicit information were parried by such cryptic remarks as, "What is age? What is time?" Clearly, he was having difficulty restraining his impatience with those of us who still thought in terms of the world of illusion.

Finally we asked him why, after having been a religious scholar, he should have elected to play the role of a Nazi pilot. To this he replied, "To see the stupidity of war." Like so many others he spontaneously selected the incarnations that were meaningful to him at a given point in his career.

The decision-making entity which determines which experiences will be recollected is no snob, inasmuch as it will overlook a person's relatively glamorous lifetimes in favor of those which cast some light upon his present situation. The lessons learned through failure, oppression, and the endurance of squalid conditions may be more educational than those which accrue from worldly achievement and hence are as often remembered.

Can a successful hypersensing session be conducted with someone who does not admit the possibility of reincarnation?

Some of our best subjects have started out as downright disbelievers. Usually they are surprised at their own performances. The skeptic who picks up one or more previous lifetimes is apt to feel like a person who, after having lived in a house all his life, suddenly discovers a new door in the midst of his bedroom wall. Looking through, he discovers a chamber he has never seen. Beyond is a corridor with more rooms opening out on either side. Little wonder that he is momentarily disconcerted.

Our hypersensing sessions have demonstrated that there can be numerous doors to reality. Hence, the facilitator should not induce the subject to conform to his expectations but should remain open to whatever comes naturally. The following account, given by a confirmed disbeliever in reincarnation, describes a way of knowing that seems alien to our usual sense-perceptions, yet is valid in its own terms.

HYPERSENSING SESSION WITH ANN BOLES—JULY 22, 1974

Marcia Moore sat beside me intoning tension from my body and encouraging the light from the spirit to shine above the supine physical being. I was in a dreamlike space, conscious, peaceful, egoless to the point of the "I" existing but not sharply separate from all else.

I wanted to be regressed after hearing the detailed accounts of others who described past lives which I felt they could not have conceived in the normal state of consciousness. Where had the stories come from? I was a skeptic, not believing in reincarnation.

After reaching a sublime state of absolute peace, I was asked what I wanted from life. At that point I wanted only to lie there suspended in that space forever, but somehow I knew that to get on with it I had to answer the question. What I said I wanted was "to participate in the world as if it were a novel—something to observe with total interest but always at arm's length, becoming involved only with those people living honestly and completely."

Marcia, through questions, brought me to a room in which there was one other person. I described a structure arched and open on two sides, allowing one to feel outside all the time. The room was furnished with many pillows. The ones I lay on were against one of the solid walls. There were tall pedestals with large pots, the curves of which seemed to please me greatly. Palms grew from the pots, their fronds bending to the floor. Ostriches grazed in the outer area and there were insects.

An old man stood beside me and we were engaged in light, beautiful conversation. His physical characteristics were not clear but he seemed to be one big smile shining through every pore. At this time and later in the session he was revealed as my companion. He knew everything and gave everything, not in the manner of a teacher speaking in words but in his presence.

Marcia took me outside to look in the pool, first to discover my own image. Physically I appeared much as I do in this life but I was dressed in sheer layers of bright scarves as a protection against the bugs. Then I was told to look deeply in the pool in order to seek another time and space. After some moments I saw a plaque of inlaid shells.

Because they were so aesthetically beautiful I could only watch them for a time. Then associations belonging to the plaques began to come. One did not read them like a book. Only after years of being with them and among the other people in the compound where they, and the people, were housed, could their meaning be felt. It was a feeling of knowing the plaques and what they symbolized with one's whole being, for they were a stimulant to all the senses, leaving little need for any other mind or body stimulation.

The compound was a very large area with small open rooms. Some were for living, others for the plaques. Each morning at the first hot light of the sun all the people went to the plaque rooms and, after a few minutes of meditation, chose the one that was to be studied that day. Each morning brought the sensation of complete rebirth. Only the people involved with the plaques lived in the compound. Outside the area were the people who didn't desire the experience. Out there were all the superficial pleasures of the senses but after becoming one with the plaques no one wished to leave the compound for there was never a feeling of being unsatisfied.

The land seemed much like a Greek Island, hot and stark. The people all had beautiful golden-brown skin that they anointed each day with olive oil. Everything was very peaceful, not stoic but wonderfully fulfilling.

Marcia asked me to read from a plaque but I couldn't. I knew how to read them but I couldn't read it for her. She asked if I could have one of the others read but I explained that this was impossible. If you took the reading of another, it was incomplete knowledge and thereby unimportant.

Marcia then tried to lead me into another time and space but there was only nothing. Finally she asked me what was on the other side of nothing, and I immediately saw the sun as if I were right on its edge. I seemed to be a spirit and not a person. She took me inside the sun and I looked out into an unlimited space. I was finally able to see a planet with no apparent life spinning at a high velocity and giving off a red gas. The only thing I could see on its surface were sparkling gem rocks.

I was brought back into the soft reality of Marcia's living room feeling very dreamy and not wanting to talk to anyone for fear that this high, this elating experience would be taken from me.

I quote this case to show that not all hypersensing sessions need involve retrotrips into past lifetimes. There are other places and spaces that can be explored without doing violence to the sensor's belief system.

How often do people change sex from one incarnation to another?

The majority of those with whom I have worked have been able to remember occupying a body of the opposite sex. Undoubtedly the number would be greater if I had gone into more depth in individual cases.

Occasionally a soul is dismayed to find itself attached to an uncongenial body. It may then retire at an early age to seek a more appropriate abode. The noted theosophist Charles Luntz once told me that as a small child he remembered having lived as a girl in the same house where he was later born as a boy. Since Charles was an exceedingly masculine individual, it is easy to see why he discarded the two-year-old female body and came back immediately as a male. Unfortunately, the mother continued to mourn for her little lost daughter, little realizing the embarrassment they had all been spared.

It may require several lifetimes for a soul to switch the polarity of its physical plane instrument. In such instances there may be one or more incarnations in which a child dies young. To some, these deaths seem like dreadful tragedies, but from a higher standpoint each brief sojourn was just a trial run.

Often there is some choice as to whether to return in a male or female form. Joyce Ween of San Francisco wrote us a letter in which she described herself as a woman in ancient Greece. In that incarnation she grew up, was educated, took a lover, married, had a child, and finally died at home in bed. Then she went on to say:

> In between dying and coming into another life I was fretting about the likelihood of consciously choosing the next persona, wondering in particular if I would choose to try being male. My recognition of identity on again

"landing" on earth felt unnatural, unchosen. I was now a very young male child in a pleasant forest encampment. . . .

It is far more common for women to remember being men than for men to remember being women, but this can be explained by our present social mores. As one dark-eyed Mexican lad explained, "I think I had a female life at one time but there is too much of the macho in me to want to go into it now."

When I began regressing people in the mid-1960s, it practically never happened that a man would admit having been a woman. Now that there is less emphasis on role-playing, the situation has changed. Especially among the younger generation it is not uncommon for men who are in all respects "masculine" to recollect female incarnations.

A case in point is that of the brilliant young chemist James Hershberger who remembered a prior existence as a wise old herb lady. At one time he founded a company called "Mother Gerd's Herbs." Next, his genius for creating sweet-smelling mixtures took him into the business of creating high quality incense. At this time his *Linga Sharira* incense factory in Austin, Texas, is the third largest producer of incense in the United States and offers a variety surpassed by none. Hersh is now happily married and the doting father of an infant daughter.

In a letter dated May 16, 1975 Hersh says:

> The hypersentient illumination was a lot like remembering a trip to the grocery store last week. I wore brown heavy clothes of Flemish or Dutch design. I married, bore and lost children, and saw the day when my husband was killed by a falling tree. I lived and did what was necessary to survive in a small house deep in the woods.
>
> You may want an idea of why I sought out the person (my other self) who lived in the snowy wood.
>
> In this life, at the age of two, I felt I should be a woman and insisted on a dress, but this feeling disappeared as the maleness of the present life prevailed.
>
> I found a strange fascination in herbals and in tales of woodland plants I had never seen. There always seemed to be a "rightness" in the trees and vines of my special childhood refuge which struggled in conflict with a Midwestern Methodist religious training. Finally, several years out of college, I was able to respond to certain intuitive urges to collect herbs and compound incense.
>
> Now, hypersentience has given me the increased confidence and direction I need to use the long remembering properly in my present life. I suspect that several other existences of mine will tie in many of the loose ends which I feel are there. Someday I want to be the old woman again in more depth and less of a quick skim.
>
> Beannaichte bi,
> Hersh

Do people ever recollect lives as animals?
The answer to this question is a conditional no.

Considering the number of times I have said, "Go back to the beginning and see if you can find out where it all started," it seems remarkable that no one with whom I have worked has ever been an ape or chimpanzee. In our society most children are taught from an early age that man evolved out of the animal kingdom. If, therefore, the tales recounted by regressed subjects were purely imaginary it should be possible to take them back to an animalistic state. Some people do see themselves as virtually mindless primitive beings, but even then their bodies were distinctively human.

Once I worked with a woman who, after describing several lifetimes, touched upon an existence in which she was in a throne room in ancient Egypt impassively watching the activities of the various courtiers. She had no feeling for anyone there but merely observed their comings and goings.

Two days after this session she phoned to say that it had suddenly flashed into her mind that she had been a very wealthy, spoiled Egyptian cat.

In her present life this lady has befriended many cats. At the time she came to me she was taking care of seven of the creatures. Moreover, she herself bears an uncanny resemblance to a cat!

While I have encountered no other subjects who saw themselves as animals, several have sensed an identification with the bird kingdom, even to the extent of having wings and feathers. These birdlike beings did not give the impression of being mentally inferior. Rather, they seemed far more sensitive and aesthetically developed than their contemporaries.

Several of these bird people felt that they were in Atlantis. The following notes from a retrotrip with Michael Matthews gives the flavor of some of this material.

> *Michael*—I'm in Atlantis. The buildings are burning—all are on fire. Things are melting and curling up into black masses much like burning plastic. What have they done?
>
> We have been so unkind to our own people. My eyes are full of tears for the unkindness that has been here. I don't feel personally guilty but am so sorry for those who must suffer, even though they bring it on themselves. I seem to be some other kind of being. Yes, this is one of my first incarnations. I came to learn about humans. To help them. I am so much wiser than they. It is hard to convey the kind of knowledge I possess. I perceive all their personality, no, their total being at a glance. By merely looking at them I have total knowledge and understanding of the place they are at and the whole of their past. They feel themselves to be so superior, yet they are behaving like spoiled children. I know where they are coming from before they open their mouths.
>
> I serve them, but don't know why I keep serving since they are so foolish. I live in a temple and do menial things for people. I feel so sorry for them. I look like an owl. I can feel my wings and feathers. I have pure white feathers and am about the size of a small man. My eyes are very large and very dark.
>
> No, this is not imagination. I am not a man in an owl suit, I am a real owl. I am so large that I can't fly. I give of myself freely in service. Yet it is making these people even more arrogant. My heart is too soft.

Marcia—Why were you born?

Michael—To learn to understand and love humanity, even at its worst. These Atlanteans are so arrogant.

Marcia—How did it end?

Michael—I see myself burnt. The place I go has beautiful colors. I'm getting larger, more radiant, resting in the light. I'm not conscious of learning anything, yet my dimensions are getting larger. There is someone there; he is talking to all of us.

Marcia—What is his name?

Michael—Ezekial. There are many of us here listening. . . .

Michael who lives and teaches metaphysics in San Francisco still gives of himself freely in service to the many people who come to him for spiritual guidance.

Do regressed subjects ever speak in other languages?

There are numerous instances of xenoglossy (speaking in an unknown tongue) in the literature of hypersensory and hypnotic regression. In my experience this is a rare but not unknown phenomenon. The problem has been that when the sensor spontaneously bursts into another language it is usually incomprehensible. (I am no linguist.) Some subjects report that they can hear another language being spoken but are unable to pronounce the syllables.

The most impressive case of xenoglossy in my experience occurred when Violet Gillfillan of Ventura, California, was visiting in ancient Egypt. Suddenly she began to speak the language of the time. One clearly repeated phrase sounded like "User maat ra meri amun."

Later when Violet was visiting her daughter in San Francisco, she chanced to meet Dr. Larry Williams, a physician who studies the language of old Egypt as a hobby. When she mentioned this phrase he immediately drew the corresponding glyphs and interpreted them to mean, "One powerful of truth in Ra, one beloved of Amun."

Dr. Williams then gave her a cartouche (an oblong figure enclosing a series of hieroglyphics) representing the message she had conveyed. This cartouche bore a remarkable resemblance to a pencil rubbing from an *ushabti* (tomb figure) which was in his possession.

Normally Violet has no knowledge of the Egyptian language.

Among commentators on the phenomenon of xenoglossy the issue seems to be whether a spiritualist or a reincarnationist interpretation should be given. Is the subject the mouthpiece of an overshadowing entity, or is he remembering words he himself once used?

Most people who claim to be psychic or clairvoyant insist that they can distinguish spirit communications from their memories of past lives. Moreover, none of the people who remembered snatches of ancient tongues have ever shown the slightest proclivity to be "taken over" by a discarnate being. Since it is extremely common for sensors to remember names out of the past, it seems logical that some who are especially adept in this procedure should also be able to recollect phrases of languages known to their former personalities.

Ultimately this debate will have to be decided on the basis of continuing research. If the practice of hypersentience becomes widespread, there can be no doubt but that the question will be resolved one way or another.

Is it possible to progress a subject into the future?

Taking people forward in time has seldom been enlightening as far as the subject's personal life is concerned. There is not the same vivid imagery, detailed reporting, or emotional involvement that characterizes our journeys into the past. In at least a couple of instances the sensor projected possibilities that might have materialized had events worked out as expected, but which in fact never came to pass.

Occasionally, subjects have tried to progress themselves. In a letter dated 20 November 1973 Claudia Barnes describes her efforts to look ahead during a self-induced hypersensing session. She writes:

> I wanted to go forward so I counted ahead as though counting years. Then I found (or imagined) myself still with long hair but somewhat more slender and seemingly very busy. I had a good job, was going many places, being confronted with many people, and was discussing things with various individuals. There were children but I'm not sure what I had to do with them. They were young, mostly between the ages of five and ten.
>
> I counted a few more years ahead and found myself married to a good-looking man with blondish-brown hair and a fine job. He was very fulfilling as a husband.
>
> I went forward again and then it seemed that I had a son. My thoughts became flighty and I began to lose interest so I decided to stop.
>
> Afterward it was hard for me to talk on a mundane level. I was still flying about half an hour afterward.

In June 1975 Claudia married John Strobel. They are now expecting their first child.

Once during a workshop attended by about eighteen people I asked a participant who was being regressed for the first time to go into the future. She was able to do so, but was distressed to see herself having a major operation. Later I discovered that she had already undergone breast surgery for cancer. Since then I have refrained from this type of speculation except for a few deliberate experiments in precognition.

It does occasionally happen, however, that people will start to have precognitive dreams after we have worked together. Thus, my friend Judy Olsen writes:

Since my sessions with you my dreams have become more vivid and prophetic. In one dream I had a clear picture of a man I knew. He was reading from a scroll and smiling at me.

Later this man called me about collaborating on a book. Last weekend we were working together on the project, seated across the table from each other. Suddenly I looked up at him and saw the exact expression and smile I had seen in the dream. This time he was reading from a paper I had written rather than from the scroll, but the smile and gaze of the eye were unmistakably the same.

This is interesting to me because I have never been good at recollecting dreams.

When it comes to predictions of world events, we have heard the same story from so many subjects that it gives pause for thought. Most of them see a vast planetary purgation culminating around the end of the century. These upheavals may include earthquakes, tidal waves, race riots, famine, economic catastrophes, and nuclear warfare. Ultimately, however, these dire happenings will work for good since only by drastic means can the earth be cleansed of its karmic overload. ·

Many subjects envision these chaotic conditions as a recurrence of the catastrophes which sealed the doom of Atlantis, and believe that history is repeating itself. However, the consensus is that there will not be a Dark Age as there was before. Once the air has cleared, humanity will move on into an era of mutual cooperation more spiritually fulfilling than any the world has known.

Shortly before this book went into print I had a reading with Isabel Buell. As usual Pelu came through, "sailing along on his dirt cloud." This time he had a message about the future of America. To illustrate his point he showed Isabel a map of the United States. Then he lifted out California as though it were a flexible plastic strip and held it up for her perusal.

The gist of Pelu's communication was that, despite the gloomy prognostications of assorted clairvoyants, California is *not* on the verge of sliding into the sea. The oft-predicted disasters, supposedly due to strike the West Coast any day, may be greatly mitigated by the redemptive energies being channeled by high-minded individuals who have been drawn into the area. Pressures which might otherwise have spelled disaster are now being creatively released.

Isabel then went on to describe how the spiritual ferment which began in California would gradually creep across the country, uplifting the consciousness of the whole continent. Increasingly, people's psychic abilities will be accepted and understood. In this way the illumination will spread, permeating the land and cleaning out the dark pockets of ignorance and greed. "There will always be quakes," she said. "But escape valves will be provided."

Isabel also predicted that over the next seventy-five years there will be a rejuvenation of our cities. "Pride will increase. We can improve our cities so that they need not be destroyed. Eventually there will be a polaric flip, but when it comes about people will be more understanding of it. They will comprehend death and know that it is just a transition. Thus they will be ready for whatever comes."

As Pelu bid us good-bye, I thought of the saintly guru of the plant kingdom Luther Burbank and of the extensive complex of greenhouses in Santa Rosa, California, where for many years he communed with the spirits of the fruits and flowers which he had so tenderly cultivated. During the 1906 earthquake when both San Francisco and its neighbor Santa Rosa were reduced to smoldering ruins, not a pane of glass in Burbank's greenhouses was cracked. Burbank himself ascribed this miraculous delivery to the protective aura of harmonious vibrations which enfolded his horticultural empire as a result of his cooperation with the forces of nature.

It may be, therefore, that the time has come to engage in some positive thinking about California, America, and the world. The coming course of events may be more pliable than we imagine. If it is true that man was placed upon this planet to learn to take responsibility for his own destiny, then it is possible that through the enlightened redirection of mental energy we still may have the chance to create a better future.

11

CONCLUSION

A young man lying on a bed with his eyes closed recollects that fifteen hundred years ago he picked a flower and presented it to a serving girl before riding off to war. He still sees the glowing pink blossom, the girl's fresh smiling face, and his horse stamping impatiently in the courtyard. These images come to mind as clearly as though he were watching them on a movie screen. Yet it is beyond his capacity to say who was the ruler of that land or what was the cause of the conflict in which he was so soon to be slaughtered.

How different is the history written in the human soul from that which has come down to us in books!

One of the most significant effects of the practice of hypersentience is an enhanced appreciation of the *quality* of the events which make up the totality of our daily existence. Almost invariably there is a drastic reassessment of the value systems to which most people subscribe. The pugnacious imperialism of monarchs, the petty disputes of theologians, the windy promises of politicians—all crumble to dust, while small tokens of love and loyalty endure like fruitful seeds ready to blossom again in fertile soil.

All that really counts, or seems worth counting, is the essence of what each individual has to give to his current situation. Thus, paradoxically, our excursions into the past provide strong encouragement to broaden the here and now of each day's experience. Our search for cosmological insights has ended up by convincing us that only by living truly and honestly in the senses can we nourish the roots of our own being—the roots from which new flowers may someday spring.

It then becomes evident that modest warmth of heart may mean more than grandiose ideals and that we must pour forth our limited resources in order to receive the unlimited abundance the higher powers are ready to bestow. This is not a moralistic issue but a simple matter of plumbing. If lifegiving energies are to flow into us, they must also flow freely out again.

THE EVOLUTIONARY PLAN

Why, if human souls existed on an exalted level even before the dawn of recorded history, must they undergo the humiliating experiences of trying to govern a succession of instinct-driven physical bodies? What is the meaning of the legend of the fall of man?

This question cannot be answered without some insight into the metaphysical concept of involution and evolution. The theory holds that all beings emanate from the divine source of Creation and will return thereto after having mastered the lessons contingent on being encased in confining sheaths of flesh. Each one of us must reenact the drama of the Prodigal Son who ventures far from his father's home but who eventually turns back to complete the circuitous journey to the land from where he sprung.

Originally, each human soul-seed was sublimely pure on its own exalted level, but lacked awareness of itself as an individualized entity. Only after many successive embodiments does the projected personal soul regain its former high estate, along with the garnered increment of total self-consciousness. From seed to plant to seed again—the process may seem redundant, yet the cosmos is enriched by each season's harvest.

In the end it must be realized that the divine essence of all being is, and always was, perfect. But we can complete the circle only by recollecting who and what we really are. That is why the art of remembering is so important. Ultimately this may be the key to our salvation—to remember our true Selves.

It can be said that the pathway of evolution does not ascend in a straight line like an escalator. Instead it repeatedly closes in on itself with a spiraling motion akin to the helix of the genetic code, the coil of a dynamo, or the serpentine motion of planets orbiting through galactic space. Although this emphasis on circularity is an oversimplification of the philosophical concept of a circulatory flow of vitalizing energies streaming from subtle to dense realms of being and back again, it may provide a context within which the events which transpire in hypersensing sessions can be placed in proper perspective.

Regardless of how many lifetimes we elect to pass on Earth, we are all obliged to materialize Spirit as well as to spiritualize Matter. In one regression session it was stated that in the economy of the solar system as a whole the Earth performs the function of Saturn. That is, Earth is a region where the law of karma reigns, where men grow through the restriction, concentration, and grounding of their energies, and where they must follow the path of duty wherever it leads.

In terms of yoga, the most direct way to the achievement of higher consciousness for Earth dwellers is Karma Yoga, the discipline of selfless service. There are other spheres in the galaxy where one can sing the praises of God the starmaker and regent of heaven, but for most of us this dense little planet is the place where we must learn to express love in action through the daily struggle for survival. Literally, we have here the opportunity to give form to divine principles and to make them concrete in the substance of our day-to-day behavior. In short, we must transfigure life in terms of accomplishment.

Once during a psychic reading the question was asked, "What is the difference between an angel and an archangel?"

After a pause the answer came back, "An archangel is one who has descended deeper into Hell."

We must understand, therefore, that just because a person gives credence to exalted ideals this does not necessarily make him a superior being. It has been my impression that there is as much selfishness among so-called spiritual people as there is among average citizens. Many who expend their energies in religious or mystical practices fail to realize that the earthly sphere provides a unique opportunity for the practice of simple human kindness.

The difficulty which some high-minded individuals encounter in confronting the unglamorous details of ordinary household obligations was brought home to me by the experience of a lady of my acquaintance who invited a group of young people to use her spacious home for several months. At the end of this time the house was to be turned over to new tenants. Since the youngsters were all dedicated to lofty ideals and were very much the "beautiful people" of the Aquarian Age, she was happy to let them use her food and furnishings and to cover many of their expenses.

As it happened, I conducted hypersensing sessions with various members of this group, including a young man with waist-long hair whom I will call Joseph. As Joseph sank into the deep state he became tearfully intense, saying:

> I pray all the time to what I call "God." All my prayers are for only one thing—let God's will be done. Use me. I give everything to God. I have nothing but what He gives me. . . . It doesn't matter how I eat or dress, I want to be used.
>
> There is nothing for me to do but to love. Just to love. I *want* uncontrolled love. Indiscriminate, undisciplined love. My heart is bursting with it. I don't care how it's done. I feel so useless; I want to be used.
>
> There's always a way of transcending myself, of going beyond what I was into.

As the session ran on for forty minutes in this vein there could be no doubt of the sincerity of Joseph's aspiration to express the quality of divine love. Unfortunately, however, he was far too preoccupied with his spiritual practices to empty garbage, carry out the trash, weed, or water the garden, even though he had been invited to live in the house free of charge in return for taking care of these chores.

Finally, when moving day came, the lady who was responsible for the house requested the group to leave the place clean for the newcomers. As it turned out, Joseph and his friends took care to depart an hour before she arrived, leaving her to cope singlehandedly with the mess they had left behind.

Distraught, she called Joseph to ask if, since they were only a five minutes' walk away, they would come and help her with the work. Sweetly but firmly

Joseph refused, saying that they had had enough to do to remove their own possessions. Incredulously she pressed the point, explaining that as a group they could accomplish in a couple of hours what would take her two days of labor. "Well," Joseph stated flatly, "if you want a clean house, that's your trip." End of conversation.

After her first shock and dismay, she took a philosophical approach to the situation saying, "I guess I'd rather be forced into scrubbing their dirty toilets than be the one to make someone else do that for me."

The point is that there are certain virtues that can be acquired only in a world where trash must be emptied, gardens weeded, and bathrooms cleaned. Presumably this educational process is as important as the enjoyment of the seraphic serenity of the celestial spheres, since souls still choose to descend into this maelstrom of human desires, and thereby become enmeshed in the snares of the world illusion.

WAS THERE A GOLDEN AGE?

Why, when sensors are asked to go back to the time when they were happiest and most successful, do they so often return to the early days of Greece, Egypt, or Atlantis? With astonishing frequency they will pick an obscure civilization or a place that does not seem native to this planet. Most people are conditioned to believe that humanity evolved from an animalistic state to its present pinnacle of achievement. Yet the dream of a long-lost golden age is so strong a component of the human psyche that we encounter it again and again, even in subjects who have never consciously considered the idea.

An illustration of this tendency to look fondly to the remote past is found in *The Search for a Soul,* Jess Stearn's account of the various lives of Taylor Caldwell. In terms of past incarnations there was little to explain this lady's talent until she went back to Classical Greece where she was an eminent lady physician. From that peak of personal attainment she dipped down through a series of dismal experiences, alternating with brief sojourns on her native planet, Melina, until finally in the present life she again came into her own as a successful author.

I too have noticed that many of the talented people with whom I have worked can find little in their recent lives to account for their obvious mental superiority. Rather than fantasizing that they were rich and famous, they have been far more likely to recollect dreary existences of poverty and frustration. When pushed back far enough, however, it is a different story. Often there is at least one early life that sounds like a Hollywood spectacular, complete with domed white marble cities, exotic religious ceremonies, flying machines, and laserlike crystals for the harnessing of solar energy.

A possible explanation for this phenomenon is that as consciousness expands it becomes too extensive to fit the framework of one personality. Consequently, it is necessary to undergo a series of fragmentary manifestations before the diverse projections of the psyche can be reintegrated into a larger whole. At present, however, the possibilities for total self-expression, especially for women, are unprecedented. As a result, many people today are able to regain their former stature with the addition of qualities developed in the interim.

To illustrate this point, the scenario for a series of incarnations might run as follows:

ACT ONE

At the height of the Atlantean civilization our protagonist is a priestess in a large and beautiful temple. She is well educated, wields much power, and identifies totally with her work and with the image she projects. At the same time she is self-centered, arrogant, and lacking in compassion for the sick and suffering.

ACT TWO

After the fall of Atlantis this entity undergoes a series of lifetimes during which she plays a variety of feminine roles. These episodes might be entitled: the Prophetess, the Slave, the Wanderer, the Housewife, the Servant, the Nun, the Prostitute, the Dancer, the Witch, the Aristocrat, the Waif, the Teacher, the Martyr, the Nurse, the Intellectual, and so forth. Some interludes may be added during which this soul incarnates in male bodies in order to balance the female component. Each scene might be called an "ego trip," and none can have an altogether happy ending since there can never be the sense of wholeness that brings real fulfillment.

ACT THREE

After millennia of pursuing specialized modes of activity, there finally ensues a series of lifetimes during which the entity that started out in the guise of the priestess endeavors to reassemble the scattered portions of her disseminated psyche. At first these efforts may be sporadic, resulting in ambivalent or paradoxical behavior, as the nun confronts the whore or the docile housewife contends with the irrepressible gypsy.

Ultimately, however, there comes a culminating lifetime when the diverse roles are recapitulated and woven into a cohesive design. The play-acting phase ends, and our heroine finally discovers the true identity which lies behind her dramatic impersonations.

For those who have arrived at the culminating phase of their earthly transactions, the technique of hypersentience can serve to synthesize the qualities garnered from diverse experiences. Consequently, people are often drawn to our work because they have a need to bind up the loose ends of many previous existences.

When there is a heavy karmic residue to be brought to the surface and dispersed, this consummating life (or lives) may be tumultuous, encompassing drastic ups and downs, failures and successes. Toward the end, however, everything starts to coalesce. At last the "bit player" becomes cognizant of the underlying intent of the author of the repertory. he has enacted. Spiritual growth has occurred, even though it may have been necessary to descend through an abysmal succession of unhappy episodes before reascending the mountain of enduring accomplishment. Then, ultimately, the liberated soul is ready to move on to new endeavors.

Recently it has become feasible for many individuals to work on lessons connected with psychic unfoldment. Available evidence seems to show that the members of early races were often in telepathic rapport with one another, almost to the point where language was superfluous. Unfortunately, these powers were frequently misused. Moreover, if people can communicate without words there is slight need to develop languages and all that verbal expression implies in terms of cultural development. One who can see into the minds and hearts and guts of others can avoid many distressing experiences. On the other hand, these same misjudgments may trigger painful but enlightening interludes in the life of the soul.

In terms of our scenario, for example, we may posit that our Atlantean priestess was clairvoyant and that she was able to bend certain powers of nature to her will. Nevertheless, she could be unthinkingly cold-hearted, cruel, and uncomprehending of the woes of others. Then, in subsequent incarnations she would have to be robbed of her generalized sensitivity in order to achieve a higher type of discernment based on pure spiritual intuition rather than on mindless instinct. The human sympathy she so sorely lacked can be distilled only from tears. In order to bring forth these tears, she had to go astray and make misjudgments. Then finally, toward the end, she might reawaken to the knowledge that was her birthright.

Because numerous men and women living today are being obliged to work out karmic patterns relating to their previous uses and misuses of psychic forces, we are now seeing a growth of interest in magic, witchcraft, and various aspects of parapsychology. It is to be hoped that by increasing their understanding of the subtle energies of nature these people can come to grips with issues which, in one lifetime or another, they must learn to resolve.

The interest in occultism of those for whom the psychic world is a reality does not stem from fantasy or frustration. Rather it grows out of an objective realization, based on sound empirical evidence, that the mind of man can tap the mind of the universe and thereby encompass formerly concealed areas of knowing. If this rattletrap society seems about to shake itself to pieces, it may be time to question its underlying value system. Hence, many people are looking for a more viable world view.

THE DESTINY FORMULA

Nowadays practically everyone knows that there is a genetic code which determines the growth pattern for the physical body. Few realize that there is also a psychogenetic code for the soul. This superordinate code, which I have elected to call the "destiny formula," prescribes the developmental plan which binds a succession of lifetimes into one coherent design.

The destiny formula is the blueprint for that portion of the cosmic plan which a particular individual has been assigned to work out. It is comparable to a grid through which primordial life energy is differentiated into specific forms and functions. Astrologers may liken it to a master horoscope which controls the lesser horoscopes of each incarnation. It is the dominant theme of which all subsidiary models of thought and behavior are variations.

Students of Oriental philosophy may see some similarities between the destiny formula and the directive energy which is known in Sanskrit as the *karana sharira*. In English, the *karana sharira* is generally termed "the causal body." *Karana* refers to originating causes while *sharira* means form or body. In brief, the *karana sharira* serves three functions:

1. It is the vehicle for the transcendent spiritual Self.

2. It contains the seeds of the purposes to be accomplished by the evolving human being.

3. It is a receptacle that preserves the essence of all that an individual garners from the experiences of many lives.

In an ancient Hindu scripture it is said:

> The influence of the antecedent actions of man forms a seed from which germinates the plant which yields good and bad fruit. This fruit is to be eaten by him in subsequent lifetimes.
>
> *Vishnu Purana I, XIX, 5*

According to the theosophical tradition the causal body is the source of the motivating impulses which manifest as desire, aspiration, and will. This radiant garment of the Divine Self exists on the higher mental plane, in contradistinction to the physical body which serves as a means of expression for the threefold etheric, emotional, and intellectual persona.

There is no real individuality until the causal body comes into existence. It is the defining factor which determines a person's unique characteristics. In this sense it is analogous to the pattern used to cut out a suit of clothing. Gradually the fabric takes on the features of the pattern. The essence of the pattern is transferred to the material that is being shaped. Until the work is done, the pattern is a necessity, but once the product is complete the pattern can be discarded. Or, as we would say, the destiny formula is shattered.

A man may use a car on land, a ship on the sea, and a plane in the air, and yet remain as he was. Similarly, he uses his physical-etheric, emotional, and intellectual vehicles as conveyances. Since these vehicles wear out they are periodically renewed and adapted to serve his changing needs. The condition of these three components of his personality reflects the growth of the transcendent body of the high Self. This higher causal body is the semipermanent structure into which is woven everything that can endure and in which are stored the germs of the qualities to be carried over from one lifetime to another. However, the causal body can absorb only the finer elements that have been built into the character. The evil is eventually discarded; the good lives on.

The causal body is the register of an individual's spiritual status. Like the physical body it can be conscientiously developed. Instead of being nourished on food and oxygen it is sustained by virtuous thoughts and deeds. At the start of the evolutionary process the newly created causal body may be clairvoyantly perceived as a pale gelatinous ovoid. Over a series of lifetimes it becomes more clearly defined until it scintillates and glows with all colors of the rainbow. Then, when the final liberation is achieved, the causal body dissolves altogether and the spiritual essence of the human being can reach directly through to the material plane with no intervening presence.

We often hear that the learning experiences of many lifetimes are analogous to the shaping of a multifaceted diamond. In actuality, it appears that a succession of embodiments may be devoted to the same basic assignment. Some people struggle repeatedly to develop one talent, such as a gift for music, healing, or science. Others concentrate upon a central quality such as loyalty, sympathy, patience, or a sense of responsibility. While many variations may be played on the same few notes, there still must be that one theme which sets the score. Thus, as the causal body matures there is a continuing revelation of its initial plan of unfoldment—the plan we call the destiny formula.

Our evidence seems to show that highly evolved people tend to adhere to a purposeful line of action, while younger souls may rush hither and yon as heedlessly as small children. In school, courses become more specialized in the advanced grades. If, therefore, the Earth is a school for souls, it follows that upon graduation those who have mastered the curriculum do not all dissolve into some tapiocalike mush—as some mystics would imply. Rather, they become more clearly defined in their crystalline purity of purpose. Then, when the destiny formula has done its work and is finally shattered, the soul no longer needs to incarnate. The liberated human being can now function freely in the subtle dimensions of consciousness.

In any in-depth application of hypersentience, it can be exceedingly important to distinguish those subjects who need to strengthen their adherence to the destiny formula from those who are preparing to dispense with this preplanned blueprint for living. Some people need to become more ambitious while others are ready to renounce the craving for worldly success. Much depends on how nearly complete the ego structure happens to be. People with schizoid tendencies and those who lack a guiding purpose must work to fortify their egos. Integrated personalities who have developed their inner resources may be ready to transcend their own egotism. Some are becoming more engrossed in worldly matters while others are endeavoring to rise beyond their earthbound natures. These two phases may even follow each other in the same incarnation as individuals recapitulate the racial evolutionary plan.

In general, the processes involved in hypersentience seem to be most helpful to people who have already demonstrated their abilities to meet the world on its own terms and who are coping adequately with the exigencies of daily living. Hence, most of our subjects have adequate incomes, charming houses, broad cultural backgrounds, and are far above average in personal attractiveness and creative accomplishment. They are not maladjusted people seeking to escape responsibilities. Rather, they are solid citizens who are bored with their own success and are, therefore, looking for new challenges. Having reached a plateau they are now ready to move on to fresh endeavors.

For those who are in process of relinquishing their ingrained egocentricity, who are disenchanted with worldly satisfactions, or who aspire to be free from the grinding wheel of repeated births and deaths, the methods outlined in this book may cast some light upon the way ahead. The rationale and mode of operation of the destiny formula must become clear in their minds before they can break its restrictive grip upon their personalities.

In a sense the destiny formula is like the shell of an incubating egg. As long as the embryo is developing, the shell is an absolute necessity. But once the inner work has been done, the bird must peck its way free, even though this act of self-liberation demands the destruction of its protective encasement. Only when the shell is shattered can the newly hatched creature spread the wings which one day will enable it to fly.

THE ISSUE OF FREE WILL

To what extent can an individual modify the destiny formula which determines his role in life's play of contending forces.

It seems evident that man must have some measure of free will, else why should he be so badly punished for his misuse of it? We are all free within limits, like a goat tied to a post who can browse where he pleases within the radius of his chain. At least we can modify the positive or negative *quality* of our responses, even to inexorable circumstances. In general, it appears that man's freedom both on the physical plane and in the subtle worlds is greater than most people imagine. Certainly it is quite enough to provide an adequate challenge in any given lifetime.

Occasionally the operations of the karmic law produce severe restrictions as, for example, a crippled body. Just as often, however, people can hardly cope with the freedom they do have. Indeed, without some master plan of action (or destiny formula), merely being at liberty to wander in aimless circles means nothing. Would the goat really be better off if the tether were cut, allowing it to meander onto the highway? All true freedom begins with self-definition, and this requires that the self be finite—which is to say that it voluntarily determines to accept certain protective limitations.

Within these limits, however, there are many ways the soul can go. Since flexibility is so prized an asset in nature it follows that it is an essential attribute of any individual's destiny formula. Fatalism is akin to rigidity; it is an inhibiting, ossifying, death-dealing compulsion of a mind that has ceased to search for alternatives. Destiny can sway and bend with the subtlest breezes of human thought. Indeed, that seems to be what men came to Earth to learn—that ultimately they can govern their own lives.

DISSOLVING THE DESTINY FORMULA

There comes a point when merely modifying the destiny formula ceases to satisfy the yearning to graze in greener pastures. Gradually the indwelling soul wearies of the same old peregrinations and, like the goat chewing on his tether, longs to be genuinely free. How then can an individual use his expanding mental faculties to burst his bonds once and for all?

In order to answer this question, it is helpful to consider the analogy of a cell within the body. Once a living cell has been built into the structure of a particular organ, it becomes more or less permanently embedded within that aggregate of physical substance. That is, if the cell comes into being within the kidneys, then no matter how admirably that minuscule intelligence plays its role it cannot avoid being conditioned by the function it is supposed to perform in the economy of the kidney as a whole. It is stuck there for the remainder of its existence.

By the same token, we who are cells in the body of humanity are conditioned by the nature and purposes of the substructures with which we choose to identify. Generally, the time of decision comes at the inception of a new course of action; hence the significance of an astrological birth chart. No doubt it is an intuitive recognition of the importance of all beginnings or birth days which inspires people to take vows and pledges, or in some way make gestures of commitment.

Why should it be necessary to enter into a covenant with some other party, be it the Lord, a coalition, a partner, or ourselves, in order to reinforce the determination to embark upon a new way of life? Why do we make New Year's resolutions? Many people say, for example, that wedding vows are useless. If two people no longer wish to enjoy each other's company, should they not be free to part? How can a youth legitimately make a pledge that will affect his entire life when he has no way of knowing what sort of person he will be in future years?

The fact remains, however, that like it or not he does exercise this prerogative. Like the driver on a superhighway he has to take one exit or another and, for a while at least, abide by the consequences of his decision.

We all have the ability to institute radical changes in our behavior patterns, but only at certain crucial junctures in the course of events. If a cell within the body has entered the tissue of the kidney, then it will have to remain in that organ and filter blood. If it joins the circulatory system, then it will become a wanderer—but again within limits. Whatever is decided at the start sets the tone for all that follows during that particular cycle.

One of the most important of these junctures is the time of death—since death is really a birth into a new realm of experience. It is, therefore, of the utmost importance that people en masse should learn the art of correct dying and that they should have some idea of what awaits them on the other side. Our work in hypersentience has impressed us mightily with the idea that an individual's attitude at the time of passing may affect his career in eons to come. If, for example, the dying person struggles to retain an outworn body, this abnormal attachment to the material plane may bring him back prematurely in a body ill suited to his needs, simply because he could not wait for the right kind of physical vehicle. Whatever unfinished business he has left behind will have to be taken care of at some future date, while sincere repentance and the desire to be at peace with God will certainly facilitate his entrance into the light.

To a large extent we inaugurate new courses of action by *making commitments*. Then, once the allegiance is formed, a hardening process takes place. The die is cast, the pledge given, the initiation taken. For the ensuing cycle we are driven by the chain of consequences that has been set in motion.

This periodic re-formation of character is accomplished not so much by deciding what we are going to do, as by deciding what we are going to be. Sometimes, in the beginning, it is necessary to play the "as if" game. That is, we pretend to be a certain sort of person "as if" it were really so. Then suddenly we realize that the mold has set, the adopted pose has taken hold, the game is for real.

When a person embarks on a policy of commitment, the first result is a conservation of mental energy. This thought power can then be directed into higher channels. For example, a man out walking picks up a purse containing one hundred dollars. If he is unsure of his own honesty, he may spend a sleepless night debating the pros and cons of keeping the money. If, however, he simply says to himself, "I am not the kind of person who takes that which belongs to someone else," the matter is thereupon closed, and he can turn his attention to more constructive pursuits. Even if he is a dedicated thief who automatically pockets the purse he is still in a stronger position than the person who dissipates energy by trying to sit on both sides of the fence.

If the laws of karma hold true, the honest man who returns the money will receive an appropriate reward. However, remuneration and retribution are not parceled out because someone upstairs is keeping a tally of good and bad deeds. Rather, the giver reaps the benefits of his virtue simply because he is the kind of man who would automatically do what he did.

The destiny formula which obliges us to grind away at the same old lessons can be dissolved only when we are able to rise to the level of total commitment to a higher guiding purpose. If we can set aside petty personal ambitions in order to produce some significant accomplishment, then we can draw upon resources as superior to those ordinarily at our disposal as the consciousness of the body as a whole is superior to the consciousness of a cell within the kidney. We can identify with a *superordinate formula* which raises us to a more spiritually inclusive plane of being where we can transcend former limitations.

There is a way out of the morass of human pettiness and greed, but it demands the relinquishing of much that people have held dear in the past. This renunciation should not be understood in terms of loss and pain. Rather, it involves an affirmation of enduring identity, an acceptance of innate divinity, and a willing acquiescence to the service of humanity in the sure knowledge that through the surrender of the small personal ego a new and more extensive sense of self is born.

12

EPILOG

All my life I have been concerned with beginnings and with the implications of these moments of inception. Now, with the increasing attention being given to the exploration of previous incarnations a significant new movement is being launched. Therefore, right at the start, I would like to say something about the way in which "hypersentience" came into being, and what my part in it has been.

Some of you may already know me from the book *Yoga, Youth and Reincarnation* by Jess Stearn which, to date, has sold more than three million copies, as well as by the books I myself have written. Nevertheless, the image which readers have glimpsed in these multitudinous pages requires some clarification. Since all that I have sought to accomplish has led to the production of this book, it seems appropriate to mention some of these antecedent developments.

In the days when I used to drive thousands of miles on lecture engagements, there were occasions when my fatigued mind would start to confuse the map of the countryside over which my wheels were rolling with the land beneath. It was easy then to slip into a hallucinatory haze in which it seemed as though the car were an infinitesimal speck creeping across a gigantic road map from one lettered dot to the next.

Sometimes when working against a deadline the same conceptual aberration would occur with regard to the calendar. Crossing off days became like taking a journey, not through experiential time, but across the face of a surrealistic calendar, weaving back and forth from Sunday to Sunday as the striped fabric of successive weeks lengthened into banners of months and years.

But this abstraction is precisely what we must overcome if we are to avoid being reduced to mere markers of consecutive events. The map is not the territory—much less the trip—nor is the calendar more than roughly congruent with the current of chronological happenings that bears us on to unknown shores. Somehow it must be possible to dig down to the bedrock of day-to-day circumstances and to anchor our dreams in this groundwork of existential reality.

For many of us there comes a point when we suddenly decide that we must begin to think our own thoughts, feel our own feelings, and be what we are, rather than reacting in accordance with standardized patterns of perception. Maps and calendars will indeed show us where we wish to go, but they can conceal as well as reveal the landscape of our true desires. Through hypersentience, therefore, we are endeavoring to shift the focus of our attention away from abstract formulas and back to the primal substance of our underlying human nature.

Ideally, this extension of normal sensory awareness should lead to a more direct interaction with the unconscious mind, which is an estuary of the mind of the universe. By remembering who we once were we also start to recollect what we *are,* in the deepest, most comprehensive essence of our being. The goal is one of self-knowing—a purpose to which all other human activities are subsidiary.

For me, this work has had many beginnings, even in the present lifetime. As far back as I can remember, my mind has been inordinately preoccupied with the subject of death. There was never any fear of it but the itch of curiosity was so great that as a small child I often toyed with the thought of jumping in front of a truck in order to find out what would happen next. Knowing that this would be disagreeable for the driver and distressing to my parents, the temptation was set aside. Finally, I settled on the concept that being dead was like being one of the dry leaves that fall from a tree when autumn comes.

The only thought that really worried me in those early days of an overprivileged childhood was the anxiety that if I ever found myself being tortured or mutilated it might not be possible to escape from the body when the pain became unbearable. Later, I learned that this concern stemmed from an experience of being put to death during the Inquisition. Somehow too, the idea seeped into my mind that existence was far brighter and more beautiful on the "other side."

One day during my ninth year while I was playing games at a friend's house I chanced to hear one of the grownups saying something about reincarnation. Immediately I left the game and, overcoming my chronic shyness, interrupted the conversation to ask, "What is that word?"

"It means that you live many lifetimes."

"Oh, but of course that's it," I thought, returning to the game without comment. My mind was now at rest. From then on I never doubted that people return to Earth again and again in order to continue their development, and that growing a body is not much different from putting on a fresh outfit at the start of the day.

That same year, while visiting my grandmother in Maine I came across a dusty old book with an entire section cut out. According to the contents page the title of the missing chapter was "The Art of Hypnosis." On asking what happened to the material, I was told that this information was dangerous, especially for children. Whatever could be so awful as to justify the mutilation of a precious book! The thought that something in print could be that bad was so intriguing that right then and there I determined to investigate the forbidden subject.

Shortly after my fourteenth birthday while browsing in my father's library I came across a book by Paul Brunton entitled *A Search in Secret Egypt*. At last I had discovered, or rediscovered, the magical realm of the occult. Again there was the ineffable satisfaction of being able to say, "This is it. This is what I was looking for all the time."

One by one I started wading through my father's excellent collection of esoteric books, giving preference to those dealing with spiritualism and psychic research. But the most sublime pleasure came when I finally gathered courage to plunge into a bulky blue and gold volume with the awesome title *A Treatise on White Magic*. Soon it became apparent that while the ostensible author of this book was Alice A. Bailey (1880–1949), actually it was one of a series of volumes authored by a mysterious Oriental adept named Djwhal Khul who dictated them telepathically from a monastery in Tibet. Little matter that I understood only the barest part of what these books contained; they proved to be an ever-fresh source of wonder and delight.

Two years later it was my good fortune to meet the redoubtable Alice Bailey herself. When she asked me what I wanted to do in life I replied, "Something connected with spiritual healing."

"That's a pretty big order," she commented, and I felt abashed at my high-flown ideas. As it turned out, however, everything I have sought to accomplish has, in my mind, come under the heading of therapy. But of course, any true student of yoga or "white magic" is per se a healer, or should be. This is the common goal of all esoteric disciplines—to mend the rifts that divide individuals, races, and nations from themselves and thereby effect a freer flow of regenerative energies throughout the body of humanity.

The autumn that I started Radcliffe College I also joined the Arcane School. This was a correspondence course in meditation based on the books of Alice Bailey. At that time, and ever since, these teachings have provided me with a coherent metaphysical framework within which it has been possible to weave a plethora of odd bits of information into a meaningful design.

Perhaps the best term for this fresh formulation of the "ancient wisdom" is *neo-theosophy* since it is so integral a part of the general theosophical doctrine. Now, thirty-three years after my first encounter with the occult, it still seems to me that the information imparted by the Master Djwhal Khul comprises the clearest, sanest, and most complete exposition of the esoteric tradition thus far presented to the world.

The most baffling sections of these books were those referring to the various living and life-bearing spheres beyond the Earth. Despite the Tibetan's oft-repeated admonitions that this recondite knowledge was being given out for future generations of inquirers, I could hardly see the point of imparting so many abstract and unprovable tidbits of information about other planetary systems. Only in recent years did I discover that many ordinary people can experience altered states of consciousness in which they appear to be tuning in on hypothetical worlds, and that these insights can be gained without drugs, fasting, or exotic rituals. I was grateful, then, that my mind had been opened to the possibilities of interdimensional communication at an early age.

Another milestone along the way which led to the writing of this book was passed during the summer of 1946 when I had just turned eighteen. My brother, Robin Moore, now a famous author, lecturer, and TV personality, had recently returned from the war in Europe. While in the army he made the acquaintance of an officer who taught him the rudiments of hypnosis. During the evenings at our summer home on Cuttyhunk Island near Cape Cod, he would amuse the young people with demonstrations of his hypnotic powers. At this time we became familiar with the usual tricks of laying a subject across two chairs from neck to ankles while a hefty young man sat on his stomach, of producing anesthesia at will, and with various methods of fabricating mental illusions. A girl could be told that she was alone with a young man while the onlookers waited to see if she would allow him to kiss her. (Generally she would.) We also found that if a subject was instructed to go back to a particular time in early childhood he or she would behave like that child, even to speaking in an infantile manner. This was my first experience with hypnotically induced age regression, or as we call it, "retrocognition."

Long before it became fashionable to make pilgrimages to India to meditate on Himalayan mountain slopes, I was privileged to enjoy this elevating experience. The years were 1955–1957. Even though my primary duty was to look after three small children and my husband, who was studying Oriental religions, the availability of servants allowed time to attend classes on rural reconstruction, to learn Hindi and a smattering of Sanskrit, and to study astrology. Since my discovery of the occult world, a few psychic experiences had come my way but nothing remarkable had occurred. Despite my efforts to practice meditation, I was feeling more scatter-minded than ever and was profoundly dissatisfied with my spiritual progress.

I had not encouraged this trip in order to seek a guru, for that need had already been met. Although we made friends with an exotic assortment of holy men, my interest lay mainly in soaking up the uncanny beauty of this land which still seems so much like home. As it happened, however, while living in a remote Himalayan hill station named Kalimpong, I encountered a man who changed my life.

His name was Ronan Dutta and we met only a few times. Although he was a man of the highest spiritual qualities, his life was that of a successful Calcutta businessman who taught yoga in his spare time. We invited him and his wife to our house one afternoon, and in his unassuming way he offered to show us some yoga postures before we partook of the elaborate English-style tea that was the high spot of our day. At that stage I hardly knew that a yoga posture was called an *asana*, that there were thousands of them, or that these apparently simple exercises could produce profound psycho-physiological changes. However, we were all impressed by the flexible limbs, supple spine, and general elasticity which enabled him to move with catlike grace through a series of extraordinary contortions. This resilience was such that he appeared far younger than his acknowledged age of fifty.

I cannot recall being overwhelmed by Ronan Dutta's offer to show me how to perform some of the postures. No thunder boomed, no lightning flashed, but just as when I first heard the word *reincarnation* or read my first book on psychic research there was a gentle dawning of the conviction that the way ahead was growing more clear. Nevertheless I was stiff and awkward at the start, and it was months before I could stand on my head or sit comfortably in the lotus posture.

For years my energies had been drawn into abstract metaphysical pursuits, while the physical body grew correspondingly devitalized. I was tired much of the time but assumed that this "housewife's fatigue" was my lot in life. Yet I had been taught that freedom was a gift we Americans enjoyed, while Oriental people tend to be fatalistic. Only at this time did the realization begin to grow that most people in the Occident are needlessly fatalistic about growing old, stiff, and infirm. It is yoga, the great gift from the East, which assumes that men and women everywhere have an inalienable right to live in healthy, self-rejuvenating bodies, and that they can transcend themselves.

The main revelation that came to me after taking up Hatha Yoga was that my efforts to meditate cross-legged on a mountain ridge overlooking the eternal snows of Kanchenjunga were in some respects comparable to prying apart the petals of an immature bud in order to make it bloom. If the flower is to blossom, one must first scratch in the dirt and dig away the weeds. People have the power to fertilize the roots, but only by grace of sun and air do the petals open wide to the light.

The roots of the personality are in the flesh. Esoteric theory has it that, physiologically, the vital functions are rooted in the area below the diaphragm. Yogic exercises nourish these underlying elements thereby supporting higher forms of attainment. To denigrate this physical discipline, as some do, because it deals with the corporeal self is like arguing that a water lily would be more pure if it didn't have to feed upon the mud. Actually, it is the fact that mud can be transformed into this exquisite flower that is so wonderful.

It seems important to make this point because the same principle is involved in hypersentience. Human beings also have roots that reach down into the instinctual depths of their being, and this extension into matter is the whole point of taking on a body. Man can link heaven and earth and make these contrasting states of being meaningful in terms of each other. Hence, we have found that it is often necessary for a person to delve into the subconscious before he can ascend to the superconscious, to look back to the past before he can create a better future, and to face the darkness before he can let in the light.

Soon after returning to the United States I resumed my interrupted college career at Radcliffe. Although my main interest was psychology, this brush with the world of academe tended to be abrasive, since most available courses offered a smattering of "psyche" and a surfeit of "ology." In those ivied halls the pronouncements of Sigmund Freud were sacrosanct and, much as I disliked the antifeminist, materialist biases of the Viennese savant, I learned to repress my true feelings about the information being poured into my head.

According to the Freudians there is a subconscious, but no corresponding superconscious, aspect of the mind. Submerged in the murky depths of the instinctual nature is a seething cauldron of biological impulses known as the id. Although these oceanic desires may undergo various transformations they are deemed to be essentially unregenerate and incapable of being sublimated. Hence, nice people keep the lid on the id lest its libidinal forces spill over and disgrace them in the eyes of polite society.

Although Freud clearly had a point when he taught that psychological problems can be traced to the suppression, repression, and distortion of instinctual drives, my own experience did not entirely corroborate his observations. Most of my friends in Harvard Square and the Boston area were relatively emancipated sophisticates. Unlike the citizens of nineteenth-century Vienna, they certainly were not sexually constricted. Yet it was clear that there *was* a subtle and insidious form of repression at work. However, the needs being denied were those not of the low but of the high self—the self that was not even deemed to exist. Powerful human urges to strive for spiritual enlightenment and to find meaning in life were being harshly rejected by the very authorities who ostensibly set themselves up as foes of repression.

These were my feelings in the late 1950s when I turned again to yoga, astrology, and occultism with a renewed appreciation of what these age-old disciplines might contribute to the wasteland of academic psychology. Since then the wave of hippiedom has risen and declined. Richard Alpert, who often brushed past me in Harvard's venerable Emerson Hall, has metamorphosed into the charismatic Ram Dass, and a swarm of swamis have streamed across the land. Particularly encouraging has been the resurgence of the humanistic and transpersonal psychologies of thinkers such as Pitirim Sorokin, Abraham Maslow, Viktor Frankl, Ira Progoff, and Roberto Assagioli. At that time, however, my request to spend the better part of my senior year producing a thesis on astrology was like asking the powers-that-be to produce a major miracle.

As it has happened, there has been no lack of miracles in my life, although most of them have required a lot of hard work. What tipped the balance in my favor was my extraordinary good luck in having as an advisor Harvard professor Gordon Allport, the world's foremost authority on prejudice. So renowned a scholar could hardly admit to being prejudiced against astrologers. Fortunately, he was as kind as he was brilliant, a true exemplar of his own teachings. Consequently, I spent many happy hours in collaboration with the eminent New York astrologer Charles Jayne composing a questionnaire, sending it to 900 astrologers around the world, and tabulating the first 250 replies. The resultant thesis was sufficiently well received to embellish my 1960 diploma with a magna cum laude, and to bring me a Phi Beta Kappa key which, appropriately enough, bore the insignia of a hand reaching for the stars.

After graduation it soon became evident that, when it came down to the nitty gritty of putting my newly acquired education to work, there really was not much I could do, especially with three children requiring most of my attention. Moreover, my mind was so weary from long nights of studying that it was a year before I could tolerate the thought of any concerted intellectual activity. Hence, I decided to work more systematically on the yoga exercises at which I had, thus far, merely dabbled. But in all New England there was no teacher to be found.

Then in the summer of 1961, I discovered Swami Vishnu-devananda's yoga camp in Val Morin, Canada. After three weeks of training under this world-famed expert my health and morale improved so dramatically that I knew the word must be spread. That fall I started teaching at the gracious home of Boston's renowned astrologer Isabel Hickey. Since then the work has grown so fast that journalists now call Boston "yoga city."

People sometimes ask me why I divide my energies among so many disciplines—yoga, astrology, parapsychology, and now hypersentience. The easy reply would be that the tendency to do several things at once comes from being born with the Sun in dualistic Gemini. In retrospect, however, it is hard to see how it would have been possible to succeed in one of these fields without the metaphysical background provided by the others. Even from a purely practical standpoint my astrological friends joined yoga classes, many yoga students took up astrology, and both groups have been loyal supporters of the work in hypersentience.

Not only did my companions upon the path of yoga provide moral and financial sustenance; the lessons learned in one discipline carried over to the others. Through yoga I was able to deepen my appreciation of the body, of the unconscious, and of the earth on which we live. Learning to respond directly to fundamental physiological feelings has given me a far greater affinity for animals, plants, stones, sunsets, mountains, seascapes, and all the wondrous gifts of nature. Indeed, my own definition of yoga is that it is the art of doing things naturally.

It was, therefore, easy to move on to work with the unconscious side of human nature via hypersentience. To me this is one more form of yoga, with the same emphasis on self-knowing.

Occasionally, people speak of going "beyond yoga" or of not wishing to limit themselves to yoga. This attitude betrays an etymological as well as philosophical misunderstanding. The Sanskrit word *yoga* means nothing more—or less—than union. As such it is both a means and an end. An individual can hardly go beyond the transcendent unity of all creation, much less be limited by it. Hence, it is feasible to refer to hypersentience as a "psycho-yoga" since it promotes the integration of all aspects of the self. Similarly, astrology, which is based on the concept that the solar system is an organic unity, can be spoken of as "astro-yoga." The factor that makes any discipline a yoga is the emphasis on health, harmony, and wholeness.

Another advantage of having a background in the occult sciences is that I have no reputation to lose. Had I spent the same time and money in pursuit of a Ph.D., the situation might be different since there would be an investment to protect. As it is, I can afford to speak out and let the chips fall where they may.

To me, it is a source of never-ending astonishment that so many reputable people are afraid to express their convictions. This reticence would be understandable if we lived in the days of the Inquisition with an ever-present danger of imprisonment, torture, or death. But even with so little to sacrifice, an astonishing number of academicians never spread their wings for fear of the disapproval of the educational establishment. My experience in talking to doctors, clergymen, professors, hypnotists, and various people in high positions has been that, if these authorities had the courage to admit what they really believed, parapsychological studies would take a tremendous leap forward.

No doubt the defensive concern which members of the male sex are particularly apt to feel for their prestige in the eyes of the world helps to account for the fact that women have been in the vanguard of many of the new spiritually oriented movements. For years derogatory remarks have been made about the "little old ladies" who become involved in theosophy, psychic research, cabalism, and astrology, and who patronize mediums, clairvoyants, card readers, and the like. But now that the psychedelic generation has experimented with the consciousness-expanding properties of various drugs, a larger proportion of men have started to investigate the world of the occult. Even though the sharply defined world of the rational ego has long been associated with the positive, masculine side of creation, while the dreamlike realm of the unconscious has been associated with the feminine side of nature, there is no longer the same compulsive need to equate skepticism with manhood and credulity with womanhood. As male-female stereotypes begin mercifully to dissolve, people are starting to realize that excessive incredulity may betray as much naiveté as excessive credulity.

For a century, however, it has been largely due to the efforts of women (and often of rather effeminate men) that the esoteric tradition survived the onslaughts of ill-informed scoffers. In my experience many of these "little old ladies," and plenty of attractive young ones as well, have had razor-sharp intellects. It is high time that someone give them a bow. Both in yoga and in hypersentience women have been the pioneers who attended classes, sponsored lectures, organized workshops, and wrote encouraging letters, even though many wonderful (and thoroughly masculine) men have also been staunch allies.

Obviously, a semiliberated female like myself is apt to be prejudiced in favor of her own kind. Nevertheless, it has been a thought-provoking experience to find myself in my forties with a fair education, three grown children, adequate means of support and, according to statistics, with thirty potentially productive years ahead, and to know that millions more are in the same position. What a mine of still largely untapped resources!

For millennia women have been kept in ignorance and servitude. Now as the karmic wheel turns, these wives, mothers, and career women who have made the effort to develop their minds constitute a highly cultivated segment of our society. They are the ones who have the leisure to read, patronize the arts, and pursue unconventional interests with scant regard for what the world thinks.

A good case can be made for the argument that the mature woman who has a pleasant home and adequate income, and whose children are more or less on their own, can, if she wishes to use her intelligence, be the most emancipated member of society today. Her influence may be exerted largely behind the scenes but it is nonetheless great.

To continue my personal chronicle, my yoga classes had been going on less than two years when I wrote a letter to the popular writer Jess Stearn suggesting that he come to my home in Concord, Massachusetts, and write a book about yoga. Amazingly enough, he did just that. Although the portrait of me sketched by Jess in *Yoga, Youth, and Reincarnation* covered an exceedingly brief cross section of my life it was an accurate description of what he saw and experienced.

People have sometimes wondered why, when there was nothing glamorous about our suburban household, this book turned out to be a best seller. I did in fact pray with fervent intensity that the book would carry the message of yoga to those who needed it. But probably the factor that made the difference was the honesty of Jess's account. Readers would say, "Well, if these ordinary people can succeed at yoga, why can't I?" That of course was the point; novices could and did gain the benefits promised. Thus the movement spread.

It may be that my greatest contribution to this work was to demystify yoga. One of the marvelous aspects of the system is that it is so intrinsically efficacious that it does not require a charismatic personality to put it across. From the start I presented the technique on an "each one teach one" basis, treating each class as a group of potential teachers.

"Everyone," I would explain, "knows someone with an aching back or an aching psyche. Show them the cat stretches, the shoulderstand, the cobra, or the locust. Let them calm their nerves with deep breathing, and maybe this will eventually open their minds to the benefits to be derived from meditation, chanting, and the study of Vedanta philosophy. There is nothing difficult or dangerous about Hatha Yoga as long as you move slowly and with self-awareness. Yoga has something for everyone."

Once a lady reporter for a large newspaper came to an outdoor class at my home. Although she enjoyed the food and hospitality without making a contribution, she never introduced herself. The first I knew of her real purpose was when a snidely written article appeared headlined "Yoga can cure everyone—so says Marcia Moore."

The quotation was, of course, manifestly untrue. The idea on which I insist is that yoga can be "helpful" to anyone, regardless of age or physical condition. My reason for dwelling on this point is that the same attitude has carried over into the work with hypersentience. Not everyone can recollect a previous incarnation any more than everyone can perform a headstand. Nevertheless, the endeavor to recollect one's body or psyche is bound to be salutary.

To date, my greatest sense of achievement lies in the fact that so many who have read my books or attended my lectures have themselves gone on to become teachers. As far as I know, I was the first to teach Hatha Yoga on a continuing basis in New England, although other instructors arrived on the scene soon after. Within the decade there was a flourishing teachers' group in Boston, Massachusetts, with similar groups springing up in other states. Sometimes it has seemed to me as though every third housewife in Newton was conducting a yoga group in her rumpus room—and for the most part doing it well. That at least is what I would like to see.

While Jess Stearn was visiting in Concord, I introduced him to Kenneth Lyon, a full-time psychologist and part-time hypnotist. My first encounter with Ken was at a meeting of a psychic research group in Canterbury, New Hampshire. In front of about two hundred onlookers Ken regressed three volunteers from the audience to previous lifetimes, using standard hypnotic techniques. It astonished me at the time, and still does, that a process with such mind-boggling implications could so easily be demonstrated to a group with no prior preparation of the subjects. Certainly it would be hard to believe that one day my friends and I would be emulating Ken with equal success.

I must confess, however, that on the afternoon I attended Ken Lyon's demonstration the occasion seemed no more momentous than that day, years before, when Ronan Dutta showed me his yoga postures. The planting of a seed is seldom a spectacular event, yet many lives have been affected because

Ken was kind enough to take time from his busy schedule to pass on the knowledge he had acquired. If I have found the incentive to sow similar seeds, even when they appeared to be falling on barren ground, it is because so many people have done the same for me.

Not until his manuscript was virtually complete did Jess add the word *reincarnation* to its title and fill out the corresponding sections. He had started out as a disbeliever and only toward the end of our collaborative enterprise did the first cracks appear in the wall of his skepticism. In this, too, the book faithfully reflects the facts of the situation.

Once Jess began to make a serious investigation of the hypothesis that souls can evolve through a succession of bodies, his inquiring mind took him to the Virginia Beach headquarters of the Association for Research and Enlightenment (A.R.E.), an organization dedicated to the promulgation of the work of Edgar Cayce. There he wrote the best seller *The Sleeping Prophet* which quickly led to a fourfold increase in the membership of this fine group. Probably more people have been won over to the idea of rebirth because of the material produced by and about Edgar Cayce than by any other factor.

In the meantime I went through a depressing period during which I became convinced that I had reached a dead end in my work as a yoga teacher. On the one hand, I felt the pressure of family obligations. On the other, I didn't have the heart to deny the benefits of yoga to those who were unable to pay the two-dollar fee for an hour-and-a-half-long class. People did come, but too few contributed enough to make these sessions financially feasible. Many staunch friends such as Shepard and Lois Ginandes, Hans and Emilie Hoffmann, and Sidney and Estelle Simons were overwhelmingly generous, but there were also negative reactions from critics who seemed determined to misunderstand everything that Hatha Yoga means.

Finally, my weariness with the situation was such that it was a relief to sell the Concord house and make a new start in Maine. In retrospect, however, I can see that this practice in becoming inured to the antagonism aroused by yoga was a valuable preparation for the far more vituperous opposition that was later directed toward our experiments with hypersentience.

Moving to Maine did indeed constitute a new start because the suggestion was made to me that I should write a book. For a month afterward I was in a quandary. How to begin? In my mind there was a vague idea about composing something on the subject of yoga and diet, because so many of the ladies who attended my classes were concerned about their weight. Since the word *diet* means literally "way of life," it seemed advisable to give as broad a scope to this work as possible.

One day while on a trip to New York City I arose early and stood alone by the window overlooking the empty streets, so soon to be teeming with people. Suddenly a gentle, deliberate voice somewhere in the center of my head seemed to say, "Let us begin where our problems begin—with appetite." The next line which followed automatically was, "What exactly do you crave, and what do you crave it *for?*"

These became the first lines of my book, which came out under the title *Diet, Sex, and Yoga*. From then on, writing has been my number one profession with an average of a book a year being produced. Recollecting this phase of unremitting writing, lecturing, and teaching, I sometimes wonder what sustained me. The answer is always the same. The vital factor which has made this continuing effort possible has been the kindness of friends and of the many unknown supporters who have written encouraging letters. I have deeply regretted my inability to compose adequate replies to these many communications, but they did feed my soul. Each and every card and letter was appreciated.

By the end of 1972 it was apparent that another seven-year cycle had run its course and that the time was ripe to make a new beginning. The books were circulating and my children, now in their twenties, were doing well. Having thus fulfilled my "kiddie karma," I acquired a camper and headed west with no special destination in mind.

On the first day of 1973 I came to the verdant Ojai Valley in Southern California. Though I have traveled many places since then, this enchanted effigy of Shangri-La remains in my memory as the place where I found the purest peace, rest, and contentment that this life has had to offer. It was also the place where most of the research was conducted which led to the writing of this book.

Some friends have described me as a butterfly that cannot sit on one flower. In actuality, I would like to set up a permanent research center and have worked hard to lay the groundwork for such an enterprise. Thus far, the closest I have come to achieving this goal was during the nine months when I rented a hilltop home in Ojai where I taught yoga, conducted hypersensing workshops, entertained a stream of visitors, and saw my first "flying saucer." We called the place Ananta Ashram. At this time Ananta Ashram is an oak-shaded grove to the west of the Ojai Valley where I have parked my motor home for an indefinite period. If, however, the work is meant to prosper, the "ashram" may one day become an information center and retreat where people can study the techniques of hypersentience.

The name Ananta derives from the beneficent thousand-headed serpent who is the vehicle of Vishnu, second person of the Hindu trinity. Rising from the sea of the unconscious, Ananta's undulating coils support the myriad forms of creation. A similar serpent appears on the caduceus, emblem of the medical profession. In India, this underlying source of power is known as *kundalini,* while in the West it is associated with the *libido.* Since Ananta is the symbol of regeneration, it is hoped that our good snake will be reborn as investigators take up the challenge of demonstrating that immortality is a fact of nature.

Shortly after coming to Ojai I read Jess Stearn's recently published *The Search for a Soul* in which he describes the past-life experiences of the novelist Taylor Caldwell. Although I had been out of touch with Jess for years, I knew he was still pursuing the line of investigation we had started in Concord. But this was something else again! The reason the account of Taylor Caldwell's experiences hit me like a lightning bolt was that her between-life sojourns were on the hypothetical planet Melina. I too had encountered subjects who spoke of places not described in history books and which probably were not of this Earth, but had discounted them as too fantastic to believe. Now I felt emboldened to pull these maverick cases out of my memory files and check them against the fresh data that were coming in.

Thus the wheel turned full circle. Originally I had introduced Jess to the technique of recollecting former lifetimes. Now it was his book which provided the incentive to launch a serious study of what appears to be an inner-dimensional network of coordinating intelligences which constitute outposts of the mind of the universe. It seems to me now that since making this decision my consciousness has expanded more than it did in all the years of pursuing more conventional yogic and metaphysical disciplines.

As I became receptive to the concept that humanoid entities may be living in concurrent dimensions of space, increasing numbers of sensors began to give independent accounts of these fabulous locales. By now I would guess that I have worked with about fifty people who have had experiences not unlike those of Taylor Caldwell, and there surely must be many more. Although some of the "planets" mentioned have sounded like a blend of Tolkien, the Oz books, and mythic Greece, they are vividly real to those who have related their adventures there. In any event, I never felt obliged to pass judgment on these experiences. They may represent alternate realities, but that does not make them any less significant than our phenomenal realm of the senses.

In looking to the future I am hopeful that someday it will be possible to produce a book describing the experiences of people who believe they have tuned in on other dimensions of consciousness. Also proposed are spin-off volumes on lost civilizations and karmic astrology. Various friends, including Kathleen Jenks and Dr. Richard Willard, are now writing books about their experiences with hypersentience and these accounts are bound to stimulate further interest.

In order to stimulate these and related projects I started the *Hypersentience Bulletin* in June 1975 with the assistance of Lynn Powell. This modest quarterly is now being published at the solstices and equinoxes in Ojai, California. The purpose of the *Bulletin* is to create a medium for the exchange of ideas pertaining to hypersentience, to coordinate research, review relevant literature, and to put interested people in touch with one another. An additional service is the compilation and distribution of periodically updated lists of facilitators. Starting in 1976 we plan to sponsor conferences in various parts of the country which will offer instruction and bring practitioners together.

At this time the work is still in its preliminary stages. Nevertheless, it takes only one small match to light a conflagration. To date, it has seemed more efficacious to light the fires of inspiration than to found an organization. To the extent, however, that interest in this subject continues to grow, an appropriate response will be given.

Now, contemplating the events of this incarnation, and knowing it to be but an eyeblink in eternity, it seems to me that the areas in which I have been able to make some contribution to human welfare have been those which involve meaning. Perhaps I have been able to see the importance of enterprises which to others appear as little more than interesting novelties. This is my purpose in writing the present book. Certainly there is nothing new about hypersentience except the name I have given it. Many others are and have been working along the same lines. If, however, this exposition can help people en masse to grasp the significance of what is happening to them, that will be satisfaction enough.

It has been my experience that persons in positions of power are usually the least able to appreciate the profound human implications of the modes of thought which are just rising over time's horizon. Most so-called authorities are too intimately identified with the established order to welcome that which is genuinely new. I am extremely grateful, therefore, that these words can go directly to the public. In the realm of psychic investigation it has been ordinary intelligent individuals who have taken the initiative in spreading the word of recent developments and who will continue to do so. I am, therefore, hopeful that enlightened men and women in all walks of life will accept what is offered in these pages and will use it for good. My love and blessings go out to them.